Philip St. George Cooke
From a photograph

EXPLORING SOUTHWESTERN TRAILS

1846-1854

by

PHILIP ST. GEORGE COOKE
WILLIAM HENRY CHASE WHITING
FRANÇOIS XAVIER AUBRY

edited by

RALPH P. BIEBER
Associate Professor of History, Washington University, St. Louis
in collaboration with
AVERAM B. BENDER

PORCUPINE PRESS
Philadelphia
1974

First edition 1938
(Glendale: The Arthur H. Clark Co., 1938)

Reprinted 1974 by
PORCUPINE PRESS, INC.
Philadelphia, Pennsylvania 19107

Library of Congress Cataloging in Publication Data

Cooke, Philip St. George, 1809-1895.
Exploring southwestern trails, 1846-1854.

(The Southwest historical series, 7)
Reprint of the 1938 ed. published by A. H. Clark Co., Glendale, Calif.
CONTENTS: Introduction.--Cooke's journal of the march of the Mormon Battalion, 1846-1847.--Journal of William Henry Chase Whiting, 1849. [etc.]
1. Southwest, New--Description and travel. 2. United States--History--War with--Mexico, 1845-1848 --Regimental histories--Iowa Infantry--Mormon Battalion. 3. Iowa Infantry. Mormon Battalion, 1846-1847. 4. Texas--Description and travel. I. Whiting, William Henry Chase, 1824-1865. II. Aubry, Francois Xavier, 1824-1854. III. Title.
F786.S752 vol. 7 917.9'04'2 74-7196
ISBN 0-87991-302-9

Manufactured in the United States of America

CONTENTS

ILLUSTRATIONS

PREFACE

PREFACE

Many explorers traveled through the Southwest searching for new trails during the decade preceding the Civil war. The journals or notes of three of these adventurers –Philip St. George Cooke, William Henry Chase Whiting, and François Xavier Aubry – are here published, describing with a wealth of detail the country traversed, the Indians encountered, and the advantages and disadvantages of the routes followed. Cooke and Whiting were commissioned officers of the United States army; Aubry was a civilian. The trails over which they journeyed were immediately used by the overland migration through the Southwest and were followed at a later time by several great transcontinental railroads.

The editor has reproduced the documents with a few alterations. He has corrected their spelling and paragraphing, and has changed their capitalization to conform to the format of the publisher. He has also occasionally altered their punctuation and word order; but such changes have been made only to avoid very awkward expressions or to clarify the meaning of the authors. All additions, with the exception of chapter headings, have been enclosed in brackets.

The editor takes pleasure in acknowledging his indebtedness to Doctor Averam B. Bender, the collaborator. Doctor Bender, who is the author of a number of articles on frontier defense and exploration, gave freely of his time and energy during the progress of the whole work, but rendered especially important service by gathering part of the material for the introduction and footnotes to the Cooke and Whiting journals. The editor wrote the introduction and footnotes to the three documents, edited the texts of the documents, collected the data for the introduction and footnotes to Aubry's diaries, and gathered part of the material for the introduction and footnotes to the Cooke and Whiting journals.

The editor desires to thank the War Department for permission to publish the manuscript journals of Philip St. George Cooke and William Henry Chase Whiting. For aid given in the preparation of this work, he is also grateful to Miss Stella M. Drumm, librarian, Missouri Historical Society; Mr. Joseph J. Hill, Bancroft library, University of California; Miss Winnie Allen, library of the University of Texas; Mr. Floyd C. Shoemaker, secretary, State Historical Society of Missouri; and Professor Lansing B. Bloom, University of New Mexico. For valuable assistance in editorial work and in preparing the manuscript for publication, the editor is grateful to his wife, Ida Parker Bieber.

RALPH P. BIEBER

Washington University
St. Louis, Missouri
June 17, 1938

INTRODUCTION

INTRODUCTION

One of the most important activities in the Southwest between the Mexican and Civil wars was the exploration of trails. The United States army, as in an earlier period, played the leading rôle, although private citizens occasionally participated. Operating over a vast area of plains and mountains, the explorers helped to bind the territory recently acquired from Mexico to the rest of the United States. Their primary objectives were to open trails for purposes of commerce, communication, migration, and defense against the Indians. They surveyed and constructed wagon roads, made military highways, and examined routes for transcontinental railroads. The army explorations were usually conducted by the engineers or topographical engineers, but a few were made by infantry or dragoons as by-products of military expeditions.[1] The journals of Philip St. George Cooke and William Henry Chase Whiting are here published as examples of surveys undertaken by the United States army, whereas the diaries of François Xavier Aubry serve to illustrate the accomplishments of private adventurers.

Philip St. George Cooke was born near Leesburg, Loudoun county, Virginia, June 13, 1809. His father was Doctor Stephen Cooke, a native of Philadelphia,

1 A. B. Bender, "Government Explorations in the Territory of New Mexico, 1846-1859," *New Mexico Historical Review*, IX, 1-32; *ibid.*, "Opening Routes Across West Texas, 1848-1850," *Southwestern Historical Quarterly*, XXXVII, 116-135; *ibid.*, "The Texas Frontier, 1848-1861," *Southwestern Historical Quarterly*, XXXVIII, 135-148.

who served as an army surgeon during the American Revolution until he was captured by the British and taken as a prisoner to the Bermuda Islands. There he fell in love with Catherine Esten, daughter of John Esten, a prominent British official; and on June 7, 1782, Stephen and Catherine were married, remaining in Bermuda to live. Some years later they moved to the Bahama Islands, where Stephen continued his practice of medicine. In 1791 they came to the United States, settling at Alexandria, Virginia. But ten years afterward they decided upon another migration, this time purchasing an estate near Leesburg, Virginia, where Philip St. George was born.[2] Little is known of Philip's early life except that he attended the academy at Martinsburg (now in West Virginia).[3] At the age of fourteen he entered the United States Military academy at West Point, and there, during his four-year course, met such famous military leaders of later years as Robert E. Lee, Jefferson Davis, Albert Sidney Johnston, and Joseph E. Johnston. Graduating from that institution on July 1, 1827, he was breveted second lieutenant of infantry, and on the same day was appointed second lieutenant in the Sixth infantry. He was assigned to duty at Jefferson Barracks, Missouri, a post then in process of erection on the west bank of the Mississippi river, ten miles south of St. Louis.[4]

From the time of his arrival at Jefferson Barracks

[2] John O. Beaty, *John Esten Cooke* (New York, 1922), 2-3; Thomas M. Spaulding, "Philip St. George Cooke," *Dictionary of American Biography,* IV, 389; Edward Preble, "John Esten Cooke," *ibid.,* IV, 384-385; *Appleton's Cyclopedia of American Biography,* I, 720.

[3] *Appleton's Cyclopedia of American Biography,* I, 720.

[4] Jones, General Orders, July 11, 1827, General Order Book, VI, MSS., Old Records Division, Adjutant-general's Office, War Department (hereafter cited as O.R.D., A.G.O.); George W. Cullum, *Biographical Register of the Officers and Graduates of the U.S. Military Academy, at West Point, N.Y.* (New York, 1868), I, 291-292, 317-318, 333-334, 338, 343-344.

until the beginning of the Mexican war, a period of almost twenty years, Cooke saw extensive service in the Far West. As early as 1829 he was a member of Major Bennet Riley's detachment of infantry which escorted Santa Fé traders from western Missouri to the Arkansas river and return, and two years afterward accompanied an Indian agent on a journey from Fort Leavenworth to the villages of the Oto and Omaha tribes. On March 4, 1833, he was transferred to the First dragoons with the rank of first lieutenant, and on May 31, 1835, was commissioned captain. In 1834 he commanded company G of the dragoons on Colonel Henry Dodge's march from Fort Gibson to the Pawnee Pict villages; in 1843 he led two squadrons of dragoons over the Santa Fé trail to protect traders, disarming Snively's band of Texans near the Arkansas crossing; and two years later he served in Colonel Stephen W. Kearny's expedition to the South pass. Meanwhile, he had been stationed, at various times, at Jefferson Barracks, Fort Crawford, Fort Snelling, Fort Leavenworth, Fort Gibson, and Fort Wayne (Indian territory).[5] At Fort Leavenworth on October 28, 1830, Cooke was married to Rachel Wilt Hertzog, of Philadelphia, the ceremony taking place at the home of the bride's sister, Mary Hertzog Dougherty, wife of John Dougherty, Indian agent. They had four children – one son and three daughters – all of whom were born at army posts on or near the frontier.[6]

At the beginning of the Mexican war in 1846, Cooke

5 P. St. G. Cooke, *Scenes and Adventures in the Army* (Philadelphia, 1857), 40-109, 225-227, 231-432; Cullum, *Biographical Register,* I, 317-318.

6 John Rogers was born at Jefferson Barracks, June 9, 1833; Flora at the same place, January 3, 1836; Maria Pendleton at Fort Wayne, February 25, 1840; and Julia Turner at Fort Leavenworth, March 10, 1842. William H. Collins, *The Collins Family* (Quincy, Ill., 1897), 160-162. See also *Missouri Republican* (St. Louis), Nov. 16, 1830; John C. Luttig, *Journal of a Fur-Trading Expedition on the Upper Missouri, 1812-1813* (Stella M. Drumm, ed., St. Louis, 1920), 151-153.

was stationed at Fort Crawford, Wisconsin territory, but was soon "ordered to the seat of war at the South." [7] In command of company K, First dragoons, which was eager to participate in the conflict, he left the post by boat and on June 26 reached St. Louis on his way down the Mississippi river. He arrived there with Captain Sumner's company of dragoons from Fort Atkinson, which had also been ordered south.[8] But in this city both Cooke and Sumner received instructions which altered their course. As soon as hostilities commenced the War Department had directed Stephen W. Kearny, colonel of the First dragoons, to organize an expedition at Fort Leavenworth to occupy New Mexico and California. On May 31, Kearny had written to Brigadier-general George W. Brooke, of St. Louis, commander of the Third military department: "I have now most respectfully to urge – to demand – (the interest of the public service admits of strong & respectful terms) that 2 companies of my regiment (Captains Sumner's & Cooke's) now stationed at Forts Atkinson & Crawford may be ordered to repair forthwith to this post [Fort Leavenworth], to follow me on my trail to Santa Fé. These companies are among the very best of my regiment, and should not be allowed to remain inactive during the present movements, when their services are so much required in the field. Each one of the companies from the captains down would consider that injustice was done to them by leaving them unemployed." [9] As a result of this request, on June 16, 1846, the adjutant-

[7] P. St. G. Cooke, *Conquest of New Mexico and California* (New York, 1878), 2-3; Cullum, *Biographical Register*, I, 318.

[8] *Daily Missouri Republican*, June 27, 1846; Cooke, *Conquest of New Mexico and California*, 3.

[9] Kearny to Brooke, May 31, 1846, Kearny Letter Book, MS., Missouri Historical Society (hereafter cited as M.H.S.).

general directed Cooke and Sumner to join Kearny's expedition, the order reaching them in St. Louis. Both officers were "inexpressibly disappointed," for they were anxious to see service in the heart of Mexico, where there was greater opportunity for action and therefore promotion. Nevertheless, on June 28 they left St. Louis aboard two steamboats for Fort Leavenworth, arriving there on the night of July 3, three days after Kearny's departure. On July 6 the two dragoon companies, with Sumner in command, marched from the post, hoping to overtake the colonel within ten days. Although they proceeded rapidly, averaging about twenty-eight miles a day, Kearny also moved fast, and consequently they were unable to join him until July 31, when they arrived at Bent's Fort.[10]

Kearny left the fort on August 1 and continued his march to New Mexico, occupying Santa Fé without resistance on August 18. Nine days later he selected Cooke's company to be part of the detachment which he would take to California and ordered it to prepare to leave Santa Fé by September 15.[11] Then, early in September, he made a tour of the country south of Santa Fé and returned to the capital firmly convinced that the natives were favorably disposed toward the United States. He established a civil government in New Mexico on September 22, when he promulgated a code of laws, issued a declaration of rights, and appointed officers for the Territorial government. Three days afterward, somewhat later than he had planned, he departed for California with a detachment of troops –

10 Sumner to Jones, July 4, 1846, Cooke to Floyd, Feb., 1859, Letters Received, MSS., Old Files Section, Adjutant-general's Office, War Department (hereafter cited as O.F.S., A.G.O); *Daily Missouri Republican,* June 29, 1846; Cooke, *Conquest of New Mexico and California,* 3-5.

11 Kearny, Order No. 18, Aug. 27, 1846, Letters Received, MSS., O.F.S., A.G.O.

"three hundred wilderness-worn dragoons, in shabby and patched clothing," according to Cooke.[12] On October 2, when encamped on the Río Grande near La Joya, Kearny learned of the death at Fort Leavenworth of Lieutenant-colonel James Allen of the Mormon Battalion, and immediately ordered Cooke to return to Santa Fé and assume command of the battalion upon its arrival there.[13]

The Mormon Battalion was organized soon after the beginning of hostilities. Forced to leave Missouri and Illinois, and refused admission to Arkansas, the Church of Jesus Christ of Latter-day Saints had decided to move to the Far West. On January 26, 1846, Brigham Young wrote a letter to Elder Jesse C. Little, of Peterborough, New Hampshire, appointing him agent of the church in the eastern states, and urging him to take advantage of any facilities the United States government might offer the Saints to migrate to the Pacific coast. Eager to aid his brethren, Little decided to go to Washington, D.C., to ask President Polk "to stretch forth the federal arm in their behalf." Carrying with him letters of introduction from the governor of New Hampshire and from others to George M. Dallas, Vice President, George Bancroft, Secretary of the Navy, and Amos Kendall, formerly Postmaster General, he proceeded to the national capital, arriving there on May 21, about a week after the outbreak of war. Two days later he called upon Kendall, who, according to Little, was of the opinion that "arrangements could be made to assist our emigration by enlisting one thousand of our men, arming, equipping and establishing them in California

[12] Cooke, *Conquest of New Mexico and California*, 69.

[13] *Ibid.*, 78; Kearny, Order No. 33, Oct. 2, 1846, Letters Received, MSS., O.F.S., A.G.O.

to defend the country." [14] What basis Kendall had for making this statement is not as yet clear, though it is known that he, together with the governor of Arkansas, visited Polk on May 25 and urged him to organize a military expedition to California.[15] The following day Kendall informed Little that the president was determined to take possession of California, that he would employ the Mormons to "push through and fortify the country," and that the whole matter of the migration of the Saints would be presented to a cabinet meeting immediately. On June 1, Little addressed a letter directly to Polk asking for federal assistance to the Mormons. Next day the cabinet unanimously decided that an expedition should be sent to occupy California, and that Colonel Kearny should be authorized to enlist as volunteers a few hundred of the Saints who were then on their way to that region, in order "to conciliate them, attach them to our country, & prevent them from taking part against us." [16] Accordingly, the Secretary of War, in his instructions to Kearny on June 3, directed him to receive into the service as many Mormons as could be persuaded to volunteer, the total number, however, not to exceed a third of his whole force.[17]

As soon as Kearny received these instructions he took steps to put them into effect. On June 19, 1846, he directed Captain James Allen, of the First dragoons, then at Fort Leavenworth, to proceed to the Mormon camps

[14] Frank Alfred Golder, Thomas A. Bailey, and J. Lyman Smith, *The March of the Mormon Battalion from Council Bluffs to California* (New York, 1928), 22-80; Hubert H. Bancroft, *History of California,* v (*Works of H. H. Bancroft,* xxii, San Francisco, 1886), 469-472; T. B. H. Stenhouse, *The Rocky Mountain Saints* (New York, 1873), 221-239; Leland Hargrave Creer, *Utah and the Nation* (Seattle, 1929), 20-22, 31-36.

[15] *The Diary of James K. Polk* (Milo M. Quaife, ed., Chicago, 1910), i, 427.

[16] *Ibid.,* i, 429, 436-440, 443-444; Golder, Bailey, and Smith, *op. cit.,* 80-84.

[17] *House Ex. Docs.,* 30 cong., 1 sess., no. 60, pp. 153-154.

and enlist four or five companies of volunteers, each of which was to consist of not less than seventy-three men nor more than one hundred and nine. The companies were to be mustered into the service of the United States and then marched to Fort Leavenworth, where they were to receive arms and prepare for the westward journey. Their pay was to be the same as that of other infantry volunteers, and their period of enlistment was to be for twelve months, at the end of which time they could retain their guns and equipment obtained at the fort. Allen, who was to command the battalion, was to have the rank of lieutenant-colonel as soon as he had mustered in the fourth company.[18] He immediately proceeded north to the Mormon camps in Iowa territory, and on June 26, at Mount Pisgah, issued a circular announcing his mission. In this document he explained the details of Kearny's order and added: "Thus is offered to the Mormon people now – this year – an opportunity of sending a portion of their young and intelligent men, to the ultimate destination of their whole people, and entirely at the expense of the United States; and this advance party can thus pave the way, and look out the land for their brethren to come after them." [19] Having no difficulty in obtaining volunteers, he soon organized a battalion of five companies of infantry, which marched from Council Bluffs on July 21 and 22, arriving at Fort Leavenworth on August 1.[20] There Allen was taken sick; but on August 12 he ordered the battalion to begin its journey and proceed to Council

[18] Kearny to Allen, June 19, 1846, Letters Received, MSS., O.F.S., A.G.O.

[19] *Daily Missouri Republican,* July 24, 1846; William Alexander Linn, *The Story of the Mormons* (New York, 1923), 371-372.

[20] *Daily Missouri Republican,* July 23, 1846; Howard R. Egan, *Pioneering the West, 1846 to 1878* (Wm. M. Egan, editor and compiler, Richmond, Utah, 1917), 14; Golder, Bailey, and Smith, *op. cit.,* 104-142.

Grove, where they were to await his arrival. However, he never rejoined his command, for, as mentioned before, he died at Fort Leavenworth on August 23. Meanwhile, in obedience to his last instructions, the Mormons left the post on August 13 and 14, and arrived at Council Grove on August 27, not having heard of the loss of their leader until the day before they reached their destination. On August 29, Lieutenant Andrew J. Smith, of the First dragoons, came to the Grove with instructions from Lieutenant-colonel Clifton Wharton, commanding officer at Fort Leavenworth, to serve as acting lieutenant-colonel of the battalion. The Mormons, with their new commander, resumed their march two days later and arrived at Santa Fé in detachments on October 9 and 12.[21]

On October 2, as previously stated, Kearny appointed Cooke to take Allen's place as commander of the Mormon Battalion. At the same time he instructed Cooke to lead it to California over the route which was then being followed by the detachment of First dragoons.[22] Kearny, with the dragoons, continued to march south along the Río Grande; but his progress was so slow that Kit Carson, the guide, predicted that at the existing rate of travel more than four months would be required to make the journey to Los Angeles.[23] Consequently, on October 9, after consultation with Carson and others, he decided to leave his wagons in New Mexico and continue the march with pack mules.[24] Writing to the adjutant-general two days afterward, he explained: "I

21 Golder, Bailey, and Smith, *op. cit.*, 146-172; *Southwest Historical Series*, III, 252.

22 Kearny, Order No. 33, Oct. 2, 1846, Letters Received, MSS., O.F.S., A.G.O.

23 Henry S. Turner, Diary, Oct. 8, 1846, MS., M.H.S.; *House Ex. Docs.*, 30 cong., 1 sess., no. 41, pp. 573-574.

24 *House Ex. Docs.*, 30 cong., 1 sess., no. 41, pp. 55, 574.

have nothing new to report further than finding the country so broken & sandy, & requiring so much time to hunt up a waggon road, that I have determined upon taking from here pack mules, so as to expedite our march to the Pacific, by which means I shall reach Monterey before the volunteers from New York can possibly get there. As we march forward, I shall have the country well examined by a corps of guides, with a view of finding the best waggon road, & will send them back to meet Capt. Cooke & his command of Mormons, so as to conduct them on without unnecessary delay. We are now about 200 miles below Santa Fé & expect in about 20 miles further to leave this river for the Gila."[25] On October 15, when Kearny left the Río Grande and marched southwest, he assigned Cooke "the task of opening a wagon road to the Pacific." The same day Lieutenant Emory, of the topographical engineers, recorded that "several intelligent guides were detached to look up a road further south" by which Cooke might "turn the mountains with his wagons."[26] Upon reaching the Copper Mines three days later, Kearny held a council with some Apache Indians and made further arrangements to provide guides for the Mormon Battalion. Captain Henry S. Turner, acting assistant adjutant-general of the Army of the West, immediately wrote to Cooke: "Red Sleeve, the Apache chief, had an interview with the general today & has promised to send some of his young men to conduct you by a good route to the Río Gila, when they meet you. The general desires that you will treat them well & make use of them as guides. They will take this note to you. As none of these young men will be able to speak the Spanish lan-

[25] Kearny to Jones, Oct. 11, 1846, Letters Received, MSS., O.F.S., A.G.O.

[26] *House Ex. Docs.*, 30 cong., 1 sess., no. 41, pp. 56, 576; Cooke, *Conquest of New Mexico and California,* 86.

guage, it is probable that Charbonneaux will understand & make himself understood by them by signs."[27] These instructions were the last which Cooke received concerning the conduct of his expedition before Kearny's arrival in California.

Meanwhile, on October 7, Cooke had reached Santa Fé and six days later assumed command of the Mormon Battalion.[28] Well qualified for his assignment by nearly twenty years of service in various parts of the Far West, he made immediate preparations for the long and tedious march. On October 19 he left the capital with 397 troops and moved slowly down the valley of the Río Grande. He took along sixty days' rations of flour, sugar, coffee, and salt, thirty of salt pork, and twenty of soap – inadequate supplies, he admitted, but all he could obtain in Santa Fé at the time. He appointed Lieutenant Andrew J. Smith assistant commissary of subsistence, Lieutenant George Stoneman assistant quartermaster, Doctor George B. Sanderson assistant surgeon, Doctor Stephen C. Foster interpreter, and Pauline Weaver guide. On the day of his departure he learned that Kearny had decided to abandon his wagons and take only pack mules to California, news which made Cooke all the more determined to get his own wagons through to the Pacific coast. Arriving at the Ranches of Albuquerque on October 24, he met some of the guides sent back by Kearny. One of them, named Charbonneau, reported that they had explored a route somewhat different from that taken by the dragoons, but Cooke concluded that their work was not entirely satisfactory. Additional guides from Kearny's detachment reached the battalion on November 2, but all of

27 Turner to Cooke, Oct. 18, 1846, Letters Received, MSS., O.F.S., A.G.O. See also Turner, Diary, Oct. 18, 1846, MS., M.H.S.

28 Cooke, *Conquest of New Mexico and California,* 83, 90.

them, with the exception of Antoine Leroux, came in "more or less drunk." Leaving the Río Grande near the site of the present town of Rincón, New Mexico, about thirty miles south of the point where Kearny had left the river, Cooke proceeded southwest to the Ojo de Vaca, or Cow spring, which he reached on the night of November 19. There, on the following day, about eight miles northeast of the present Wilna, Grant county, New Mexico, he had a long consultation with the guides about the proper route to take and finally decided that the only one practicable for wagons lay considerably south of the trail which Kearny was following. In his journal Cooke recorded the conclusions he reached and the reasons for them: "I have reflected long and anxiously. The general wished me to come the Gila route, that a wagon road might be established by it. The guides which he sent me would not attempt it, and aim to go some three hundred miles and then strike the San Pedro, its tributary, and this at a distance of from fifty to a hundred miles from the Gila – the whole distance. What difference if this distance is doubled, if it is a better route? I shall strike the Gila all the same by either, at the same point. . . I have determined to follow the Janos road until I can turn off (probably two days on this side), as the best road, or route, to the same point of the Gila which I should strike in any route; all my guides agree in its being so."

Cooke's journal relates in detail the story of the Mormon trek from Santa Fé to California; hence the rest of the journey needs only to be outlined here. Marching southwest from the Ojo de Vaca, the battalion made its way over the mountains near the Guadalupe pass to the San Pedro river, where it turned north and proceeded down the valley of that stream about fifty-five miles before going west to Tucson. From this *presidio* it continued northwest to the Pima Indian villages on the Gila river. There it picked up Kearny's trail and moved west along the south side of the Gila and across southern California to San Diego, reaching that point on January 29, 1847. The following day Cooke issued an order congratulating the battalion upon the successful termination of its journey of more than two thousand miles. "History may be searched in vain for an equal march of infantry," he asserted. This order was read to the Mormons on February 4 and "was cheered heartily by the battalion." [29] Indeed, the Saints and their commander had reason to be proud of their achievement, for they had opened the first wagon road through the Southwest to California. It was used by thousands of emigrants in the following years, and, as a practicable railroad route, was one of the principal reasons for the Gadsden purchase of 1853 and 1854.[30] Today it is followed in a general way by the Atchison, Topeka and Santa Fé Railway from Rincón to Deming in New Mexico, and by the Southern Pacific Company's lines from Vista, New Mexico, by way of Douglas, Tucson, and Yuma, Arizona, to San Diego, California.

Cooke's resignation as commander of the Mormon Battalion was accepted by Kearny on May 13, 1847; he then hurried east in time to serve at Vera Cruz and Mexico City during the latter part of the war. Remaining in the service for about twenty-five years after the end of the conflict, he participated in practically every important activity of the army during that time. In the Civil war his only son, John, and his son-in-law, J. E. B. Stuart, espoused the cause of the South, but Cooke,

29 Bancroft, *History of California*, v, 487.

30 Paul Neff Garber, *The Gadsden Treaty* (Philadelphia, 1923), 17-63.

though born in Virginia, remained loyal to the Union. In fact, he spent all of his active life in the United States army. On October 29, 1873, after forty-six years of continuous, conscientious, and efficient service, he was placed on the retired list, "being over the age of 62 years." [31] A recent biographer has stated: "Cooke was a stern disciplinarian, with a high sense of honor and sincere religious feeling. He did not lack a sense of humor, and was notably fond of young people." [32] He was the author of two books: *Scenes and Adventures in the Army: or Romance of Military Life* (1857), and *The Conquest of New Mexico and California: an Historical and Personal Narrative* (1878). At the direction of the Secretary of War he also revised *Cavalry Tactics,* a two-volume work which he published in 1861. He died at his home in Detroit, March 20, 1895, at the advanced age of eighty-five years.[33]

William Henry Chase Whiting, the author of the second journal here published, was born in Biloxi, Mississippi, March 22, 1824. His parents, Levi and Mary A. Whiting, were natives of Massachusetts. His father had been in the United States army since 1812 and at the time of William's birth was captain of the First artillery.[34] At the age of twelve William entered the

[31] *From Everglade to Cañon with the Second Dragoons* (Theo. F. Rodenbough, compiler, New York, 1875), 175-193, 437; Cooke, *Conquest of New Mexico and California,* 305; Beaty, *John Esten Cooke,* 75; Cullum, *Biographical Register,* I, 318, III, 69; *Detroit Free Press,* Mar. 21, 1895.

[32] Spaulding, "Philip St. George Cooke," *Dictionary of American Biography,* IV, 389.

[33] Cooke to Cooper, Jan. 11, 27, Oct. 3, 1860, Letters Received, MSS., O.F.S., A.G.O.; *Detroit Free Press,* Mar. 21, 1895.

[34] C. B. Denson, *An Address Delivered in Raleigh, N.C., on Memorial Day (May 10), 1895* (Raleigh, 1895), 10; Francis B. Heitman, *Historical Register and Dictionary of the United States Army* (Washington, 1903), I, 1030; Joseph Mills Hanson, "William Henry Chase Whiting," *Dictionary of American Biography,* XX, 136.

English High School in Boston, the first public high school in the country, and two years later enrolled at Georgetown College, D.C., graduating from both institutions with the highest honors. He became a student in the United States Military academy in 1841, where he met Ulysses S. Grant, George B. McClellan, Winfield S. Hancock, John Pope, Ambrose E. Burnside, William S. Rosecrans, Fitz John Porter, George E. Pickett, and others who became prominent during the Civil war. Porter was his classmate and roommate. On July 1, 1845, he was graduated at the head of his class of forty-one, attaining a higher average than any previous student at West Point.[35] He was immediately promoted in the army to second lieutenant, corps of engineers, and assigned to duty at Pensacola, Florida. There, as assistant engineer, he helped to supervise the repairs and improvements to Forts Pickens, McRee, and Barrancas between 1845 and 1848. In the latter year he was ordered to Texas, where he was placed in charge of an expedition to locate a route for military and commercial purposes between San Antonio and El Paso.[36]

Even before the United States army made plans to open a highway between San Antonio and El Paso, a number of citizens of the former city had attempted to do the same thing. Eager to divert the Santa Fé-Chihuahua trade from Missouri to Texas, the merchants of San Antonio, during the summer of 1848, raised about $800 to defray the expenses of an expedition to discover a route between their city and Chihuahua by way of El

35 Denson, *op. cit.*, 10-12; Cullum, *Biographical Register*, II, 42, 49, 85, 108, 112, 118, 140, 179, 191.

36 *Senate Ex. Docs.*, 29 cong., 1 sess., no. 1, pp. 259-260; *ibid.*, 29 cong., 2 sess., no. 1, pp. 127-128; *House Ex. Docs.*, 30 cong., 1 sess., no. 1, p. 265; Cullum, *Biographical Register*, II, 112.

Paso. John C. Hays, colonel of the Texas Rangers during the Mexican war and a surveyor by profession, was placed in charge of the party.[37] He asked Colonel Peter Hansborough Bell, of the Texas Rangers, for an escort of troops and received prompt assurance of support. Accordingly, on August 22, Bell ordered Captain Samuel Highsmith with a small detachment of Rangers to accompany the exploring expedition, instructing each man to conduct himself "in a manner creditable as a soldier, and like a gentleman."[38] Hays and a small party of citizens and Indian guides set out from San Antonio on August 27 and marched north to a military camp on the Llano river, where, on September 1, they joined Highsmith with thirty-five Rangers. Four days later the combined forces proceeded westward, and, after suffering intensely from lack of food and water, were forced to march into Mexico to prevent starvation, crossing the Río Grande from the southern part of the present Brewster county, Texas, on October 15. Moving a short distance up the west bank of the river, they reached the settlement of San Carlos in an emaciated condition. They apologized to the natives for trespassing upon Mexican territory but asserted that the need for food left them no alternative. After resting there a day and feasting upon bread and milk, they continued up the west bank of the Río Grande and arrived at Presidio del Norte on October 22, more than fifty days since the beginning of the expedition. Again expressing regrets for stepping upon Mexican soil, they recrossed

[37] *Texas Democrat* (Austin), Aug. 16, 30, 1848; *Texian Advocate* (Victoria), Aug. 31, 1848; Walter Prescott Webb, *The Texas Rangers* (Boston, 1935), 67-69, 94.

[38] Hays to Bell, Dec. 13, 1848, *Democratic Telegraph and Texas Register* (Houston), Dec. 28, 1848; Highsmith to Bell, Dec. 15, 1848, *Western Texian* (San Antonio), Jan. 12, 1849.

the river into the United States at that place and marched to a camping ground just beyond Fort Leaton, a trading post and ranch on the Río Grande about five or six miles southeast of Presidio del Norte. Too fatigued to complete the reconnaissance to El Paso, Hays decided to return home. Proceeding northeast to the Pecos river and thence southeast to San Antonio, he arrived at the latter place on December 10, 1848, after an absence of 107 days. A ball was given in his honor. Highsmith, who had separated from the rest of the party at Devils river on November 25, reached Camp Llano with his Rangers sixteen days later.[39] Hays reported to Colonel Bell on December 13 that the best route for a wagon road extended north from San Antonio to the San Sabá river, and thence northwest across the Pecos river to El Paso.[40] Highsmith, in a report to Bell dated December 15, expressed the same opinion, claiming that a "first rate road" could be established, "with the necessary requisites of wood, water and grass, over a fine and level country, unobstructed by mountains or any natural opposing difficulties." [41]

Although these accounts were somewhat optimistic, Major Jefferson Van Horne, of the Third infantry, then stationed at San Antonio, wrote a letter to the adjutant-general on December 19, 1848, accepting them at their face value and enclosing a copy of Hays's report.[42] The War Department, however, had already taken steps to

39 John S. Ford, Memoirs, 477, MS., University of Texas Library; Samuel A. Maverick, Chihuahua Expedition, 1848, MS., *ibid.;* Mary A. Maverick, Memoirs, 102-104, MS., *ibid.*; Hays to Bell, Dec. 13, 1848, *loc. cit.*; Highsmith to Bell, Dec. 15, 1848, *loc. cit.; Texas Democrat,* Sept. 20, 1848; *Weekly Herald* (New York City), Jan. 6, 1849.

40 Hays to Bell, Dec. 13, 1848, *loc. cit.*

41 Highsmith to Bell, Dec. 15, 1848, *loc. cit.*

42 Van Horne to Jones, Dec. 19, 1848, Letters Received, MSS., O.F.S., A.G.O.

open routes of communication in Texas. On December 10, William L. Marcy, Secretary of War, ordered Major-general William J. Worth to proceed to that state and explore the country along the left bank of the Río Grande, in order to discover whether there was a practicable route for "troops, munitions of war, etc.," between San Antonio and Santa Fé.[43] The major-general immediately went to Texas, where he became commander of the Eighth and Ninth military departments, with headquarters at San Antonio. Under the authority of Marcy's instructions, and with the reports of Hays and Highsmith before him, Worth, on February 9, 1849, issued an order directing Lieutenant William H. C. Whiting of the engineers and Lieutenant William F. Smith of the topographical engineers to proceed "with an escort" to reconnoiter the trail to Presidio del Norte followed by Hays, so as "to ascertain if there be a practicable and convenient route for military and commercial purposes between El Paso and the Gulf of Mexico, passing by or near Austin or San Antonio de Béxar in Texas." Failing to find a suitable wagon road by that route, they were to return by a more direct one via the Pecos and San Sabá rivers. Worth believed that a road to El Paso by way of Presidio del Norte, though somewhat farther, would be preferable to a more direct one, inasmuch as the former, running parallel to the frontier, would attract settlers to a region where they could be of great assistance in furnishing the contemplated military posts with necessary supplies.[44]

[43] Marcy to Worth, Dec. 10, 1848, Military Book, XXVIII, MSS., O.R.D., A.G.O.; Bender, "Opening Routes Across West Texas, 1848-1850," *Southwestern Historical Quarterly,* XXXVII, 119.

[44] Worth, Order No. 10, Feb. 9, 1849, Letters Received, MSS., Chief of Engineer's Office, War Department (hereafter cited as C.E.O.); Whiting to Totten, Feb. 10, 1849, *ibid.*

The expedition which was thus authorized left San Antonio on February 12, with Lieutenant Whiting in command, the escort consisting of nine men "well versed in frontier life and experienced as woodsmen and hunters." Whiting, who was only twenty-four years of age, had no previous experience with Indians or in prairie travel. The party also included Lieutenant Smith, Richard A. Howard the guide, two Mexicans, and Whiting's servant – fifteen men all-told.[45] Howard had been one of Hays's guides the year before.[46] Because of inclement weather and unruly mules, the expedition did not reach Fredericksburg until February 19, when another man was added to the escort. Leaving that German settlement on the evening of February 21, Whiting and his command proceeded northwest across the Llano river to the San Sabá, and thence southwest across the Pecos to the Río Grande. West of the Pecos, while passing through the Apache country, they barely escaped with their lives during a thrilling adventure with the Indians. On March 24 they reached Fort Leaton, near Presidio del Norte, and remained there several days to recruit their strength. They resumed the journey on March 29 and traveled up the east bank of the Río Grande, arriving at Ponce's Ranch, opposite El Paso del Norte, on April 12. There they rested for about a week, crossing the river to purchase supplies. On account of the scarcity of water between the San Sabá and Pecos rivers on their outgoing trip, Whiting and Smith decided to return home by a somewhat different route. Departing from Ponce's Ranch on April 19, they traveled down the east bank of the Río Grande for over one

45 *House Ex. Docs.*, 31 cong., 1 sess., no. 5, p. 281; *Senate Ex. Docs.*, 31 cong., 1 sess., no. 64, p. 4. When Whiting's journal is used as a source of information, the editor considers it unnecessary to refer to it in the footnotes.

46 Maverick, Chihuahua Expedition, 1848, MS., University of Texas Library.

hundred and twenty miles and then turned east to the Pecos river, whose course they followed to the southeast for about sixty miles. From that point they crossed over to Devils river, along which they moved to within a few miles of its mouth; and then journeying almost due east, they crossed Las Moras creek, the Nueces river, and the Río Seco, arriving at San Antonio in two parties on May 21 and 24 (or 25). Whiting reported that the object of the reconnaissance had been attained, as his return route could be made into a practicable wagon road for military and commercial purposes between San Antonio and El Paso.[47] The San Antonio *Western Texian* was very enthusiastic about the results of the survey: "They have explored a large section of country of which little has been hitherto known, and have succeeded in surveying an excellent wagon route from this place to El Paso, in nearly a direct line. . . The importance of this information, both for military and commercial purposes, can hardly be calculated. . . The popular impression heretofore has been that the face of the country was of such a character as to render a practicable wagon route on this side of the Río Grande totally out of the question. This delusion, however, has entirely vanished by the return of this party." [48]

The route located by Whiting and Smith on their return from El Paso to San Antonio was extensively traveled in later years. During the summer of 1849 a wagon road was constructed over it by Brevet Lieutenant-colonel Joseph E. Johnston, then chief topographical engineer of the Eighth military department.[49]

[47] *House Ex. Docs.*, 31 cong., 1 sess., no. 5, pp. 281-293; *Senate Ex. Docs.*, 31 cong., 1 sess., no. 64, pp. 4-7; *Nacogdoches Times* (Nacogdoches, Tex.), June 16, 1849; *Daily Missouri Republican*, July 7, 1849.

[48] *Western Texian,* May 24, 1849, in *Nacogdoches Times,* June 16, 1849.

[49] *Senate Ex. Docs.*, 31 cong., 1 sess., no. 64, pp. 26-29, 40-54.

Known as the lower, or southern, road, it was followed by California-bound argonauts in the same year. Before the day of the railroad it was used by the United States army, the overland mail and stage, Texas cattle drovers, and settlers migrating to New Mexico, Arizona, and California. Today it is followed in part by the Southern Pacific Company's tracks from San Antonio to El Paso, Texas.

Whiting continued in the engineer service during the fifties, superintending river and harbor improvements and the construction of fortifications in California, Texas, North and South Carolina, Georgia, and Florida.[50] In April, 1857, he married Miss Kate Davis Walker, daughter of Major John Walker, of Wilmington, North Carolina.[51] On February 20, 1861, at the outbreak of the Civil war, he resigned from the United States army and espoused the cause of the South. Very active throughout the conflict, he was considered one of the most able engineers in the Confederate service.[52] A biographer has written: "Below average height, Whiting was, nevertheless, of martial bearing, handsome, and sinewy. He was idolized by his troops, who affectionately called him 'Little Billy.'"[53] On January 15, 1865, during an attack by a federal fleet on Fort Fisher, near Wilmington, North Carolina, he was severely wounded; he was then taken as a prisoner of war to Fort Columbus, Governor's Island, New York, where

50 Cullum, *Biographical Register*, II, 112-113.

51 W. H. C. Whiting, "Diary of a March from El Paso to San Antonio" (Marcus J. Wright, ed.), *Publications of the Southern History Association*, VI, 284; James Sprunt, *Chronicles of the Cape Fear River, 1660-1916* (Raleigh, 1916), 121; Denson, *op. cit.*, 33.

52 Denson, *op. cit.*, 12-35; *New York Times*, Mar. 11, 1865.

53 Hanson, "William Henry Chase Whiting," *Dictionary of American Biography*, XX, 137.

he died of his injuries, March 10, 1865. He was buried in Oakdale Cemetery, Wilmington.[54]

François Xavier Aubry, whose diaries are published in the concluding chapter of this volume, was a Santa Fé trader, an explorer, and the most famous long-distance rider of his day. He was a French-canadian, having been born in Maskinongé, Quebec, December 4, 1824. His father was a farmer of small means, whose family had originally come from Abbéville, France; his mother's name was Magdeleine Lupien. He received an elementary education in his native town, but at the age of twelve or thirteen, because of financial necessity, left school to accept employment with a Maskinongé merchant, Monsieur Clément. Not long afterward he obtained a similar position with Monsieur Marchand in the near-by town of St. Jean, where he remained about three years. Meanwhile, his parents had been deprived of their small farm at a forced sale and had moved to the new settlement of St. Maurice, a short distance northwest of Three Rivers. Grieved to see his father and mother in straightened circumstances, François, in 1843, decided to migrate to the United States in order to aid them. "I must leave," he wrote, "not because I am forced there by any misconduct, but to earn more in the hope of helping my parents." [55]

On May 1, 1843, at the age of eighteen, François left home to seek his fortune in a foreign land. After traveling for some time, he came to St. Louis, then rapidly becoming the commercial metropolis of the West. There he was fortunate to secure employment as a clerk in the store of Lamoureaux and Blanchard, 14 South First street, dealers in dry goods, groceries, hardware,

[54] *Ibid.;* Denson, *op. cit.,* 35-56; Sprunt, *op. cit.,* 296.

[55] Joseph Tassé, *Les Canadiens de L'Ouest* (Montreal, 1878), II, 179-181.

queensware, boots and shoes, hats and caps, etc. The members of the firm were Moses Lamoureaux and Elzear Blanchard, who, like himself, were French-canadians, having settled in St. Louis a few years before.[56] But clerking in a store did not provide an adequate outlet for the tremendous energy of young François; so he finally decided to cross the prairies of the Far West and engage in the overland trade with Santa Fé. The exact date of his first journey has not been ascertained, but it is known that he made a trip in 1846. Obtaining credit from his former employers, Lamoureaux and Blanchard, he purchased goods suitable for the "commerce of the prairies" and arranged to have them freighted over the plains by Webb and Doan, Santa Fé traders. On May 9, 1846, traveling with the prairie schooners of this firm, he left Independence, Missouri, and reached Santa Fé after a short trip of about forty-five days. The traders had hastened westward because they had received news of the outbreak of war between the United States and Mexico and of the proposed expedition of Colonel Stephen W. Kearny to New Mexico. Early in July, according to the account books of Webb and Doan, Aubry paid them $117.60 for freight and $15.00 for board. After a short stay in Santa Fé, he disposed of his merchandise with profit, and on July 16, accompanied by a small party of traders, began his return trip to Missouri. Starting a practice which he continued on most subsequent travels, he kept a brief diary, noting the trains met, the number of wagons in each, the names of their proprietors, the conditions of travel, and other similar items. Aubry and his companions reached Inde-

[56] *Ibid.*, II, 181; *Daily Missouri Democrat* (St. Louis), Sept. 12, 1854; *Green's Saint Louis Directory for 1845*, pp. 23, 103; *St. Louis Business Directory for 1847*, p. 24.

pendence on August 17 and St. Louis five days later, bringing with them the proceeds of their venture – $100,000 in silver coin! Excerpts from his diary were published in the newspapers.[57]

During October, 1846, Aubry journeyed up the Mississippi river, visiting Galena, Illinois, Prairie du Chien, Wisconsin, and other towns, where he met a number of fellow Canadians. After remaining a few months in one place, where he did a fair business, he decided to return to St. Louis and engage permanently in the Santa Fé trade.[58] His craving for almost constant activity was already manifesting itself, a marked feature of his character which was to exert a dominating influence upon his meteoric career.

In his very first year as an established Santa Fé trader Aubry broke precedent by making two trips to New Mexico instead of the customary one. As early as April 17, 1847, he informed the citizens of St. Louis and vicinity, through the medium of the *Daily Missouri Republican,* that he was about to depart for Santa Fé, and that he would take along all letters and papers addressed to that city if left at the *Republican* office on or before April 20.[59] Since the only postal service to New Mexico was an irregular military express which ran between Fort Leavenworth and Santa Fé, his announcement was welcomed by many people who were desirous of communicating with that far-away territory. At the stated time he departed for the town of Kansas (now Kansas City, Missouri), whence, on April 27, his goods

[57] Webb & Doan, Daybook, 1846-1848, Webb MSS., New Haven, Conn.; *ibid.,* Cashbook, 1846-1847; *Täglicher Anzeiger des Westens* (St. Louis), Aug. 24, 1846; *St. Louis Daily New Era,* Aug. 24, 1846; *Daily Missouri Republican,* Aug. 24, 1846; *Southwest Historical Series,* I, 29.

[58] Tassé, *op. cit.,* II, 181-182.

[59] *Daily Missouri Republican,* Apr. 17, 1847.

were freighted by another trader; Aubry himself, with the mail, left western Missouri three days later. Arriving in Santa Fé early in July, he quickly disposed of his merchandise and by the twenty-eighth of that month was on his way to "the States," again carrying some mail. About August 31, in advance of his companions, he reached Independence after a journey of approximately thirty-four days, in the last four of which he traveled three hundred miles.[60] This fast ride for four days, during which he averaged seventy-five miles for every twenty-four hours, was Aubry's first burst of speed, a feat which may have given him confidence in his ability to cover even greater distances at an equally rapid pace. By September 6 he was in St. Louis, where, despite the lateness of the season, he purchased merchandise and made immediate preparations for a second trip. He left western Missouri on September 25, and, after a brush with Indians near the New Mexican settlements, reached Santa Fé on October 29, in advance of the cold and snow of the winter season. He at once inserted advertisements in the recently established newspaper, the *Santa Fé Republican,* describing himself as a wholesale dealer in dry goods, groceries, and liquors, and featuring gin, brandy, port wine, and Havana sugar. Aided by this publicity, he sold all of his goods by the latter part of December, when he was again ready to depart for Independence and St. Louis.[61]

Between December, 1847, and September, 1848, Aubry made three fast trips from Santa Fé to Independence, each of which was completed in record time. On November 27, 1847, about three weeks before beginning

60 *Weekly Reveille* (St. Louis), May 10, Sept. 13, 1847; *Daily Missouri Republican,* Sept. 6, 7, 1847.

61 *Daily Missouri Republican,* Sept. 7, 9, Dec. 20, 1847; *Santa Fé Republican* (Santa Fé, N.M.), Oct. 30, Nov. 13, 1847.

the first of these journeys, he announced in the *Santa Fé Republican* that he would leave for Missouri about Christmas day and would willingly take along all papers and letters destined for "the States." Before departing he declared his intention of covering the distance in eighteen days, a feat which the *Republican* was certain he could accomplish, because, it asserted, "he is one of Nature's most persevering children." [62] Leaving three days earlier than had been announced, he rode away from the capital early on the morning of December 22, accompanied by five men who expected to travel with him the whole distance. But he moved at such a fast pace that they dropped behind, the last one, his servant, becoming exhausted sixty miles west of Council Grove. Along the way he was attacked by a gang of Mexican robbers, was delayed a half day by Indians, experienced four days of severe cold weather, lost a half day because of a snowstorm, and killed three mules by hard riding. Dashing eastward during the last three days at the rate of one hundred miles for every twenty-four hours, he rode into Independence on January 5, 1848, just fourteen days from Santa Fé – four ahead of his schedule.[63] This was the quickest trip on record between these two points, surpassing the best previous time by ten and a half days.[64] A correspondent of the *Daily Missouri Republican* at Independence wrote on Janu-

[62] *Santa Fé Republican,* Nov. 27, Dec. 11, 25, 1847.

[63] *Ibid.,* Dec. 25, 1847, Jan. 1, Feb. 12, 1848; *Daily Missouri Republican,* Jan. 11, 18, 1848; *St. Louis Daily New Era,* Jan. 11, 1848; *Saint Louis Daily Union,* Jan. 12, 1848; *Weekly Reveille,* Jan. 17, 1848; *Jefferson Inquirer* (Jefferson City, Mo.), Jan. 22, 1848.

[64] Norris Colburn, a Santa Fé trader, left Santa Fé on August 3, 1846, and arrived at Independence the following August 27, making the trip in twenty-four and a half days. "This journey eclipses in speed any other ever performed between the two points," asserted the *Daily Missouri Republican* (Sept. 2, 1846).

ary 5: "Such a rate of travel is unprecedented in Prairie life, and speaks much in favor of Mr. A.'s indomitable courage and perseverance." [65]

Before Aubry made his second rapid journey from Santa Fé to Independence, he broke precedent by transporting goods from Missouri to New Mexico earlier in the year than had ever been done prior to that time. Following his first quick trip, he proceeded to St. Louis to purchase merchandise for the New Mexican market, reaching there on January 17, 1848.[66] Hoping to avert any more difficulties with the Indians along the Santa Fé trail, he wrote a letter to the War Department on February 16 requesting permission to borrow a six-pounder cannon and ammunition from the St. Louis Arsenal to protect his property *en route* to New Mexico.[67] But the Secretary of War, after consulting with the Ordnance Department, replied on March 7 that "in view of probable contingencies the loan requested cannot properly be authorized." [68] Leaving St. Louis for Independence before receiving this reply, Aubry made preparations for an early start across the plains. On March 11, when the *Western Expositor* of Independence announced his intention of departing from that point in a few days with a train of fifteen wagons, it remarked: "This is much earlier than usual to leave for the plains, but we have every confidence in the dauntless zeal and indomitable enterprise of Mr. Aubry to overcome every obstacle. He will start with corn enough to feed his animals as far as Fort Mann, by which time the grass will be sufficient to subsist them.

65 *Daily Missouri Republican*, Jan. 11, 1848.

66 *Ibid.*, Jan. 18, 1848.

67 Aubry to Marcy, Feb. 16, 1848, Index to Letters Received, No. 143, MSS., O.R.D., A.G.O.

68 Marcy to Aubry, Mar. 7, 1848, Military Book, XXVIII, *ibid.*

Such energy and perseverance deserve, as we hope it will meet with, the most consummate success."[69] Upon recording the news of his departure on March 16, the same newspaper once more expressed confidence in his ability to achieve his purpose: "He seems to have adopted, 'fortune favors the brave and the enterprising,' as his motto, and thus goes ahead. We shall not be at all surprised should he make three trips across the plains the present season. He incurs heavy expenses by starting so early, but will possess many advantages by reaching that market so much earlier than the more tardy. Many are disposed to predict the failure of his present adventure, but we have no fears."[70] Nor was the *Expositor's* confidence in Aubry misplaced, for on the morning of April 21, when most traders were still at St. Louis or Independence, he arrived in Santa Fé, his wagons following a few days later.[71] "He is a young trader," asserted the *Santa Fé Republican* on April 22, "has made but few trips to this country, but on all occasions has met with good success, and may he still continue, as no person is more deserving than he is. His wagons will be here in a few days, when our market will again be supplied, for he has a large and extensive stock of goods. Merchants who wish to replenish their stock, will do well to call on him, as he intends to sell out at wholesale, and return immediately to the States."

As a result of this publicity, as well as of some advertising, Aubry sold his stock of goods at wholesale before his wagons reached Santa Fé, and at once began to make arrangements for a second fast trip to Independence. The *Santa Fé Republican* congratulated him upon his

69 *Weekly Reveille,* Mar. 20, 1848; *Santa Fé Republican,* May 3, 1848.

70 *Jefferson Inquirer,* Mar. 25, 1848.

71 *Santa Fé Republican,* Apr. 22, May 3, 1848.

good fortune and added: "He is prompt in all his contracts and his word is as good as the State Bank of Missouri." [72] When he announced his intention of making the journey to Independence in the seemingly impossible time of ten days, the *Republican's* faith in him remained unshaken: "We do not doubt that he will; for if energy and perseverance can accomplish a feat of that kind, Aubry is the man." [73] Accompanied by six men, he left Santa Fé on May 19, galloping toward the Great Plains at high speed.[74] Three days and twenty-one hours afterward he passed Fort Mann.[75] His companions broke down from exhaustion before they had covered three hundred miles, and Aubry performed the rest of the trip alone. On the way he was attacked by Indians, walked about thirty or forty miles, killed three horses and two mules by fast riding, and traveled three days without provisions. But before sunrise on May 28 he rode into Independence, eight days and ten hours after leaving Santa Fé.[76] He had beaten his previous record by about five and a half days, having averaged nearly a hundred miles a day during the whole trip! "Such traveling is unexampled," recorded the *Daily Missouri Republican,*[77] and other newspapers were equally laudatory of his tremendous energy and unparalleled endurance. After purchasing merchandise in St. Louis for the third time in 1848, he transported it across the plains in thirty wagons, reaching Santa Fé

[72] *Ibid.*, May 3, 1848.

[73] *Ibid.*, May 13, 1848.

[74] *Ibid.*, May 23, 1848; *Daily Missouri Republican*, June 3, 1848.

[75] *Santa Fé Republican*, June 8, 1848.

[76] *St. Louis Daily New Era*, June 3, 1848; *Daily Missouri Republican*, June 3, 1848; *Jefferson Inquirer*, June 3, 1848; *Weekly Reveille*, June 5, 1848; *Missouri Statesman* (Columbia), June 9, 1848.

[77] June 3, 1848.

ahead of his teams on August 5.[78] Three days later the *Santa Fé Republican* undoubtedly expressed the opinion of many when it asserted: "This gentleman travels with a rapidity almost super-natural."

But Aubry's supreme riding effort was still to come. Because of the slow progress of his wagons, he concluded not to await their arrival but to intrust Joseph Mercure with the sale of his merchandise, which had already been advertised for disposal at "wholesale at reduced prices for Cash." Meanwhile, he devoted his energies to making preparations for a strenuous trip. This time he decided to travel alone. Likewise, he made no predictions about the number of days he expected to consume in reaching Independence, except that they would be fewer than on any previous attempt. By September 12 all arrangements had been made.[79] He was intrusted with a letter dated on the same day, written by some one in Santa Fé to the editors of the St. Louis *Reveille,* which stated: "Allow me to introduce to you the man to whom the telegraph is a fool. He leaves here this morning very early, and I write this letter the night before. I think he will be in St. Louis suddenly." [80] The *Santa Fé Republican* considered the occasion of sufficient importance to issue an extra edition on September 12, which was given to Aubry to carry to "the States." "Mr. F. X. Aubry," it asserted, "who has this moment left our office, and who has just informed us that he has to leave for the U. States in a few moments; therefore we strike off a few items of the latest dates and news

[78] *Daily Missouri Republican,* June 3, 1848; *Saint Louis Daily Union,* July 15, 1848; *Santa Fé Republican,* Aug. 8, 1848; G. Douglas Brewerton, *Wars of the Western Border* (New York, 1860), 123-124.

[79] *Santa Fé Republican,* Aug. 8, Sept. 12, 1848; *Saint Louis Daily Union,* Sept. 23, 1848.

[80] *Weekly Reveille,* Sept. 24, 1848.

about town etc., for the benefit of our exchanges in the States, as we are informed by him that his business compels him to reach the States as soon as he possibly can. We wish him a safe trip, and a safe return, as we would be happy to see our country settled by just such men as Mr. Aubry, – energy and perseverance is what we know is wanted in a new country like this. We would not be surprised to hear that Mr. A. has made the quickest trip this time that ever was made, as his anxiety for his business will induce him to travel at the utmost speed." [81]

Before dawn, on September 12, Aubry left Santa Fé in a swinging gallop on his solo ride to Independence.[82] "In the yellow morning sun and under the slant rays of autumn noon" he raced down the mountains toward the Great Plains. Dashing eastward at a terrific pace, he obtained fresh horses from passing wagon trains and at Fort Mann, Council Grove, and other places where he had stationed them. A yellow mare named "Dolly," his favorite mount, carried him about two hundred miles in twenty-six hours. He traveled constantly, day and night, listening to the monotonous creaking of the leather of his dragoon saddle. For nearly six hundred miles the trail was muddy, and for twenty-four consecutive hours he rode through a driving rain. On his journey he broke down six horses, walked twenty miles, slept only a few hours, and ate but six meals. He swam most streams, which were swollen by heavy rains. On Sunday night, September 17, "his foaming horse half ran, half staggered" into Independence. He had made the trip in only five days and sixteen hours, about two

81 *Santa Fé Republican—Extra,* Sept. 12, 1848, in *Saint Louis Daily Union,* Sept. 23, 1848.

82 *Santa Fé Republican,* Sept. 12, 1848; *Weekly Reveille,* Sept. 24, 1848; *Daily Missouri Republican,* Sept. 23, 1848.

and a half days less than his previous record. He had traversed about eight hundred miles of plains and mountains at an average rate of one hundred and forty miles a day.[83]

When he stopped in front of the Noland House, he was so exhausted that he had to be helped from his saddle and carried into the hotel. After consuming a hasty meal of ham, eggs, and coffee, he went to bed, leaving instructions with the proprietor to wake him after three hours. But he was permitted to sleep for six hours before he was aroused. "He was rather wrathy," wrote an eyewitness, "telling them he preferred taking his food and rest in broken doses, and that they were working against him with their intended kindness." [84] He immediately boarded a Missouri river steamer then at Independence landing and left for St. Louis, a trip of four hundred miles by water. On the night of September 21, near St. Charles, the boat was brought to a standstill by fog, a delay that exasperated Aubry. Reaching the town on the following day, he went ashore and took a buggy for St. Louis. Arriving there that night,[85] ten days from Santa Fé, he immediately went to the office of the *Daily Missouri Republican* and recounted the details of his fast ride. Next day the editor wrote: "Yesterday evening, we were very much surprised to see in our sanctum Mr. F. X. Aubrey, direct from Santa Fé. If an apparition had sprung up, it would not have as-

[83] Spruce M. Baird to Governor George T. Wood, Dec. 18, 1848, Santa Fé Papers, MSS., Texas State Library, Austin; *Daily Missouri Republican,* Sept. 23, 1848, July 8, 1850; *Saint Louis Daily Union,* Sept. 23, 1848; *Weekly Reveille,* Sept. 24, Oct. 1, 1848; *Missouri Statesman,* Sept. 29, 1848; *Jefferson Inquirer,* Sept. 30, 1848; *Odessa Democrat* (Odessa, Mo.), Feb. 23, 1917; Alexander Majors, *Seventy Years on the Frontier* (Chicago and New York, 1893), 185-186; J. Frank Dobie, "The Saga of the Saddle," *Southwest Review,* XIII, 130-133.

[84] *Odessa Democrat,* Feb. 23, 1917.

[85] *Daily Missouri Republican,* Sept. 23, 1848.

tonished us more, for it was but the other day we bade him good by on his way out, and here he is again, in less time than is usually allowed to make the trip out or in, not saying any thing of the attention to business and incidental delays." [86]

Aubry's spectacular dash from Santa Fé to Independence was widely acclaimed by his contemporaries as a marvelous performance, and has since been adjudged the fastest and most remarkable long-distance ride on record. Under the headlines "Unprecedented Feat," "Most Extraordinary Trip," and "Extraordinary Feat," the newspapers of the day described the details of the journey. "The performance seems almost incredible," asserted the *Daily Missouri Republican*.[87] The *Weekly Reveille* stated: "The extraordinary feat of this gentleman . . . transcends the history of travelling." [88] Alexander Majors, who knew Aubry and had extensive experience with horses and riders on the frontier, wrote at a later time: "The man who attempted to ride 800 miles in the time he did took his life in his hands. There is perhaps not one man in a million who could have lived to finish such a journey." [89] A modern scholar of the Southwest, who knows how to write as well as to ride, has stated: "Not one man in a hundred thousand could ride like Aubry. The strain of hard horseback riding is terrific. Buffalo Bill knew whereof he was speaking when he declared that 'fifteen miles an hour on horseback would in a short time shake any man all to pieces.' " [90]

Leaving St. Louis for Santa Fé on September 26,

86 *Ibid.*

87 *Ibid.*

88 *Weekly Reveille*, Sept. 24, 1848.

89 Majors, *op. cit.*, 186.

90 Dobie, *loc. cit.*, 135.

1848, Aubry continued in the Missouri-New Mexico trade but made no more record rides between the two points.[91] In 1849 and 1850 he extended the scope of his mercantile activities to Chihuahua, Mexico, and San Antonio, Texas. During the spring and summer of the former year he traveled from Santa Fé to Chihuahua and return on a successful trading venture.[92] On December 1, 1849, after receiving a consignment of goods from Missouri, he left Santa Fé for Texas with twenty large wagons and about two hundred and fifty mules. He passed through El Paso del Norte and over the trail located by Whiting and Smith, reaching San Antonio in advance of his wagons on January 12, 1850. Commenting most favorably upon the excellence of the road he had traversed, he asserted that it was the best route for the Santa Fé Mail, that traders who used it could supply New Mexico with merchandise at lower prices than could those who purchased goods in St. Louis and Independence, that it was less liable to Indian attacks than the Santa Fé trail, and that it was the best way for the Chihuahua trade.[93] The arrival of another merchant from El Paso at about the same time caused a citizen of San Antonio to boast: "The whole Santa Fé trade must come this way; it cannot be helped. These two large traders are but the forerunners of what is to come." [94] On February 15, Aubry departed from Victoria, Texas, and twelve days later left San Antonio with eighteen wagons "loaded with merchandise for the Chihuahua market." He encountered a severe snow-

[91] *Daily Missouri Republican*, Sept. 26, Nov. 14, 23, 1848, Feb. 13, 1849.

[92] Webb & Doan, Daybook, 1848-1849, Webb MSS.; *ibid.*, Ledgerbook, 1848-1849; Webb, Daybook, 1849-1850, Webb MSS.; *Daily Missouri Republican*, May 17, Aug. 25, 1849; *Saint Louis Daily Union*, May 17, 1849.

[93] *Democratic Telegraph and Texas Register*, Jan. 31, 1850; *Daily Missouri Republican*, Mar. 13, 1850.

[94] *Democratic Telegraph and Texas Register*, Jan. 31, 1850.

storm beyond the Pecos, losing forty mules in one night. By April 27 he was in El Paso.[95] Whether he proceeded to Chihuahua before or after he reached El Paso has not been ascertained, but it is known that he left the latter place on June 1, 1850, and was back in Santa Fé eleven days later.[96] During the fall he made another journey from Santa Fé to Texas, and by that time additional experience and probably financial pressure from Missouri forced him to admit the fallacy of his earlier predictions. Writing from San Antonio on November 23, 1850, he informed the *Daily Missouri Republican:* "The Indians often come within a few miles of this place, to remind the citizens that they are still in the wild country. Several depredations have recently been committed within fifteen miles of this place. It is likely that the subsistence stores for the posts at El Paso, Doña Ana, and all those south of the Jornada del Muerto, will be brought from Missouri. The freight would cost the Government at least fifty per cent less. With the Government it is a question of dollars and cents, and there is no doubt that the Quartermaster General will discover that the Missouri route is the best, safest, and cheapest." [97]

Aubry never went to Texas again. In 1851 and 1852 he confined his mercantile activities to the trade between Missouri and New Mexico, and during that time attempted to discover new routes, or cut-offs, for parts of the Santa Fé trail. Most of his exploring trips were devoted to an examination of the country between the Cimarrón and Arkansas rivers, in order to lay out a new road which would shorten the Santa Fé trail and

95 *Ibid.*, June 13, 1850; *Daily Missouri Republican,* Mar. 14, 1850; *Saint Louis Daily Union,* June 20, 1850.

96 *Daily Missouri Republican,* July 8, 1850.

97 *Ibid.*, Dec. 14, 1850.

eliminate the terrible hardships of crossing the Cimarrón *jornada*. Between April, 1851, and October, 1852, he traversed that district nine times with wagons loaded with merchandise. On May 2, 1851, when he reached the Arkansas river after the first of these explorations, his animals had gone for two days and his men one day without water; they had traveled "through sand and a hot sun, and had to drink the blood of the Antelope," according to a summary of Aubry's journal.[98] Upon arriving in St. Louis he gave an account of his experiences to a friend, who later wrote: "He closed his narration to me, quietly saying, what my own journeyings in the wild West had taught me: 'There is no suffering like that for water.' "[99] During another exploring trip – in January, 1852 – he traveled through deep snow and in intense cold, the thermometer registering twenty degrees below zero on two successive nights. "He is certainly the most daring traveler on the prairies," declared the *Daily Missouri Republican* after hearing about this journey. "No season or weather stops him."[100] Despite numerous hardships, he eventually located a route which became known as "Aubry's trail." Leaving the Santa Fé trail two miles northeast of Cold spring, a short distance northwest of the present Boise City, Cimarrón county, Oklahoma, it extended northeast across the Cimarrón river into the present Baca county, Colorado, thence in the same direction along Bear creek into the present Stanton county, Kansas, and thence north to the Arkansas river, crossing it near the boundary line between the present Kearny and Hamilton

98 *Ibid.*, May 19, 1851.

99 *Saint Louis Daily Evening News*, Sept. 27, 1854. See also Max Greene, *The Kansas Region* (New York, 1856), 50-52.

100 *Daily Missouri Republican*, Feb. 16, 1852.

counties, Kansas.[101] That place was called "Aubry's crossing," to distinguish it from the Cimarrón, or Arkansas, crossing, fifty-eight miles farther east. In August, 1852, when the Santa Fé Mail traveled Aubry's trail and pronounced it excellent, the *Occidental Messenger* of Independence stated: "Aubry deserves praise for marking it out so successfully, and in spite of all opposition and danger opening up a way so useful to all who cross the plains. We sincerely trust that the honor so justly merited will not be given to another." [102] Although occasionally used by traders, travelers, the Santa Fé Mail, and United States troops, Aubry's trail never superseded the regular Cimarrón route of the Santa Fé trail.

But Aubry grew weary of trading and exploring between Missouri and New Mexico, and soon turned his face to the Far West to engage in a new type of activity. Between November, 1852, and August, 1854, he made two journeys from Santa Fé to San Francisco and return, driving New Mexican sheep westward to the California market, and exploring the country for possible railroad and wagon routes on his eastward trips. Continuing the practice which he had started some years before, he combined his private business with a project of public interest.

Aubry left Santa Fé on the first of these journeys, November 16, 1852, taking along 10 large wagons, approximately 3,500 sheep, about 100 mules, and a number of horses.[103] Four days afterward the *Santa Fé*

101 *Ibid.*, May 18, 1852.

102 *Occidental Messenger*, Aug. 28, 1852, in *Daily St. Louis Intelligencer*, Sept. 6, 1852.

103 *Santa Fé Gazette* (Santa Fé, N.M.), Nov. 20, 1852; *San Francisco Daily Herald*, Feb. 25, 1853; *Daily Alta California* (San Francisco), Mar. 31, 1853; *Daily Missouri Republican*, July 4, 1853.

Gazette stated: "He expects, if successful, to return early in the spring, with two or three wagons, in the attempt to explore a Rail Road track. Should he find a good road, he informs us he will not hereafter be a Santa Fé, but a California trader. Success attend him." [104] Aubry wrote in his journal: "I set out, in the first place, upon this journey simply to gratify my own curiosity as to the practicability of one of the much talked-of routes for the contemplated Atlantic and Pacific railroad." At that time the desirability of constructing a transcontinental railroad was a subject of discussion in all parts of the country, although congress did not authorize the survey of all available routes until almost four months later. Aubry moved south along the Río Grande until he reached the beginning of Cooke's wagon road, which he followed to a point twelve miles beyond the Ojo de Vaca. There, pioneering a new trail, he left the road and took a west southwest course directly to Tucson, a cut-off that saved him about ten days and one hundred and fifty miles of travel.[105] At Tucson he again picked up Cooke's trail and followed it to the Colorado river, whence, on February 10, 1853, he wrote a brief description of his journey to that point: "We traveled a long and very bad road and crossed several *jornadas,* or deserts, of one hundred miles in length, without water, and of course suffered much. It is not probable we shall retain any pleasant recollections of this trip; and still we had good luck, for we have only lost one of the flock since we left the Del Norte." [106] Early in March he reached Los Angeles and on the fifteenth of the same month left for San Francisco,

[104] *Santa Fé Gazette,* Nov. 20, 1852.

[105] *Daily Missouri Republican,* Jan. 21, Mar. 29, Apr. 18, Sept. 26, 1854; *Daily Alta California,* Mar. 6, 1854.

[106] *Daily Missouri Republican,* Mar. 25, 1853.

where he found a ready market for his stock. There he announced his intention of exploring a route for a railroad along the thirty-fifth parallel, and obtained information about the various passes of the Sierra Nevada from Vincent Haler, the leader of Frémont's disastrous winter expedition of 1848-1849.[107] On June 20, 1853, he departed for Stockton, whence, six days later, at the head of a party of twenty men with thirty pack animals, he started his return journey.[108] At Kern river early in July he met Alexander Godey, a famous mountain man and guide of Frémont, who gave him additional information about his proposed route.[109] He crossed the Sierra Nevada by way of the Tejón pass, near the southern boundary of the present Kern county, California. Leaving the pass on July 11, Aubry journeyed east across the Mojave desert and along the Mojave river, and thence northeast to the Colorado river, crossing it a short distance south of the present Boulder Dam. From that point he traveled southeast and east, passing through what are now Mojave, Yavapai, Coconino, Navajo, and Apache counties, Arizona, and thence east to Zuñi and Albuquerque, arriving at the latter place by September 10. "I am satisfied that a railroad may be run almost mathematically direct from Zuñi to the Colorado, and from thence to the Tejón pass in California," he reported.[110] Although traversed in part by trappers before and immediately after the Mexican war, and for some distance by Captain Lorenzo Sitgreaves in 1851, the thirty-fifth parallel route was first

107 *Daily Alta California*, Mar. 31, 1853; *Santa Fé Weekly Gazette*, May 21, 1853; *Daily Missouri Republican*, July 4, Aug. 7, 1853.

108 *Daily St. Louis Intelligencer*, Aug. 9, 1853; *Daily Missouri Republican*, Aug. 7, 1853.

109 *Daily Missouri Republican*, Sept. 16, 1853.

110 *Santa Fé Weekly Gazette*, Sept. 24, 1853.

examined in its entirety from California to New Mexico by François Xavier Aubry.

Aubry returned to Santa Fé on September 14, 1853, and was soon busy making preparations for another journey to San Francisco.[111] Indeed, he had already begun to plan a second expedition before he left California, for on May 4, when at San José, he had written to Manuel Álvarez of Santa Fé requesting that merchant to order several thousand sheep for his next drive to the Pacific coast. "I shall take money to New Mexico to pay for all the sheep I may wish to buy," he assured Álvarez.[112] Since arrangements for the purchase of much of his stock had been made previous to his return, Aubry was soon able to gather together about 14,000 head. A few prominent men of Santa Fé decided to accompany him and drive sheep to California, thus making the total number about 50,000. He and his fellow drovers left Santa Fé about October 10 and proceeded down the Río Grande to Albuquerque.[113] There they met Lieutenant Amiel W. Whipple, of the topographical engineers, who was in charge of an official government expedition to explore the country near the thirty-fifth parallel for a railroad route. The lieutenant was busy getting as much information as he could about the region through which he expected to travel and naturally sought an interview with Aubry's party. Whipple wrote: "Mr. Tully, a companion of Mr. Aubry in his recent trip from California, has given a description of the country over which he passed. Mr. Aubry himself has since confirmed the statements of his friend, caution-

[111] *Daily Missouri Republican,* Oct. 18, 1853.

[112] Aubry to Álvarez, May 4, 1853, Álvarez MSS., Historical Society of New Mexico.

[113] *Santa Fé Weekly Gazette,* Sept. 24, 1853; *Daily Alta California,* Jan. 25, 1854; *Daily Missouri Republican,* Mar. 29, Apr. 18, 1854.

ing us to avoid his trail as unsuitable for our operations."[114] Mr. Baldwin Möllhausen, topographer and artist of Whipple's expedition, recorded in his diary: "The only one whose information seemed at all authentic was a certain Aubry, who had been in California with his flocks of sheep and had several times come into serious conflict with the Club Indians. All the reports could not be called very encouraging for the object of our journey, yet, as a result of the varied accounts, we anticipated all the more new and interesting experiences that we would find an opportunity to have in the western regions."[115] It may be that Aubry was willing to recommend his route as an excellent one for a railroad but considered it very undesirable for a party of explorers. Nevertheless, Whipple took along a copy of Aubry's journal.[116]

Following the conference with Lieutenant Whipple, Aubry and his companions departed from Albuquerque and traveled his route of the previous year, arriving at Los Angeles on January 10, 1854. Shortly afterward they journeyed to San Francisco.[117] There he announced that the object of his return trip would be to make a wagon road from California to New Mexico along or near the thirty-fifth parallel. On July 1 he left for San José, whence, five days later he began his journey to New Mexico in command of a party of approximately sixty men, about eleven of whom had been with him the year before. He took along a wagon to make a trail

114 *House Ex. Docs.*, 33 cong., 2 sess., no. 91, vol. III, p. 48.

115 Baldwin Möllhausen, *Wanderungen durch die Prairien und Wüsten des Westlichen Nordamerika von Mississippi nach den Küsten der Südsee* (Leipzig, 1860), 235.

116 *House Ex. Docs.*, 33 cong., 2 sess., no. 91, vol. III, p. 106.

117 *Daily Missouri Republican*, Apr. 18, 1854; *Daily Alta California*, Jan. 25, 1854.

and a boat with which to cross the Colorado.[118] He traveled his route of 1853 until he crossed the Colorado, when he proceeded a little south of it for some distance. Then, occasionally crossing his own trail, as well as Whipple's, he journeyed eastward through the same general region he had already explored and arrived at Santa Fé on August 18, 1854, forty-three days after his departure from San José. Aubry was still of the opinion that the thirty-fifth parallel route was the best one for a railroad, although he now recommended that it be constructed by the way of Cañon de las Uvas instead of over the Tejón pass. He also believed that the trail he had just traveled was practicable for a wagon road.[119] Today the routes he pioneered are followed in a general way by the Atchison, Topeka and Santa Fé Railway from Albuquerque, New Mexico, to Bakersfield, California.[120]

118 *San Francisco Daily Herald,* July 1, 1854; *Daily Alta California,* July 3, 1854; *Daily Missouri Republican,* July 15, 1854.

119 *Daily Missouri Republican,* Sept. 26, Nov. 4, 1854. Between August 27 and October 18, 1857, Lieutenant Edward F. Beale, who used one of Aubry's men as a guide, surveyed a wagon road from Fort Defiance to the Colorado river. In his report to the Secretary of War on April 26, 1858, he stated: "I presume there can be no further question as to the practicability of the country near the thirty-fifth parallel for a wagon road, since Aubrey, Whipple, and myself have all travelled it successfully with wagons, neither of us in precisely the same line, and yet through very much of the same country." *Uncle Sam's Camels* (Lewis Burt Lesley, ed., Cambridge, 1929), 97-98, 142, 186-261.

120 The following references to Aubry's career, none of which is very reliable, have not been cited in the footnotes of the present volume: Albert D. Richardson, *Beyond the Mississippi* (Hartford, 1867), 331; *Memoirs of General William T. Sherman* (New York, 1875), I, 89-90; Samuel Woodworth Cozzens, *The Marvellous Country* (Boston, 1876), 201; James Lee Humfreville, *Twenty Years Among Our Hostile Indians* (New York, 1899), 425-426; Frank A. Root and William E. Connelley, *The Overland Stage to California* (Topeka, 1901), 54, 425; William Elsey Connelley, *Doniphan's Expedition* (Topeka, 1907), 628-629; Thomas Edwin Farish, *History of Arizona* (Phoenix, 1915), I, 99-102; R. M. Wright, "Personal Reminiscences of Frontier Life in Southwest Kansas," *Kansas State Historical Society Collections,*

Aubry had no sooner reached Santa Fé than he became involved in an altercation that brought his career to a sudden end. Shortly after two o'clock on the afternoon of Friday, August 18, he rode into the plaza, very tired after his strenuous journey. He immediately went to the store of his friends, Joseph and Henry Mercure, where he asked for a glass of water and ordered a toddy. When the news spread that he had returned from California, a number of citizens hastened to greet him. Among them was Richard H. Weightman, a veteran of the Mexican war and a practicing attorney, who had previously aroused Aubry's ire by vigorously advocating the thirty-second parallel route for a railroad. Upon entering the store he found Aubry drinking a toddy and jokingly remarked, "Hello, Aubry, are you at that yet! When I last saw you at Albuquerque, you were at it." Aubry placed his glass upon the counter, shook hands with Weightman, and invited him to have a drink. Weightman declined and took a seat upon the counter about five feet away.[121] According to the *Santa Fé Weekly Gazette,*[122] "a general conversation then took place between them about the journey of Mr. Aubrey from California, which lasted a minute or two, when Aubrey began to talk about the newspaper called *El Amigo del Pais,* which Weightman had formerly edited

VII, 51; William R. Bernard, "Westport and the Santa Fé Trade," *ibid.,* IX, 561-562; Walker D. Wyman, "F. X. Aubry: Santa Fé Freighter, Pathfinder, and Explorer," *New Mexico Historical Review,* VII, 1-11; Frank C. Lockwood, "Arizona Pioneers: 1854 to 1864," *Arizona Historical Review,* V, 327-332.

121 *Daily Missouri Republican,* Sept. 10, 13, 21, 26, 28, Oct. 28, 1854; *Daily Missouri Democrat,* Sept. 12, 1854; Ralph Emerson Twitchell, *Leading Facts of New Mexican History* (Cedar Rapids, 1912), II, 306-307.

122 The *Gazette* stated: "The facts within our knowledge we obtained from the witnesses to the transaction, as they related them, under oath, before His Honor Judge Davenport, who sat as the committing magistrate, and therefore may be relied on." *Santa Fé Weekly Gazette,* in *Daily Missouri Republican,* Sept. 26, 1854.

in Albuquerque. He asked Weightman what had become of his paper, who replied that it had died for want of subscribers. Aubrey then said that any such lying paper ought to die. Weightman asked him what he alluded to, when Aubrey replied and said: 'Last fall you asked me for information about my trip, which I gave you, and you afterwards abused me.' Weightman replied that it was not so; whereupon Aubrey brought his fist down upon the counter with considerable force and repeated, 'I say it is so.' Weightman then got off the counter, and took in his right hand a tumbler of about one-third full of liquor and water, which was standing by him, and pitched the contents into the face of Mr. Aubrey; he (Weightman) then put the tumbler back upon the counter, stepped back a pace or two, and placed his hand upon his belt. When Aubrey received the contents of the glass in his face, he immediately drew a five shooter from his left side, and as he brought it up in front of him, one barrel prematurely discharged (supposed while he was cocking it) before it was on a level with Weightman's person, and the bullet went into the ceiling. When Weightman saw Aubrey draw his pistol, he drew a Bowie knife he wore in his belt; they clinched, and before Aubrey had time to bring his pistol down and fire a second time, Weightman stabbed him in the abdomen."[123] Bystanders immediately separated them, but Aubry collapsed in the arms of a friend. "Let me bleed," were the only words he was heard to utter. Ten minutes later he was dead.[124]

Great excitement prevailed throughout the city after this tragedy. On the following afternoon burial services were held for Aubry in the parochial church, and his

---

123 *Ibid.*

124 *Ibid.; Daily Missouri Republican,* Oct. 28, 1854.

body "was followed to the grave by a large concourse of friends." Meanwhile, Weightman had given himself up to the United States marshal, who put him in the *calabozo*. The feeling against him was so intense that a guard had to be stationed around his place of confinement. He was indicted for murder, but his trial did not occur until September 21, when the excitement had subsided. The jury then brought in a verdict of "not guilty," since the defendant had "committed such an act in defense of his person." [125]

Aubry was widely and favorably known in his day. The *Daily Missouri Republican* described him as "the most intrepid traveller the world has ever produced." [126] He was "the most energetic and indefatigable trader connected with the Santa Fé trade," according to the *St. Louis Daily New Era*.[127] Among the sobriquets given him by the newspapers were: Skimmer of the Plains, Prairie Telegraph, Lightning Traveler, Great Plains Courier, The Telegraph, Little Aubry, Fleet Traveler of the Prairie, and Intrepid Aubry. The Indians called him "White Cloud." [128] As for his personal appearance, several men who knew him have left us good descriptions. Alexander Majors wrote: "Mr. Aubry was a Canadian Frenchman of low stature, short limbs, built, to use a homely simile, like a jack-screw." [129] The English traveler, George D. Brewerton, stated: " 'Little

125 *Daily Missouri Democrat*, Sept. 26, 1854; *Daily Missouri Republican*, Sept. 26, 28, Oct. 28, 1854; Twitchell, *Leading Facts of New Mexican History*, II, 305-309.

126 *Daily Missouri Republican*, Sept. 10, 1854.

127 June 3, 1848.

128 *Daily Missouri Republican*, Mar. 30, 1849, Feb. 2, Aug. 31, 1852, Sept. 10, 21, 1854; *Santa Fé Republican*, Aug. 8, 1848; *Saint Louis Daily Morning Union*, May 26, 1851; *Saint Louis Daily Evening News*, Sept. 11, 1854; George D. Brewerton, "In the Buffalo Country," *Harper's New Monthly Magazine*, XXV, 456.

129 Majors, *op. cit.*, 186.

Aubry,' like my friend Kit Carson . . . is . . . a man of medium stature and slender proportions, with keen eyes, iron nerve, great resolution, and indomitable perseverance."[130] A Missouri river steamer completed in April, 1853, was named after him,[131] as were Aubry Cliffs and Aubry Valley, Arizona, Fort Aubry, Kansas, and towns in Missouri, Oklahoma, and Texas. Of the various encomiums published at the time of his death, the one that appeared in the *Daily Missouri Democrat* came closest to being the historian's estimate: "His explorations have added largely to our knowledge of the country, for which he should be gratefully remembered; while his intrepid conduct, in the midst of constant perils, challenge our highest admiration. Monuments have been raised to men of inferior character and less renown. Ought not St. Louis to pay such a tribute of respect to his memory?"[132]

130 Brewerton, *loc. cit.*

131 *Daily Missouri Republican,* Jan. 26, Apr. 18, 19, 1853.

132 *Daily Missouri Democrat,* Sept. 12, 1854.

COOKE'S JOURNAL OF THE MARCH OF THE MORMON BATTALION, 1846-1847

COOKE'S JOURNAL OF THE MARCH OF THE MORMON BATTALION, 1846-1847

SANTA FÉ, OCTOBER 13, 1846.[133] The rear of the battalion arrived last evening, and this morning I assumed command; it is four hundred and eighty-six strong; but about sixty are invalids, or unfit for service, and for much of the march from Fort Leavenworth have been transported in wagons. Captain Higgins [134] and a small detachment were sent from the crossing of the Arkansas in charge of a large number of women and children, who are to winter at a temporary settlement of the Mormons at Pueblo, near its headwaters; nevertheless, there are here twenty-five women and many children. Colonel Doniphan, commanding in New Mexico, has ordered those pronounced by the surgeons unfit for the march to California to be sent to winter at Pueblo; and as I believe women would be exposed to great hardships on my exploring winter march (beside being a serious encumbrance) and many of them being willing, I have

---

133 Cooke's journal is published from the manuscript copy in the old files section of the adjutant-general's office, because the printed document (*Senate Ex. Docs.*, 31 cong., special sess., no. 2, pp. 1-85) is not an accurate reproduction of the original. The manuscript is entitled: "Journal of the march of the Mormon Battalion of infantry volunteers under the command Lieut. Col. P. St. Geo. Cooke, also captain of dragoons, from Santa Fé N.M. to San Diego, Cal. – kept by himself by direction of the comd'g. General Army of the West." Cooke's report to General Kearny, dated San Luis Rey, California, February 5, 1847, was a brief summary of his journal. *House Ex. Docs.*, 30 cong., 1 sess., no. 41, pp. 551-562.

134 Captain Nelson Higgins, of company D. Golder, Bailey, and Smith, *op. cit.*, 285.

ordered all the laundresses to accompany the detachment for the Arkansas. Captain Brown [135] will command it, and it will consist of First Lieutenant Luddington [136] and eighty-six rank and file, embracing only a few efficient men – husbands of the twenty laundresses.[137] Captain Higgins was ordered to join the battalion here with his party.

Contrary to the general's expectation, the paymasters have brought out so little specie that a payment of troops cannot be made. In consequence Captain Hudson's [138] new company, ordered to join my command, cannot mount themselves, and it has been broken up by order of Colonel Doniphan. Another consequence is that the quartermaster's department remains without a dollar and can with great difficulty furnish transportation for my reduced numbers. The mules that came

135 Captain James Brown, of company C. *Ibid.*, 284.

136 Lieutenant Elam Luddington, of company B. *Ibid.*, 282.

137 The detachment reached Pueblo on November 17, 1846, and during the spring and summer of 1847, together with other Mormons who had arrived there, journeyed to the Great Salt Lake. B. H. Roberts, *The Mormon Battalion* (Salt Lake City, 1919), 32-33.

138 Captain Thomas B. Hudson, of St. Louis, formerly in command of company E (Laclede Rangers), First regiment of Missouri mounted volunteers. On September 18, 1846, Kearny, before leaving Santa Fé for California, issued the following order: "Capt. Hudson of the Laclede Rangers, will select from his own co. such men as he may think well fitted for the purpose, & with the consent of Col. Doniphan & Maj. Clark, of the Mo. Mounted Vols. & Horse Artillery, will receive from those corps, Volunteers, to make up his co. to 70 or 80, & will hold them in readiness to join Capt. Allen's Battalion of Infantry, on its arrival at this place, & to accompany it to California." This new company was called the "California Rangers." John T. Hughes asserted that it was dissolved by Colonel Doniphan "as soon as he learned that California was in the hands of the Americans"; but Cooke maintained that it was broken up because the men, having received no pay, could not mount themselves, and "the quartermaster's department, which could scarcely command a dollar, could hardly have furnished the transportation." Kearny, Order No. 26, Sept. 18, 1846, Letters Received, MSS., O.F.S., A.G.O.; John T. Hughes, *Doniphan's Expedition* (Cincinnati, 1848), 141; *House Ex. Docs.*, 30 cong., 1 sess., no. 41, p. 551.

with the battalion are utterly broken down. Those that have been procured here are quite unfit for such an expedition, and they deteriorate every hour for want of food. Beyond a temporary aid of ox wagons, the assistant quartermaster only calculates to furnish transportation for a pound and a half per day for each man for sixty days. The rations should amount nearly to that; and thus officers' baggage, the company equipage, ammunition, tools, packsaddles, sick men, etc., etc., are by no means sufficiently estimated for – but particularly if I shall be forced to leave the wagons. I have just heard that the general's expedition has left theirs, and in common prudence have provided packsaddles.

On the sixteenth and seventeenth [of] October the battalion was paid on the August rolls by Major Cloud,[139] who accompanies me; the payment was made in checks, under a special agreement and arrangement. The night of the sixteenth salt pork arrived – there had been none in Santa Fé for two weeks. On the seventeenth my beef cattle (previously contracted for) and packsaddles were received. On the eighteenth the issue to companies of sixty days' rations, packing, etc., were nearly completed. I have reluctantly consented to take five women – the wives of officers and sergeants. They are transported and provisioned at their own expense.

OCTOBER 19. I sent the battalion by companies to Agua Fria, about six miles – its aggregate strength three hundred and ninety-seven. Second Lieutenant Gully's[140] resignation has been accepted by Colonel

139 Jeremiah H. Cloud, of Missouri, was appointed additional paymaster of volunteers, July 2, 1846. He died on August 4, 1847. Heitman, *Historical Register*, I, 311.

140 On August 6, 1846, Lieutenant Samuel L. Gully, then at Fort Leavenworth, was appointed assistant quartermaster to the Mormon Battalion by Lieutenant-colonel Allen. He served in that capacity until his arrival in Santa

Doniphan. First Lieutenant A. J. Smith [141] and Brevet Second Lieutenant George Stoneman,[142] of the First dragoons, whose companies have marched for California, have joined my command. The first will perform the duties of commissary of subsistence; and he has eight hundred dollars for the purchase of beeves and sheep. Lieutenant Stoneman will act as assistant quartermaster. Assistant Surgeon George Sanderson,[143] of Mis-

Fé, when he was removed by Cooke. On October 18, 1846, Captain Jefferson Hunt and three other Mormon officers wrote a letter to Brigham Young blaming the dismissal on Adjutant George P. Dykes, first lieutenant of company D. Gully died on July 5, 1849, while crossing the plains from Iowa to the Great Salt Lake. Golder, Bailey, and Smith, *op. cit.,* 151, 176, 178-179.

141 Andrew Jackson Smith, a native of Pennsylvania, was graduated from the United States Military academy on July 1, 1838, when he was promoted in the army to second lieutenant in the First dragoons. During the six years immediately preceding the Mexican war he served, at various times, at Jefferson Barracks, Fort Gibson, and Fort Leavenworth. He was a member of Colonel Kearny's expedition to the South pass in 1845. On March 4 of that year he was commissioned first lieutenant and on February 16, 1847, captain. He fought in the Union army during the Civil war and resigned from the service, May 6, 1869. He died on January 30, 1897. Cullum, *Biographical Register,* I, 566, III, 128; Heitman, *Historical Register,* I, 894.

142 George Stoneman was born in the state of New York. Graduating from the United States Military academy on July 1, 1846, he was promoted in the army to brevet second lieutenant, First dragoons. His first service was in the Army of the West during the Mexican war. He was acting assistant quartermaster of the Mormon Battalion from October, 1846, to February, 1847. During 1853 and 1854 he was a member of several military escorts for topographical engineers engaged in surveying routes for a transcontinental railroad. He saw extensive service on the side of the North during the Civil war, making a number of spectacular raids into Confederate territory. He retired from active duty on August 16, 1871, on account of "disability contracted in the line of duty." Between 1883 and 1887 he was governor of California. He died on September 5, 1894. Cullum, *Biographical Register,* II, 160-162, III, 179; Heitman, *Historical Register,* I, 930.

143 Doctor George B. Sanderson, of Missouri, was born in England. On August 20, 1846, at Fort Leavenworth, he was appointed assistant surgeon of volunteers, being assigned to the Mormon Battalion. A lot of friction developed between Sanderson and the Mormons, because the latter believed, probably unjustly, that the physician was guilty of "arrogance, inefficiency and petty oppressions." Sanderson resigned on August 31, 1847. Roberts, *op cit.,* 28-29; Heitman, *Historical Register,* I, 858; Golder, Bailey, and Smith, *op. cit.,* 152, 163-164, 216; Bancroft, *History of California,* V, 480-482.

souri, is attached to the battalion. I have sixty days' rations of flour, sugar and coffee, and salt, thirty of salt pork, and twenty of soap. There are three mule wagons to each company, beside six large ox wagons; also four other mule wagons for the field and staff, quartermaster property, hospital department, and the paymaster; and there are four or five private wagons.

After dispatching a multitude of last duties, I left town and arrived in camp at sunset. Here I found all huddled in the sandy creek bottoms; no grass; the thirty-two extra mules arriving at dark, and, like some of the others, without ropes and picket pins; they and the beeves and oxen were to be herded under rather difficult circumstances. I have no muleteers. Some fodder has been procured and fed. The battalion were never drilled, and, though obedient, have little discipline. They exhibit great heedlessness and ignorance and some obstinacy.[144] This afternoon I met Lieutenant Love, First dragoons, on his way to "the States"; he brought me a note from General Kearny. I am informed that the wagons have been left rather as a matter of convenience. I have brought road tools and am determined to take through my wagons. But the experiment is not a fair one, as the mules are nearly broken down at the outset. The only good ones (above twenty, which I bought near Albuquerque) were taken by Mr. Fitzpatrick,

144 Thirty-two years later Cooke wrote: "Every thing conspired to discourage the extraordinary undertaking of marching this battalion eleven hundred miles, for the much greater part through an unknown wilderness without road or trail, and with a wagon train. It was enlisted too much by families; some were too old, – some feeble, and some too young; it was embarrassed by many women; it was undisciplined; it was much worn by travelling on foot, and marching from Nauvoo, Illinois; their clothing was very scant; – there was no money to pay them,– or clothing to issue; their mules were utterly broken down; the Quartermaster department was without funds, and its credit bad; and mules were scarce." Cooke, *Conquest of New Mexico and California*, 91.

who brought an order for the twenty-one best in Santa Fé. My guide is a Mr. Weaver,[145] sent to me by the general, who met him coming by the Río Gila from California.

OCTOBER 20. My staff being behind, necessarily engaged, I determined to make the day's march some ten miles to the last water on this side of the river, to which there must be a hard march. I have but twenty-eight beeves, ten less than the number I made every effort to get of the commissary at Santa Fé. When I overtook the drove this morning, I found but eighteen and learned that the corporal had turned the ten over the day before to a teamster of the battalion on a misdelivered, undirected order of Captain McKissack.[146] I took them out of the wagon and sent back eight miles to Santa Fé for the oxen, leaving the wagon in the road under charge of a party. The whole train of wagons watered the mules by driving into a small stream and waiting upon each other until they drank (with much difficulty). This kept them an hour whilst I was waiting for them, and I learned that they had brought no buckets – that none

145 Pauline Weaver, a half-breed, was born in White county, Tennessee, early in 1800. His father, Henry Weaver, was a native of England; his mother was a Cherokee squaw. At an early age Pauline left home and entered the employ of the Hudson's Bay Company as hunter and trapper. Not liking the rigor of the northern winters, he finally migrated to the Southwest and during the fall of 1830 began to trap along the Gila and Colorado rivers. Thereafter, he spent much of his time in that region, where he became acquainted with the habits, character, and dialects of the Apache Indian. For a number of years he served the United States army as scout and guide. He died at Fort Lincoln, Arizona, about October 1, 1867. Edmund Wells, *Argonaut Tales* (New York, 1927), 253, 256-257, 260, 267, 277-278, 290, 471-477; Alpheus H. Favour, *Old Bill Williams* (Chapel Hill, 1936), 15, 111, 183; Frank C. Lockwood, *Pioneer Days in Arizona* (New York, 1932), 124-127, 199.

146 Captain William M. D. McKissack, a native of New Jersey and a graduate of the United States Military academy, was assistant quartermaster of the Army of the West and was then stationed at Santa Fé. He died at Pittsburgh, Pennsylvania, January 27, 1849, at the age of thirty-six. Cullum, *Biographical Register,* I, 482; *Southwest Historical Series,* VI, 36.

could be had at Santa Fé! I have taken every pains to equip them fully and wrote a form for a requisition for my approval; but the quartermaster frequently assured me he would give them not only what they ask for, but what they wanted, and issued on a simple receipt. It took them six hours to make the eleven miles. There is no grass, and I obtained, with great difficulty, four cartloads of cornstalks and fodder. The staff officers are still in the rear. I issued a long order of regulations for the march this evening, and put the command on twelve ounces of flour and a pound and a half of beef; sugar and coffee at three-fourths rations. I require that they should turn out under arms at reveille roll call.

OCTOBER 21. I ordered an early reveille and march to accomplish the long day of twenty-four miles. I shall give a detailed account of the difficulties of twenty-four hours. I got the wagons ready before eight o'clock, having ordered, to spur them, that each company should send off its baggage as soon as the whole of it was ready, and that they should march in the order in which their baggage got off. When all were ready I learned for the first time that nineteen of the beeves and fourteen mules were missing. I had arranged that the guard, increased to twenty-seven privates, should guard both, by night, and that a corporal and four butchers should drive the oxen; and a corporal, on daily duty, should, with six of the guard, drive and take care of (except during the night) the extra mules. I had broken up yesterday evening an old wagon I found here, for the axles, etc., and ordered the spokes made into picket pins; still they were missing, and I found myself without mounted men to send after them. I immediately assembled the old guard, and sent the officer of the day and [the] officer and non-commissioned officers of the guard, with four divisions of it, in pursuit, with orders not to leave the ground until all were found – then to bring them on. But this consumed an hour.

They were all recovered. I passed the whole column and reached the Galisteo at eleven o'clock. I then stopped until all had passed, directing them to move on down the shallow stream, and, with the assistance of men of the companies, to take the animals from the wagons, so that all should drink at the same time. I was on the ground an hour and three-quarters before the last wagon had passed. Each company marches in rear of its baggage. On this terrible piece of road down the stream, several oxen fell in the wagons, and they had to be rolled out of the road by main force, they making no motion; the feet of others are so sore that they have to be turned out! The last of the command have got into camp at nine o'clock at night, several wagons not getting nearer than a mile. I had a little wood brought two or three miles from the last hilltop. There is none here. I had sent forward my interpreter, who could only succeed in buying twenty-four bushels of ears of corn. Lieutenant Smith and Lieutenant Stoneman, acting assistant quartermaster, arrived about nine o'clock this evening.

OCTOBER 22. I got the companies under arms this morning nearly by the time the music ceased; yesterday they commenced at that time. I got off at nine o'clock and marched about eleven miles to the village of San Bernalillo [147] and encamped near some cornfields,

[147] The present Bernalillo, Sandoval county, New Mexico. "The town of Bernalillo is small, but one of the best built in the territory," recorded Lieutenant Emory on September 4, 1846. Captain Abraham R. Johnston described it in his journal on September 27, 1846: "At Bernalillo the wealthy cultivate the grape, and make a delicious wine. The grape grows upon small bushes on the flats, and is irrigated like the other products. We found peaches there

which, having been just gathered, stalks and all, there was good gleaning of broken fodder. I obtained also ten *costales* of ears of corn. The rear came up near sundown. Many mules gave out and oxen also. These I attempted to replace by hiring oxen or a mule wagon, but it was not accomplished; the rich men are ill-disposed. I released this evening Captain Hunter,[148] whom I arrested forty-eight hours ago for leaving my camp and going back to Santa Fé without asking permission.

OCTOBER 23. Our camp ground last night was on coarse sand and stone and little hillocks of bunch grass. There was wind and some rain, and I slept under a fallen tent. All my servants, too, are sick, and many of the men. Notwithstanding every exertion on my part, eight mules were missing this morning. I left back the old officer of the day with his whole guard, and now, near sundown, they have not come up. I am encamped on the road, extending half a mile along strips of grass. Hitherto I have encamped by regulations. I made an effort today to hire oxen, but it failed. The road is excessively bad, and it has taken one company seven hours to come eleven miles. I have killed beef every day but one. I have determined, as a matter of utter necessity, to purchase mules if I fail in exchanging. I met today a number of volunteers going back, and passed, a mile or two from here, their camp, of three companies of Price's regiment under Major Edmonson. He marched from Santa Fé four days before I did, to relieve Lieu-

inferior to any in the United States, as also any grape cultivated in the open air. Fences are made of clay, by putting the mould on the wall and filling it, and leaving the large brick thus formed to dry there. They appear to be rather used to keep men out than horses or animals, as in many places the top of the wall was covered with prickly cactus." *House Ex. Docs.*, 30 cong., 1 sess., no. 41, pp. 39, 567-568.

148 Captain Jesse D. Hunter, of company B. Golder, Bailey, and Smith, *op. cit.*, 282.

tenant-colonel Jackson, under orders to march against the Navajo Indians. I recovered there two mules belonging to my company. The men I had met were hunting cattle. The major said [that] after making a day's march it took him two or three to collect his animals. That is far worse than my battalion. The Navajo, it is to be feared, will escape lightly this season! We heard by Lieutenant Smith that Colonel Dougherty, with a regiment of infantry, would be in Santa Fé in a week. Yesterday, the twenty-second, Major Sumner was to set out with Lieutenants Love and Stanton for Missouri; it is a hazardous trip.

I am directed to keep a journal. I have not one minute of time unoccupied and am unwell. An influenza is prevailing. For several days before today, the heat and dust has been great, whilst I have been kept awake at night (sleeping under three blankets) by cold. The old guard came up at sundown.

OCTOBER 24. I sent forward the assistant quartermaster and interpreter to exchange or purchase mules, and made arrangements to borrow from the pay department treasury drafts, if they could be used. About ten o'clock, in the Ranches of Albuquerque, I exchanged my three worst mules for good ones, giving sixty-five dollars, and bought two others, a great bargain for seventy dollars. I met here Charbonneau,[149] one of the guides left for me, who reports that he had examined a route different in part and farther than that taken by the general, *viz.,* to descend the river farther and fall into a road from El Paso to the Copper Mines. The report is favorable; but they did not make a thorough examination by

[149] Cooke called him a "half-breed guide." Cooke, *Conquest of New Mexico and California,* 105. Charbonneau was probably a son of Toussaint Charbonneau, interpreter of the Lewis and Clark Expedition. Stella M. Drumm to the editor, May 1, 1938.

any means; and the practicability of the route from the Copper Mines to the Gila is still a problem.

In the Ranches of Albuquerque I received a message from the assistant quartermaster that he should like to see me in a village, and there I found [that] there was a prospect of getting mules. I left him there, and he succeeded in exchanging thirty of my mules, broken down and utterly worthless to the expedition, for fifteen good ones, and also in purchasing ten at forty dollars. At Albuquerque I bought twelve *fanegas,* or *costales,* of ears of corn, and put them in the wagons and crossed the river, and making my way through three miles of excessively deep sand, encamped a quarter of a mile from the road, at good grass comparatively, and near Captain Burgwin's [150] camp, where he had arrived this

150 John Henry K. Burgwin, a native of North Carolina, was graduated from the United States Military academy on July 1, 1830, when he was promoted in the army to brevet second lieutenant, Second infantry. On March 4, 1833, he was commissioned second lieutenant in the First dragoons, on June 30, 1835, first lieutenant, and on July 31, 1837, captain. Between 1833 and 1846 he was stationed, at various times, at Fort Leavenworth, Fort Wayne (Indian territory), Fort Gibson, Fort Towson, and Fort Croghan (Iowa). He accompanied Colonel Kearny's expedition to the South pass in 1845. At the outbreak of the Mexican war he joined the Army of the West, being sent ahead of the main body of troops to overtake the trading caravans of Armijo and Speyer. He was selected by Kearny to accompany him to California, but on October 6, after learning of the occupation of that province, the general ordered him to remain in New Mexico "at some point in the Río Abajo country . . . suitable for obtaining supplies for the winter, & for giving protection to the inhabitants from hostile Indians." In January, 1847, following the Taos insurrection, Colonel Price ordered him to proceed with the expedition which marched northward to put down that revolt. Joining the colonel's command on January 28, he participated in the assault upon the Pueblo de Taos on February 3 and 4, when he was mortally wounded while "gallantly leading, and skilfully directing the attack." He died of his injuries on February 7, 1847, at the age of thirty-six, and was taken to Santa Fé for burial. Shortly afterward his body was exhumed and brought to Fort Leavenworth, where it was reinterred, September 22, 1847. Kearny, Order No. 34, Oct. 6, 1846, Letters Received, MSS., O.F.S., A.G.O.; Cullum, *Biographical Register,* I, 372; Connelley, *Doniphan's Expedition,* 74, 80, 138-139, 270, 317, 517.

afternoon. Here I purchased of officers eight mules, giving treasury drafts. Captain B. was also kind enough to exchange eight of his best public mules (very indifferent indeed) for eight of my worst, which were worthless to me. I also obtained twenty oxen. Also exchanged a very heavy and two nearly unserviceable wagons for two ponton wagons and another. I found some of my sheepskins spoiled. There was rain last night. The march about eleven miles. I have had today excessively hard and unremitting labors.

OCTOBER 25. Captain Burgwin received by express this morning, from five or six most respectable American merchants, a letter asking for protection, as they had reason to believe General Armijo was marching up to seize their property, which they estimate at half a million. The captain is very crippled in means and had almost determined to do nothing but forward the express. I advised him, if satisfied of a strong probability of the truth of the report, to go down, even if dismounted, and I left him disposed to do so. In the multitude of my engagements last evening, I forgot the two packs of Indian goods which General Kearny wrote me he had left for me. This morning, after marching a mile, I sent back a pack mule for them. The men have come up with one very poor pack, which "was all they could find." This may be a great misfortune, but is not all.

At a village above I saw a large herd of good mules going out to grass; and having seen that still several of my teams were broken down, or likely soon to be so, I sent the quartermaster and interpreter to the owner, a Chávez, to exchange or buy. He has come up this afternoon utterly unsuccessful; they treated his offers with contempt. It was great good luck to obtain those yesterday from a merchant in want of money. The bargain for exchange, two for one, was made before he saw mine. After that, he was so disgusted that Mr. Stoneman was forced to leave in the lot a good mule with a sore shoulder to make up the number, etc., as agreed upon, or he would have broken the bargain. To complete the series, a pair of wagon hounds were found this evening to be broken. I have ordered an issue of pork every fourth day. I also issued an order of further regulations. I assembled the captains this morning at reveille and earnestly exhorted them to lend me a more efficient assistance in requiring the mules to be properly grazed and fed, or else the expedition must very soon fall through. They made excellent promises. I reduced to the ranks this day a first sergeant for failing to form his company at reveille and giving the excuse that it was not light enough to call his roll. I have made a short march of nine or ten miles, because I expected the mule trade to take much time, and because Captain Burgwin reported that there was no grass elsewhere within reach. We encamp on uneven sand and without fuel, or even thinking of it; such are the resources of this country. I could obtain but five bags of corn (ears). The mules were herded loose this afternoon; the oxen are all unyoked at halting for the night.[151]

OCTOBER 26. Marched at eight o'clock. Passed several villages. Beside sand, found deep mud from the breaking of irrigating canals. I sent across the river to Otero's store at Valencia for some pack blankets, for which the assistant quartermaster had an order, and

151 On October 25, 1846, William Coray, first sergeant of company B, recorded in his journal: "This was Sunday, but we continued our march, stopping for nothing. Marched 15 miles, camped on the Río Del Norte. The Spaniards brought to us apples, grapes, corn and wine for sale though at an exorbitant price. They seemed much delighted at the sight of our women and would crowd before us in such multitudes that I could hardly press my way through . . . and give them apples." Golder, Bailey, and Smith, *op. cit.*, 180.

directed him to purchase or exchange mules. Otero, like Chávez, both malcontents, asked unreasonable prices. He had lost yesterday evening five or six thousand sheep – [and] two shepherds killed – by the Indians. He had been riding all night, hiring some villages of Indians to pursue them. I stopped some time among the Lunas (great sheep holders). All the effective males of the village had gone after the Navajo, who also had stolen 6,600 yesterday, and, it was said, killed two shepherds. I wrote then a note for Captain Burgwin, informing him of this robbery, for the lady to send. She thought they, mostly women, were in an exposed situation. This was about eighteen miles only from the dragoon camp. But what can they do with broken-down mules? All the best [were] selected by General Kearny, and horses cannot work and live here. The day quite cool; wore my greatcoat all day; still sick of a cold, which is very prevalent. We are exposed to black frosts nightly, without fuel. Encamped near a village; pretty good grass, but bought about eighteen bushels of corn and a cartload of fuel. I find some of the mules getting sore shoulders. I called up the company commanders and gave them a lecture on the subject, such as to fitting and cleaning collars, shortening hames, lengthening bearing chains, etc., and above all in relieving mules about to become galled, for I have assigned all the mules, giving two extra ones for every team. The march thirteen or fourteen miles. Saw mother and daughter today; the latter thirteen, and married, as usual here, at that age; both fine looking, with the large liquid eye of the *señora*.

OCTOBER 27. A cold day with some rain. Marched about eight, as usual. Yesterday morning one of the Chávez's claimed a yoke of oxen received of Captain

Burgwin, which he did not get from me. It appears he returned to Captain B.'s camp, left there about sunset with a note on the subject, and overtook us early this morning. Captain B. adds to the subject of the oxen that an intelligent man had arrived from Santa Fé, which he left in the morning yesterday, bringing intelligence of an arrival just before he left, from the United States, with a report of a battle of General Taylor with the Mexicans, with the result unknown further than a loss of killed of 1,000 Americans and 1,500 Mexicans. The captain adds that the report was believed in Santa Fé, that Colonel Doniphan had marched with his whole regiment for El Paso, and finally that the captain himself would march today down the river with many of his men afoot. We passed through a very handsome, straggling village with many cottonwoods. The church is very large, with steeples and bells. The road was good. I encamped early, having come about twelve miles. The assistant quartermaster has failed all day to purchase or exchange a mule either on the route or a mile or two below at the Alcalde Chávez. It seems that many persons, as usual, are setting out with their best mules on a buffalo hunt. I herded all the animals above three hours this afternoon in some old cornfields strewed with broken fodder. I obtained a cartload of wood. There is scarcely a large weed within a mile or two of my camp. There is plenty of grass, but very dry and frosted. I engaged twenty-two bushels of corn, which have not yet come – near sundown. The arrival may be Mr. St. Vrain, expected daily when I left Santa Fé, twenty days from Independence. I look for an express.

OCTOBER 28. It rained all night and this morning till after nine o'clock. The priest disappointed me in the corn. I marched about nine o'clock. At one o'clock the advance guard had come to this ground, a mile below Sabinal; the last wagons were two hours later, so deep and heavy was the sand and mud. The sun came out about twelve, but it is now cloudy and very cold. The mountains opposite are covered with snow. I got a large cartload of wood and have engaged corn. We have obtained no mules, cattle, or sheep today. I sent Charbonneau on to La Joya, after a man with mules for sale who is a day in advance, and have directed the assistant commissary to proceed tomorrow a day in advance to purchase 300 sheep, 14,500 pounds of beef (in the hoof), which, together with the twenty-eight beeves, will make sixty days' rations from Santa Fé. All the mules, as usual, and all the cattle were herded a half mile from camp until near sunset.

OCTOBER 29. Marched about ten miles to the bottom below La Joya; the road still heavy from the rain; found there my two dragoons and property all safe; mules improved. Lieutenant Smith, acting assistant commissary of subsistence, and the interpreter have gone on. I have bought here one indifferent mule. With the Mexican, with wagons and mules, no bargain could be made; his mules poor and price extravagant. Bought some corn. We have the pleasure of encamping here in a cottonwood grove, with plenty of fuel for the first time. The mountains all round are white with snow. Reports are rife that General Kearny has been taken prisoner, and others as outrageously improbable. Two Mexican oxen, strays from Captain Burgwin, were recovered today. The weather is clear and cold. Last night a number of the battalion went off and spent the evening in the town a mile off, and this morning a Mexican complained of wood being stolen. Lieutenant Stoneman's horse received a bayonet wound, and a favorite shepherd's dog of my personal attendant was also wounded last night. I have extreme difficulty in causing the mules to be picketed properly; there is a great *vis inertiae* in such a command; they tie two together and picket them by short ropes, and *will* put them too close together. The guard has, [for] several days, consisted of one subaltern, one sergeant, two corporals, and thirty men. A sergeant and twelve of them guard the beeves and oxen unyoked. Since two or three guards were left back half the day to hunt strays, it has nearly stopped straying. The officers of the day seem to exert themselves very commendably.

OCTOBER 30. Marched early; encountered the sand bluff; spent two hours in ascending it, doubling teams, and in addition about twenty men assisted in drawing up each wagon.[152] I suspect [that] a road, a quarter of a mile lower, is better. I depended upon the known route of the regiment of dragoons and the word of a guide who had returned. About six miles from camp, a fine camp ground was passed; and I came on to Polvadera, where I found no grass, unless by passing an immense canal. I determined to do so at a gap. My men worked well with spades and large hoes furnished by some Mexicans (who worked well with them) unasked, but it was a difficult job. I broke one wagon hound. The camp was thus established about three o'clock in a pretty bottom, where the grass is as good as usual. I bought corn. The men went half a mile or more for

152 Corporal Daniel Tyler, of company C, wrote: "We had to leave the river for a time, and have twenty men to each wagon with long ropes to help the teams pull the wagons over the sand hills. The commander perched himself on one of the hills, like a hawk on a fence post, sending down his orders with the sharpness of – well, to the Battalion, it is enough to say – Colonel Cooke." Roberts, *op. cit.*, 35.

cottonwood fuel on the river bank. The sand hill was very severe on the animals; it was three or four hundred yards long. The day has been cloudy with a southerly wind, which reminded me of snow almost as much as the white-capped mountains everywhere visible at no great distance, or height – some of them.

OCTOBER 31. As cold and cloudy as ever. Lieutenant Smith, with the interpreter, arrived last evening from below; he had engaged three hundred sheep some twenty-five miles lower down, and also a sufficiency of cattle, but mostly heavy American beeves, which I think will not do near so well as the Mexican breed. I marched at eight o'clock precisely. The road was good until I encountered the spot where it has fallen into the river at a bluff point. The river was higher than when the dragoons passed there. Six teams got through with difficulty, many men being forced to get into the cold water and remain there a long time. I then ordered the rest over a steep hill, and a mile round, as I was told. I think they did better. We passed several companies of American merchants who have come over to this side. We learned by an unusually reliable source this morning [of] a report that General Armijo had just written to his wife to lend as much money as was wanted for our army, that he had set off under guard for Mexico, that about a thousand volunteers were at El Paso for the purpose of coming up to attack and rob our merchant caravans, and that General Wool when last heard of was near Chihuahua, etc.

The assistant quartermaster and commissary of subsistence have been out all day attending to their department wants. I encamped three miles below Socorro at two o'clock, and mustered and inspected the battalion. It is now dark. Mr. Stoneman has just come in; he has purchased five mules for $170. Mr. Smith has just arrived. We are but two or three miles above the last settlement. The march was thirteen miles; the weather cold, but it has cleared up. There is more variety and beauty in the scenery; the broken bluffs and mountains hem in the river more closely, and there is more woods. I am encamped on the border of a forest. I have determined to send back tomorrow two of the ox wagons; there are six; and but five men were sent to drive them back; one of these, who has been and is very ill, was left in a village today. Yesterday and today ten oxen have been left on the road, unable to move. I shall send about six yoke of the worst back with the empty wagons. I also heard today that the trading company below were sending up mules to assist Captain Burgwin, on his march for their protection.

NOVEMBER 1. Five o'clock P.M. I have just encamped on the river, five hundred yards from the road, after a march of about fourteen miles. Lieutenant Smith came in late last night; he had bought his beeves, which he could not get nearer than Socorro, and where I had to send for them this morning. I sent back this morning three ox wagons; one with a broken tongue and pair of hounds, tied behind another, to be left in care of the alcalde of Socorro. I sent seven yoke of the worst oxen. It took me until half past nine o'clock to make these arrangements, which I had repeatedly ordered eighteen hours before, and then had to do it myself. A dumb spirit has possessed all for the last twenty-four hours, and not one in ten of my orders has been understood and obeyed. All the vexations and troubles of any other three days of my life have not equalled those of the said twenty-four hours. Weaver was very dangerously ill in the night. Mr. Smith is off with the interpreter after sheep. My guide has been absent the whole day. The assistant quartermaster has been endeavoring to exchange broken-down mules. Captain Burgwin is encamped two or three miles above me. Weaver is much better this evening. We have corn this evening; it was one of my disappointments that none was brought last night. My attention is constantly on the stretch for the smallest things. I have to order and then see that it is done. There is a wonderful amount of stolidity, ignorance, negligence, and obstinacy which I have to contend against.

NOVEMBER 2. Lieutenant Smith came up last night with the sheep, which this morning I found to be very poor – about half of them lambs, almost worthless. His cattle, too, are much too poor. I marched before eight o'clock; the *jornada* was before me; here the river sweeps off to the southwest. Mountains fill the bend, and the great trade road passes to the south over an elevated plain, with a good road but no water very near it for eighty-five miles; halfway it passes within five or six miles of a spring. Here the road I have followed crosses the river, and we turned to the right on the slightly broken tracks of General Kearny. In the wide bend to the left are several hundreds of the merchants' wagons; they are ruinously waiting the progress of events; it will one day be found out that they are not "Santa Fé traders," and that the breaking up [of] the lawless custom-house there has ruined *their* business.

Behind me, within a mile or two, came Captain Burgwin's squadron half mounted upon mules. On his march, near Luna village, some inhabitants came at speed to him, reporting that the Navajo had just robbed them and taken off a woman – the very incident that I apprehended, and wrote the captain a letter in the village to warn him of. Captain Grier's company, being much ahead, he was sent instantly to the rescue – his men half afoot. He overtook and recaptured the cattle and sheep; and following on about sixteen miles, the mules of his company exhausted and left, and his men following at long intervals afoot, the captain, Lieutenant Wilson, Corporal Price, and one private (on horses got of Mexicans) overtook four Navajo; then uprose from a ravine fifty others, who surrounded the captain and party. These killed two Indians outright and then retreated in good order under a shower of arrows, and were pursued in their turn a quarter of a mile until they fell upon a few of their footmen, and thus came off unwounded. In this bottom I saw a herd of many thousands of sheep and sent Mr. Smith with one hundred dollars to purchase eighty, to make up for the lambs; I ordered him, if the owner was not there, as a case of necessity to tell the foreman that we must have them, giving them a fair price – the same we gave yesterday.

Of the guides sent me by the general, only Leroux[153]

[153] Antoine Leroux was one of the famous mountain men of the Far West. He was a French-canadian who came to New Mexico during the early twenties, made his home in Taos, and became a Mexican citizen. His wife, who was a Mexican, was Juana Vigil Leroux. Before 1846 he had trapped in all parts of the Southwest. After helping to direct the march of the Mormon Battalion in 1846 and 1847, he was employed as a guide by Captain Sitgreaves in 1851, by Captain Gunnison in 1853, and by Lieutenant Whipple in 1854. He supplied some geographical information for a map of the territory of New Mexico compiled in 1851 by Captain John G. Parke, of the topographical engineers. On February 4, 1853, when he wrote a letter to William H. Seward recommending the thirty-fifth parallel route for a railroad, he stated: "I have crossed from New Mexico to California by four different routes, namely: Cook's Sonora route, the Salt River route, that recently followed by Capt. Sitgreaves' party, and the old Spanish trail. . . I have trapped on nearly every stream between Cook's route and the Great Salt Lake, and am well acquainted with the region of country between these places." He was still living in Taos in 1861. L. Sitgreaves, *Report of an Expedition down the Zuñi and Colorado Rivers* (Washington, 1854), 4; *House Ex. Docs.*, 33 cong., 2 sess., no. 91, vol. II, pp. 40, 59; *ibid.*, vol. III, p. 48; *House Ex. Docs.*, 37 cong.,

joined me this afternoon; the others have come up to-night more or less drunk.[154] Weaver continues to improve, although very sick and feeble yet. Leroux said I had very poor animals to start to California, "not half so well fitted out to carry wagons as the general was." He asserts that it is twelve hundred miles and at least ninety days' travel from here. Very discouraging. It further appears from his account that it is perhaps four hundred miles from where we leave the river (seventy or eighty miles below this point) to where we can strike the Gila, this distance, for the most part, unexplored and unknown by any of the guides. I send him forward in the morning with all the guides but Charbonneau and Weaver (sick), to explore the plains beyond the point we leave the river (perhaps not more than fifty miles) and return to meet me there.

Mr. Smith got the eighty sheep, but I have now but little more than seventy-five days of meat (at one and one-half pounds of beef to the ration), or ninety days from Santa Fé according to the general's advice, and will, if possible, use about ten of the oxen for beef. Nothing is more certain than that if I had continued with no better outfit of mules than I received at Santa Fé, I should now be broken down. I have hired three Mexicans and put the three hundred and eighty sheep under their exclusive charge. I have this night commenced herding the whole of the mules and beeves and oxen, putting all of the sentinels, ten in number, to

2 sess., no. 112, p. 28; *Daily Missouri Republican,* Feb. 17, 1853; D. S. Stanley, *Personal Memoirs* (Cambridge, 1917), 29-30; Tassé, *op. cit.,* II, 229-248; Favour, *op. cit.,* 107, 118, 177, 199, 206.

154 Cooke's report to Kearny, February 5, 1847, stated: "The numerous guides and hirelings you sent to me, I found at the lowest village; they had been idle for weeks; and I found I was to venture, with my wagons, into a wide region, unknown to any of them." *House Ex. Docs.,* 30 cong., 1 sess., no. 41, p. 553.

guard them exclusively. We passed this afternoon some very bad road. I found that we could improve on the track made by the regiment of dragoons. Making about eleven miles. The camp is in an open grove of the river bottom. We rejoice once more in plenty of fuel and good fires; for the last twenty-five or thirty miles the timber on the fine wide bottoms of the river has been quite a striking feature in the landscape, otherwise picturesque, with lofty mountains in every direction, blue from distance or haze and capped with snow fields. The weather is more moderate.

NOVEMBER 3. Captain Grier,[155] Lieutenant Wilson,[156] and Mr. Houck [157] visited us this morning. Captain G. confirms the statement of his skirmish with the Navajo and praises Lieutenant Wilson. By a person who left Chihuahua October 14 a paper of that city of the sixth has been received, containing an account of Santa Anna's installation and his inaugural address (or, perhaps, a proclamation); in it he calls us "audacious and perfidious Americans," promises vigorous war, and to head the army. This man confirms the report of a battle near Monterrey and gives some particulars, *viz.*, that

---

155 Captain William Nicholson Grier, First dragoons, a native of Pennsylvania, was graduated from the United States Military academy in 1835. On March 16, 1848, he was breveted major for "gallant and meritorious conduct in the Battle of Santa Cruz de Rosales." He died on July 8, 1885. Cullum, *Biographical Register,* I, 491-492, III, 111; Heitman, *Historical Register,* I, 478.

156 Clarendon J. L. Wilson, a native of Virginia, was graduated from the United States Military academy on July 1, 1846, when he was promoted in the army to brevet second lieutenant, First dragoons. On February 4, 1847, he was breveted first lieutenant for "gallant and meritorious conduct in the conflicts at Embudo and Taos, N.M." He died at Albuquerque, New Mexico, February 21, 1853, at the age of twenty-eight. Cullum, *Biographical Register,* II, 146; Heitman, *Historical Register,* I, 1045.

157 Probably Solomon Houck, of Boonville, Missouri, a Santa Fé trader. *Southwest Historical Series,* I, 129.

there were 5,000 Americans, that the Mexicans lost 1,300 killed and wounded, [and] that during the battle other American forces took possession of the city, where, at the last accounts, they were invested by a superior Mexican force. There has been a strong suspicion amongst the merchants down here of a conspiracy to rise and throw off the American rule in this territory, connected, perhaps, at the moment, with the advance of seven hundred men who certainly did march from El Paso north; and there is no doubt but they had emissaries or spies, and most likely, I think, above the *jornada.* I learn that the volunteer who brought the report to Captain Burgwin of the arrival and news from the United States also states that at that time there was a talk in Santa Fé of the rising of the people. As for myself, I believe that the priests and a few of the millionaires would like to put forward others to attempt to regain their despotic sway and grinding oppression of the people; but, take them altogether, I think the cowardly barbarians – too well off to have a decent government forced on them – are selfish enough to refrain from any risk in the world.

I marched today about fourteen miles. Some bad bluffs of heavy sand were passed. The camp is on a high plain covered with grama grass, apparently entirely dead but said to be nearly as good as corn. For the last forty miles the flat river bottom occupies perhaps two miles in width, some of it richer than above. There is, however, a white efflorescence rather more frequent here than there, which is said to contain much carbonate of potash and to render the soil unfit for agriculture. This district, entirely unoccupied, has the great superiority to that above (so thickly inhabited), of forests covering perhaps one-fourth of the bottoms; and the mountains also, covered with cedar, are very near. Fear of the Indians has made it a desert. A man of company A has died this evening. His death was very sudden; he walked to the surgeon's tent this morning. The last two nights have been very cold, with severe frost. Today the sun was disagreeably hot. I have reduced the ration to nine ounces of flour and ten ounces of pork. At this rate I have eighty-six days' [rations]. Our course today has been about southwest. Mr. Leroux left me this morning, with four other guides, to descend the river to the point where it is practicable to leave it with wagons, to explore beyond. After advancing several miles, I met one of the party that he had sent back ostensibly to settle upon signals by smoke, but really, I believe, because he had no use for him.. This fellow, who weighs about two hundred, has been drunk for a week or two; his gun is broken past use. I have directed the assistant quartermaster to discharge him.

It took a cow and twelve of the lambs to make the ration tonight; the lambs, not the smallest I fear, weighed eighteen pounds. We came in view this afternoon of a distant, lofty mountain running off to the east from the range east of the great Chihuahua road; the *jornada* (literally "day's journey") – which, far down, as far as we could see – was an unbroken mass of snow. Doctor Foster, the interpreter, calls a bush which I pointed out to him, the mesquite; this same bush, of a small growth, is common on the Missouri and Platte prairies. I could never find out a name for it there. We passed cactus plants ten feet high and saw a specimen of an extraordinary variety – a bush of many small stems bearing long thorns and also the usual fruit, covered with a full allowance of the minute prickers.

NOVEMBER 4. Marched at eight o'clock; passed

some very bad sand and stony hills. The men are distributed to the wagons, fifteen or twenty to a wagon. Near two o'clock, as I sat on a hill watching the difficult ascent, two dragoons rode up, and in dismounting, the carbine of one went off and was very near hitting me. They handed me a letter from Captain Burgwin to the amount that he had received information that some troops were coming from the south by way of the Copper Mines. It seems very improbable, but it is certainly possible; they may, by this route, attempt to surprise the traders' wagons. The last three miles of road were excessively bad – many steep ascents, with loose stone and sand. I encamped near a great rock where there is a small prairie of grama grass. The march about eleven miles, which took from seven to eight hours of work so hard that the teams can scarcely stand many such, if in succession. This evening one of the party detached by Lieutenant Smith at the crossing came up (in four days he says – probably six days) from Santa Fé. He brought no news at all. The report of the battle not yet confirmed; the infantry regiment not arrived but expected daily. The captain, quartermaster sergeant, and rest of the party, he reports, went back from Santa Fé by permission of Colonel Price. He reports Colonel Doniphan and his regiment on their march down, within ninety miles of this point; said that Colonel Doniphan said he was going against the Navajo Indians with a small part of his regiment, whilst the rest continued the march. The country today very broken, wild, and poor.

NOVEMBER 5. This morning being stormy and the draught animals very fatigued, I determined to rest today, having marched seventeen days without stop. I am told that a Mexican in Sonora will sometimes make powder in a day for use the next. There are said to be extinct volcanoes to the east, on the Órganos range of mountains beyond the *jornada* road. Saltpetre is a very common efflorescence on the surface of the soil. About sixty miles to the east of Albuquerque, and at a point one hundred and fifty miles to the south of it, are salt lakes with a plentiful deposit of pure salt. The day turned out clear. I saved an ox with its shoulder out of place, by staying today; it could not come up last night. Today I sent for it and had it slaughtered for beef, but although it weighed four hundred it took sixteen of the commissary's lambs to make out the ration. I have ordered, in case of alarm at night, that the companies should turn out on the battalion parade ground where they habitually form, and that all the teamsters, two to a team, should proceed to the assistance of the guard in securing the animals. My camp is surrounded by a singularly broken and wild country. In the small open space near the mouth of a dry creek, lofty and irregular hills and bluffs jut in on three sides, and on the fourth is a narrow cottonwood bottom; and a high mountain rises from the opposite bank of the river, and their blue and white tops are visible in every direction. These hills are covered with the dry yellow grama grass and are dotted with cedars. On a little hill which juts into the camp stands a large rock of square proportions above thirty feet high, inaccessible in any part; it is a sandy conglomerate and precisely the color of the adobes; has a striking resemblance to the ruins of a church or other large building.

NOVEMBER 6. Marched eight or nine miles over the gravel bluffs, incessantly up or down hill. I struck the river where the general crossed to a wide bottom in a semicircle bend and waited for his packsaddles.[158] Now

[158] Kearny had encamped there from the evening of October 9 to the

we had our first practice at breaking a wagon road for a mile and a half round the bend of the river. I encamped at the lower end. The mules are herded half a mile up the flat ravine. The hills passed today are well clothed with grama grass, but there is no bottom land for ten miles. The weather is becoming warmer by day and less cold by night. I shall march from here tomorrow (my twentieth day from Santa Fé), as did the general, he having remained here three days. The march was about eleven miles today, as much as can be well made over such a rugged country. Charbonneau, the guide, caught a fine large beaver on the river last night.

NOVEMBER 7. We found a tolerable road four or five miles today, but then struck lofty hills of sand that were barely passable; the last, particularly, almost a mountain. The advance reached this camp near the river after above six hours' march, scarcely eight miles; and the rear were near nine hours, being for the last two hours within a mile of the camp. There is every few miles a small bottom in a bend of the river; none other. Yesterday the weather was quite hot until near sundown. In the night, water froze about one-fourth of an inch in thickness. We have tonight plenty of cedar for fuel, also the mesquite bush. If the route should con-

morning of October 14. The camp was located in the present Sierra county, New Mexico. On October 9, when Kearny decided to leave his wagons behind, Captain Johnston wrote: "A number of mules gave out in the teams to-day, indicating that our rate of travel must be very slow to reach California with wagons. Upon due consultation, the general determined to remain in camp, and send to Major Sumner for mules to take back the wagons and other property which we could not need in packing, and resort at once to packing as a means of transportation. This he resolved upon, knowing what he had passed over; and, upon the report of Carson, who represents the country as worse rather than better in front. Leaving, then, to Captain Cooke the task of opening a wagon road, he determined as above. A Mexican, Tones, and Corporal Clapin were despatched at midnight, and ordered to ride to Major Sumner before stopping – 60 miles." *House Ex. Docs.*, 30 cong., 1 sess., no. 41, pp. 574-575.

tinue any great distance as difficult, no animals could stand it. Mine are poor to commence. I had a pioneer party out. From ten to twenty men march with every wagon. Pushing and pulling through deep sand and up hill, with musket and knapsack on, is very severe work. No animal is now ever staked. The country begins to look outlandish. The flickering fires tonight reveal around strange plants and bushes; the Spanish bayonets look like colossal statues with their cap of luxuriant leaves, and other nameless bushes we have seldom seen before. We have got among wild animals – turkeys, deer, and bears.

NOVEMBER 8. It blew hard and rained last night and this morning till after sunrise. The animals, too, have had little rest from yesterday's excessive labor, when the teams were in some instances doubled. I marched at nine o'clock with the tents wet; the road as bad for three or four miles; the wind very high and cold. After five miles I encamped on a second bottom, where there was plenty of grama grass. It took many of the wagons from three to four hours to make this short march. It is very discouraging. There is not a loose mule now that is fit for work. Doctor Sanderson and Mr. Hall, who came ahead, have accidentally fired a cottonwood bottom a mile below this camp, and it is now burning with a great smoke. I fear that Leroux, the guide who is exploring, will, by his self-made convention, take it as a signal to return. Three nights ago a teamster lost a mule, which he did not report till evening; so yesterday morning I sent him and his assistant back the day's march afoot. They came up last night without finding it. This morning a mule was found in a sand pit exhausted. I left two of the guard to allow it to rest and endeavor to bring it up. A pair of wagon hounds were broken as we came into this camp. I have some spare ones. From the last hilltop we had a view of another range of mountains off to the southwest; they are covered with snow, and the high wind blew directly from them. It is to pass around their southern point that we still continue on the river to the south.

NOVEMBER 9. Leroux came back last evening; he went down about fifty miles, struck off where the river turns east at San Diego, and in fifteen miles found some water holes. Then he saw from a high hill a creek running out of the mountain at an estimated distance of thirty miles (the next water), over a rather level plain. We marched early and had immediately to ascend an exceedingly difficult, long hill, and so for four or five miles, winding very much and just able to pass – very broken and difficult ground. At two o'clock the first wagons reached a good camping ground on the river, just where General Kearny struck off, and there I have encamped. It has now become evident to all that we cannot go on so, with any prospect of a successful or safe termination to the expedition. The guides say that most of the mules would not go to California driven *loose*. I examined the mules and found that whole teams are poor, weak – nearly broken down. The three ox teams and wagons were to go back about this time at the latest; three have already gone. Twenty-two men are on the sick report; quite a number have been transported in the wagons, and the knapsacks and arms of others. Many of the men are weakly or old or debilitated or trifling. Besides all this, my rations are insufficient.

I have then ordered that fifty-five of the sick and least efficient men shall return to Santa Fé, taking with them twenty-six days' rations of flour at ten ounces, and pork at half a pound. I shall thus get rid of 1,800 pounds' weight of rations, and by means of what they leave, particularly the live stock, increase my rations for the remainder, seventeen days of meat and thirteen of flour. But I have also determined to send back, if possible, only one team of oxen, so as to use on my mule wagons the ten other yoke. This requires that the other two ox wagons should be left here, which I have ordered; they can be sent for. Captain Burgwin is encamped about fifty-eight miles above. There are also some thirty extra mules, which, some think, to pack with sixty or eighty pounds would do nearly as well as loose. I have also determined to pack, if possible, ten extra oxen, which are nearly broken down, two hundred pounds each. I have ordered the upright tent poles to be left and muskets to be used as substitutes, and the tents to be reduced to one for nine men – which they will hold, if opened and lowered to the height of a musket. This all accomplished, I hope by patience and perseverance and energy to accomplish the undertaking, though in a very few days I commence a route of above three hundred miles to the San Pedro river, of which the guides know little or nothing – know not if there be water sufficient, Leroux thinking himself fortunate in finding water at an interval of thirty miles at the outset. No one doubts but that I could not have made this commencement of the march with the mules furnished at Santa Fé. The march undertaken is now said to be three hundred miles longer than then believed; and such is its character that, making the road as we go, ten miles is sometimes a very hard day's march – equal to at least twenty-five miles of a good road.

November 10. I was forced to remain in camp today. It took until near three o'clock to get off the party of fifty-five invalids under Lieutenant Willis, notwithstanding my constant efforts.[159] Thirty-one tents, twelve camp kettles, twenty-six mess pans, and one hundred and forty-nine tent poles have been put in one of the extra ox wagons and the two partially concealed. The two citizens who came to take them back were sent afoot to inform Captain Burgwin of the fact by tomorrow night. Meanwhile they are put in charge of a beaver-trapping party, who expect to be in the vicinity for eight or nine days. I have had the packs prepared today for mules and oxen, under the instructions of the guides and other Mexicans, and some of the animals packed in each company, so that it can be well done and early tomorrow morning. Weaver is getting well fast. Leroux with two guides, Mr. Foster the interpreter (volunteer), and one of the Mexicans hired to herd sheep (an excellent woodsman who has been on the Gila) go ahead early in the morning. They will explore beyond the point lately examined by Leroux and return to meet me, or, what is better, send two back from there and continue the exploration. Charbonneau's trap was sprung by a beaver last night, but it left a forefoot and was missing.

NOVEMBER 11. We encountered a very bad, rocky bluff this morning within a mile of camp; otherwise meeting with less obstacles than usual, coming chiefly in river bottoms. After marching fourteen miles, I encamped on hilly ground a half mile from the river; a woody bottom between; but standing water in a dry slough was found a quarter of a mile from the ground. Three more men went to join the party returning this

159 On November 10, Henry Standage, a private in company E, noted in his diary: "This morning 50 of the Battalion were sent to winter at Santa Fé, or if possible to go to Pueblo, including the sick. This does in reality make solemn times for us, so many divisions taking place. May the God of Heaven protect us all." Golder, Bailey, and Smith, *op. cit.*, 182.

morning – two sick, and one as the only active, efficient man of the whole detachment (this makes fifty-eight). There was an evident improvement in our means today. Thirty-six mules were very lightly packed, besides some oxen; but still the last wagon was eight hours making the fourteen miles. Some of the packed oxen performed some antics that were irresistibly ludicrous (owing to the crupper perhaps), such as jumping high from the ground many times in quickstep time, turning round the while – a perfect jig! For the last eighteen miles we have found fine river bottoms interrupted by points of bluff, on this side chiefly, for a mountain rises abruptly beyond. They are more than a mile wide, and, what is best, with much timber upon them – a wide strip invariably. We are in sight now of the point of mountain at El Paso. The weather is fine; the country grows more flat; the bottom grass is dead, but good grama grass on the bluffs. A deer and turkeys were killed today. A difficulty is that I cannot encamp on a regular bottom, the grass being dead. This afternoon while Charbonneau, who is very active, was making rather a remote exploration for water, giving it up, I came on a mile, guiding myself through weeds, willows, and reeds above my head, found water in the densely timbered and brushy bottom, and established the camp on the bluff, with fine grass near. The tents are pitched with muskets, somewhat lengthened by a peg that enters the muzzle; the backs are opened and a gore inserted; so they are stretched out nearly into a circle and are very capacious.

NOVEMBER 12. Fifteen miles today and a tolerably good road; it is very cheering! It has been a fortunate day. The pioneers were several times just ready for the wagons as they arrived, and I discovered that we had got into a *cul-de-sac,* just in time to set the wagons right. It is a difficult thing to hit grass and water, as the river generally has half a mile of tangled wooded bottom on this side. I have done it tonight after some perseverance and difficulty. There were fine rich river bottoms nearly all day. This forenoon we turned up on the bluff, however, at a canyon, where there was a fine view of a rapid in the river below and apparently a good pass through the mountains to the road on the other side – most probably where the *jornada* road approaches within three or four miles of the river; if so, there the future road should fall into the one I make. This morning I was awakened at four o'clock with a report that horses had been crossing the river in the vicinity for half an hour. I had the mules, etc., driven close; got up and became soon convinced that it was the sound of rapids, or the water against snags. I heard it as a breeze came from the direction of the river. I sent a small party, however, into the bottom. I have calculated that I lightened the wagons above twenty per cent by the late operation, whilst my rations were increased eight days; and it is confirmed by the facility of motion.

NOVEMBER 13. After following the river this morning a mile or more, we found a pole and note from Leroux, but met at the same time two of the guides, who directed us short to the right to leave the river, stating it was fifteen miles to water.[160] I followed a smooth inclined plain (between two bluffs) three miles and then had a steep ascent; then following ridges and making ascents occasionally, we reached another inclined bed of a rainy-weather stream; from this we wound up a long valley to a ridge which bounds it, following that over a

160 The battalion left the Río Grande about fifteen miles northwest of the present town of Rincón, Doña Ana county, New Mexico.

very rocky prairie. Charbonneau had gone to the head of the inclined plain and found, he thought, an outlet. The water is at its head; but he did not return in time to direct all the wagons; and it is doubtful with me if it would have been better. The wagons arrived at this ground about an hour by sun, having come fifteen or sixteen miles and all uphill, the prairie usually being gravelly and not rough. The water is about one hundred feet lower than the camp, in a rocky chasm difficult of descent for animals; the chief supply is a natural rock-bound well thirty feet in diameter and twenty-four feet deep. It contains about fifty-five thousand gallons. Many feet below it are two smaller holes, which the animals can get at, two or three at a time. There is no fuel, save a few bushes and Spanish bayonets. The country is well covered today with grama grass, and also I saw buffalo grass. We came over a high point, and had a fine view of the Órganos and the El Paso mountains, and the mound called "San Diego," where the river turns to the east. For a road coming up the river, there is a very fine valley gradually ascending to this point. The course today, allowing for a variation of the needle of 12° E., was southwest. Some antelopes were seen.

NOVEMBER 14. Expecting to march thirty miles (to the Mimbres) without water, and after the hard and late march yesterday, I lay [by] until near ten o'clock and cooked a ration; then all the animals were watered, and I got off twenty minutes after eleven o'clock. We proceeded in a direction 35° west of south. After a mile of ascent over rolling ground, we struck the margin of a vast plain surface extending indefinitely to the southwest and slightly inclined toward us. After coming about four miles, we met one of the guides, who stated that Leroux was at a stream seven or eight miles more to our right, near the mountain range, that the Mimbres had not been found, etc. I then took his course, southwest, proceeded about five miles, when he bent more to the right, and finally nearly a mile short to the right, into a valley, where a stream running from the hills and mountain to the right loses itself in the sand; near-by, above, is a fringe of timber – cottonwoods, ash, etc. The prairie today was generally covered thick with large gravel, with intervals of clay, all well covered with grass, both grama and buffalo, in places quite green and luxuriant. We came through prairie dog villages, always found with buffalo grass.

Thus Leroux on his second trip (or third, if he had attempted the exploration promised by the general) has only reached about forty miles from the river! I have no guide that knows anything about the country; and I fear such exploring, as we go, will be very slow or hazardous work. Leroux goes tomorrow with six men, and he is to send back one, every day's journey (for me), to meet me (he going that day double) until his party becomes too small. It is cold and cloudy, with a high southwest wind. Some expectations of snow are entertained. Lofty mountains, distant and isolated, rise here and there from the great smooth plain I have mentioned. Such is the general characteristic, I am told, of Mexico. The Mimbres, which I was led to believe we would reach tomorrow, it is now thought by the guides may not be reached the day after! Just in the camp is apparently the foundation of a house; the stones, though large, are rounded; it rises a foot or two from the ground. This is the plan. . . Close by, besides fragments of earthen pottery, is a broken mortar of a very hard red stone resembling a buhrstone. All the exterior is apparently in its natural rough state; there seems to be no other similar stone near.

NOVEMBER 15. Eight o'clock A.M. The guides are behindhand. It rains a little, and there is no fuel at the next camping ground. There being good grass and fuel here, I have reluctantly concluded to lay by today; but I have no doubt of its being for the general advantage. Leroux, Mr. Hall, Doctor Foster the interpreter, Charbonneau, and three Spaniards have gone, and I have urged the necessity of an active and more distant examination of the country.

Evening. It has blown a gale all day, raining, snowing, and shining alternately; it is very cold, although the wind is but little west of southwest. I sent for an ox which was left yesterday "given out," and had it slaughtered, and, together with the smallest and poorest beef, [had it] issued as a ration, gaining thereby about a third of a ration.[161] I have calculated now, at the rate of issue, that we have, after today, ninety days of meat and eighty-six of flour.

NOVEMBER 16. A clear, cold day, with a high west wind blowing directly from the snow in sight on the low mountains close to our right. Our course today S. 15° E., bending slightly to the right into a curve, or shallow cove, of the mountains. Here, at their feet, after coming about thirteen miles, we find a small swampy hole of water, apparently insufficient, with plenty of black mud close to the surface.[162] Many old Indian trails concentrate here, and the grass is unusually poor.

161 On November 15, Henry Standage wrote: "Laid by encamp'd in a valley waiting for the old ox to come up. . . About 3 o'clock P.M. we received our share of the white ox. It is really the poorest beef that can be imagined and not only is there a lack of fat, but it is covered with sores caused by the blows received from day to day in order to get the poor thing along through the deep sands. Some complain a little at this kind of meat." Golder, Bailey, and Smith, *op. cit.*, 183-184.

162 "This has found its way to some of the maps as Cooke's Spring," recorded Cooke some years later. Cooke, *Conquest of New Mexico and California*, 126.

The road today generally level, but with a few stiff rises and hollows to pass. Country well covered with grass; the soil seems good, with less gravel and stones. Charbonneau has returned and reports the gap just before us to be practicable, and that there is water six miles from here. He went with the others about twelve miles beyond it without finding other water. It was found to be about twenty miles round the point of the mountain to the south, and that way the guides went. Charbonneau reports favorably of the appearance of the country beyond the mountain; an open plain to the west, a little north. There is an irregular enclosure of rocks piled up (about three feet) on a hill near camp, probably a temporary defense of some of the Indians of the country. Very pretty, partially crystallized siliceous cinders are very common. There is no wood, but with brush, Spanish bayonets, etc., we make out pretty well. I felt yesterday almost confident that we might have crossed the mountain to the west of our last camp, where Leroux has been twice exploring. This evening I am told that one of the men went over yesterday hunting and reports it passable (too late). It would have saved much distance, and Leroux should have examined it.

November 17. Another bright morning, with a cold northwester. I marched to the southwest, up a winding valley and over the ridge, down to near the verge of the open prairie beyond; up a ravine to the right of the road (going to the north) is the water. In this mouth of the pass I was compelled to encamp a little after ten o'clock, having marched only three miles (which Charbonneau had called six). We saw today a new variety of oak – a large luxuriant bush eight to ten feet high, with leaves about an inch long; they are still very green. Also a new and beautiful variety of the Spanish bayonet, very large and spherical in shape, the largest leaves near three feet long and indented like a fine saw, with a pole eighteen feet high from the center. Tesson killed in the mountain two of the domestic goats with cropped ears; they were very wild; stolen, I suppose, and then lost, by the Indians.[163] I have been on a peak three hundred feet high; a view of our exact course was obstructed by a higher mountain close by; but in that direction – west – only slight and smooth (looking) elevations could be seen. But alas, where shall the water be found? To the south it is a vast level, from which, irregularly, rise conical hills, mountains, and short ridges, evidently from volcanic eruptions. This ridge was covered with brown sandstone, hard and fine. I saw there a flock of partridges of a new species; they are rounder, smoother, have longer necks, and a beautiful plume to the head, and are slate-colored. Two new splendid varieties of the cactus are found here: one a solid hemisphere, with ridges and horny hooks three inches long; the other with the leaf seven inches long, also round and ridged, but velvety and variable in color from pink and purple to nearly black.

November 18. After a severe night, with a very high north wind, we had a bright calm morning. Water, however, froze solidly over in vessels after sunrise. One of the Mexicans whom I hired as a shepherd came back yesterday at three o'clock afoot and reported the Mimbres eighteen miles distant. I march this morning before eight. About two miles disengaged me completely of the defile, when we followed a course 40° north of west over a tolerably smooth, firm prairie, a little rolling

163 The battalion was still without adequate food supplies. "I eat guts today for the first time though many have eat them before," noted Standage on November 17. Golder, Bailey, and Smith, *op. cit.*, 184.

and occasionally sandy, but generally a good soil. After making ten miles from a hill, we saw the Mimbres's timber 25° nearer the west, and down a smooth descent, apparently about five miles; we found it eight. I have observed that rising ground, particularly if it bounds your horizon, and descending ground are both very deceiving. In the first case an object will appear more distant, and in the latter much nearer, than the reality. The prairie this afternoon is more gravelly and covered with small stones. The wagons came in after eight and a half hours' steady pulling.[164] This is a fine, clear, bold stream, and is in places fringed with trees – amongst others, walnut – and with thickets of osiers (whence its name).[165] It is a pleasant camp ground; but no guide is here for tomorrow. There is a mountain before us – to the west – tapering to a distant point on the left and sinking to a high ridge on the right; but where is water or our most advisable course? Heaven knows! We are exploring an unknown region with wagons. It is believed that our camp three days ago is within a day's march (a long one), but the guide differs from me as to the direction of the gap; he thinks it northeast of this camp. The next traveler on this road, I hope, will pass the ridge at that camp, as my guides doubtless should have done, and cut off fifteen miles. There were thirty mortars found this morning cut into a solid rock, for corn or ore.

NOVEMBER 19. After a warm day, the sun blistering the face, water froze last night an inch thick. Doctor Foster, the interpreter, came in last night and reported the Ojo de Vaca, on the Copper Mine and Janos road,

164 Standage wrote: "Very much worn out today. The brethren are daily growing weak." *Ibid.*, 185.

165 The battalion crossed the Río Mimbres near the northern boundary of the present Luna county, New Mexico.

at eighteen or twenty miles. I marched this morning soon after seven o'clock, but in crossing the river, an hour and a half was lost, and a second road was cut through the saplings and brush; a pair of wagon hounds were snapped off. Our course was 25° south of west. The prairie was pretty firm and very little rolling; but the march was mostly an ascent, and we did not reach camp with the wagons until dusk; the mules were in harness eleven hours. Here there is only a little brush for fuel.

NOVEMBER 20. It was exceedingly cold last night; water froze in my hair this morning whilst washing. Leroux, Mr. Hall, etc., came in about seven o'clock last evening. They report that they found a hole of water about ten miles in the direction of San Bernardino (which they consider our course, and which is about 30° south of west), [and] that they went ten or twelve miles farther without finding any indications of water. Having come thirty-six or thirty-eight miles in two days, I deemed it almost necessary to halt a day, in the condition of the mules.

This morning I took the guides with me up a hill three hundred or four hundred feet high, to look at the country. Whilst there a Mexican trading party arrived from the vicinity of San Bernardino. After a close examination the following is the amount of their information: that it is seventy or eighty miles there; and that it is above thirty miles from the water hole discovered (and out of the route) to the next water, which they believed certainly insufficient for our stock; and that there is one more watering place between that and the vicinity of the old ranch San Bernardino. I had a long and anxious consultation with the guides. They agree that if there (at San Bernardino), it would be still very uncertain whether we could reach the Gila on our course. They say (and Doctor Foster, the interpreter, who was there in July last, agrees with them) that Janos is southwest of this point; that there is a wagon road leading there, and beyond to Fronteras; that from Janos, six or seven days' travel from here, the route is direct to the San Pedro and Gila – a traveled one where there is a trail, and that it is certainly better and surer than the more direct course; that it would make not more than four days' difference in the whole route – four days farther; and finally they advise that that course be taken (I have no guide for the other).

I have reflected long and anxiously. The general wished me to come the Gila route, that a wagon road might be established by it. The guides which he sent me would not attempt it, and aim to go some three hundred miles and then strike the San Pedro, its tributary, and this at a distance of from fifty to a hundred miles from the Gila – the whole distance. What difference if this distance is doubled, if it is a better route? I shall strike the Gila all the same by either, at the same point. I think there will scarcely be a wagon road for commerce between Santa Fé and the Pacific. If the continent is thus crossed in this vicinity it will be through El Paso, from which my road may be available. I have traveled a month with ten or fifteen men to help each wagon, and I am now nearly south of Santa Fé. If I had been supplied with *good* fat mules, it might be safe to keep directly on in this wilderness. But it should be noticed that making a wagon road for thirty or forty miles without water, is equal to going fifty or sixty with a road. This is done, with good mules, once or twice in a long journey. I have determined to follow the Janos road until I can turn off (probably two days on this side), as the best road, or route, to the same point of the Gila which I should strike in any route; all my guides agree in its being so. An Indian was in the vicinity, when Tesson arrived yesterday, alone; but he would not allow himself to be approached. This trading party report that they parted with a party of Apache sixty or seventy miles from here. I sent for the two senior captains and told them all the information on the subject of the routes; they agree with me as to the best; in fact I find now that there is no difference of opinion amongst all the staff officers.

Mr. Hall,[166] who was with the guides, thinks the country impracticable for us. This water is a spring in a quaking bog, where there is danger of animals falling through. I discover that the maps are worthless; they can be depended on for nothing. Mitchell's and Tanner's, both published this year, disagree two degrees of longitude in the relative positions of Santa Fé and San Diego. Some of the officers represent that the ration is insufficient, etc., and I find that the stealing of provisions has become very troublesome. I have increased

166 Willard Preble Hall was born at Harper's Ferry, Virginia, May 9, 1820. Graduating from Yale College in 1839, he moved to Missouri during the following year and studied law in the office of his brother, William A. Hall, of Randolph county. Later he removed to St. Joseph. At the outbreak of the Mexican war he enlisted as a private in company C, First regiment of Missouri mounted volunteers. In August and September, 1846, at the direction of General Kearny, he collaborated with Colonel Doniphan in compiling the "Kearny Code" of laws for New Mexico, which was proclaimed on September 22. During his absence from Missouri he had been elected a representative to congress. After receiving news of his election, he resigned from the army, and, pending the meeting of congress, traveled with Cooke to the Pacific coast. He was lieutenant-governor of Missouri from July, 1861, to January, 1864, and governor from January, 1864, to January, 1865. He died at St. Joseph, November 3, 1882. *Messages and Proclamations of the Governors of the State of Missouri* (Grace Gilmore Avery and Floyd C. Shoemaker, editors, Columbia, 1924), IV, 3-40; *Missouri Republican,* Nov. 4, 1882; Connelley, *Doniphan's Expedition,* 238-242.

it to ten ounces flour and twenty-eight ounces of fresh meat. That leaves me, by calculation, seventy-seven days' rations of meat and seventy-nine days' of flour. Of this party I have obtained eight tolerably good mules, six by exchange and two by purchase. Of six, the owner being not here, he was given his own price, which was fair, and a certificate that he was required to sell to us. The mules we disposed of were worthless to us, and unfortunately we have quite a number more of the same sort.

NOVEMBER 21. I marched this morning by the road, of which the guides had pointed out the course. I found it took a different one: 25° east of south, going over a ridge and leaving smooth prairie to the right. Whoever reads what I wrote yesterday will perceive that, relying upon the information of my guides and interpreter that Janos was to the southwest, I was balanced in my judgment as to my best course and followed their advice. I have followed them in almost every direction but east. After going a mile and a half toward that point, I decided to turn to the right [167] and go to the hole of water they had found ten miles on the way to San Bernardino. I then sent back to get the Mexican as a guide, on the terms he agreed to yesterday. At half past one, coming ten miles towards the west, I encamped at the foot of the mountain, the water being two miles up a narrow valley right away from my course. Whilst encamping, some

[167] Corporal Tyler wrote: "On the morning of the 21st the command resumed its journey, marching in a southern direction for about two miles, when it was found that the road began to bear southeast instead of southwest, as stated by the guides. The Colonel looked in the direction of the road, then to the southwest, then to the west, saying, 'I don't want to get under General Wool, and lose my trip to California.' He arose in his saddle and ordered a halt. He then said with firmness: 'This is not my course. I was ordered to California,' 'and,' he added with an oath, 'I will go there or die in the attempt.' Then turning to the bugler, he said, 'Blow the right!'" Roberts, *op. cit.*, 37.

servants, to my great relief, found enough water for cooking, etc., within a quarter of a mile; the animals are herded near the holes of water and there guarded. Leroux and Charbonneau arrived at the same time from the spring, without the Mexican; he would not come. Their information is very obscure, if not contradictory. They can convey no ideas of distance, but it would seem that my greatest risk is not to find enough of water the day after tomorrow, after encamping tomorrow night without any. I have directed Leroux and Weaver and three others to go on to the second water tomorrow and send back to the first, information; also to keep on to the creek which the trading party left a day and two halves of days before we met. There they left other Mexicans trading with Apache who were in the mountains close by. He will endeavor to speak to them to get information (guides), and to induce them to trade with us.

NOVEMBER 22. At half past seven I sent up the teamsters to water and bring down the animals as soon as possible, calculating to march at ten o'clock. Four or five different holes of water were found within a mile or two of camp, which, altogether, supplied a deficiency. Five minutes before ten o'clock I marched. Mr. Hall had gone an hour before with three men (with a spade) to dig at a dry creek which he reported to me he had found about eight miles westward of this camp, and where the sand was full of water. Leroux said it would not be more than three miles from our course. At eight o'clock Leroux, with his four assistants, went ahead. Winding out of our narrow valley, I found that Charbonneau and the pioneers had taken a course about 22° west of south. Reaching the head of the long column of men and wagons, I found that the trail of the Mexican trading party had not yet been struck, and that the guide had given Mr. Stoneman a point of mountain to go toward and was absent looking for the trail and for water far to the left. Much dissatisfied with the course, I kept a constant watch for the trail and became convinced we should see nothing of Mr. Hall. At ten o'clock, on a flat mound near our direction, Charbonneau came to us. He assured me that Leroux was still to our left, that he had not found the trail, but [that] he had found an old one which he was sure would lead to water. He left us to continue the same course and went off again to the left to renew his researches. Thus we continued until near four o'clock, following always a straight course toward the hills and mountains in our front, the great plain directly on our right lying in our true course. I was very much discouraged. Certain of finding no water tonight, I feared for tomorrow night.

Suddenly, at four o'clock, exactly before us, at perhaps fifteen miles, we saw a white smoke spring up. I knew then it was Leroux, who had spoken of making a smoke at the little water hole. I kept on, better satisfied, until sundown, when I encamped in a smooth low place, with the usual grama grass and enough Spanish bayonet for fuel, but no water. Since dark, Charbonneau has come in, having found the trail leading to the smoke, and he says it is still six miles to our left; he says he saw Leroux and party a moment before the smoke arose; he thinks it not more than twelve miles from this place. His mule give out, he says, and he stopped for it to rest and feed half an hour, when, going to bridle it, it kicked at him and ran off. He followed it a number of miles and finally shot it, partly, I suppose, from anger, and partly, as he says, to get his saddle and pistols, which he brought into camp. Mr. Hall also came up after dark. He found, by digging, probably a plenty of water and in a good course; then, seeing nothing of the column for a long time, he, supposing we had not marched, went back to the old camp. He got separated from the men and they have not yet come (eight o'clock). Two oxen gave out and were left today; two wagons with ox teams have just come up.

The road, or rather country, was smoother than usual today; the same gravel and clay, well covered with grass. It has been mostly a gentle descent. After all have passed, we leave a very good road. I directed today that the three wagons of each company and those of the staff should lead alternately an hour and a half, each set stopping, after leading so long, until all passed; it has answered very well. The old guard was, very provokingly, caused an unnecessary search of some hours for a mule which Weaver took off, leaving his own in its place without giving information of it. The weather has been unluckily rather warm today and very calm. The march about fifteen miles. The country in this direction is much smoother than that examined by the guides more to the west and in our proper direction.

NOVEMBER 24. Morning. A severe trial has been undergone – forty miles without water! Yesterday morning, reveille and breakfast was before daylight. The march had begun when the sun rose; and all admired its singular and unusual beauty. But once or twice before on this march had the mirage been observed; it results in part from heat and moisture. Now the sun rose over a distant range of mountains, and the mirage formed a vast luminous sea, or lake, to which the outline of the mountain gave a far shore; and then the higher mountains became a grand city, fortified and castellated, and with churches and spires, and the masts and sails of shipping which rested upon the bright and placid bosom of its bay. Our course, as I said, bore yesterday directly for the white column of smoke which rose from amidst the hills at the base of a small mountain; so we proceeded again from our dry camp. About nine o'clock a very strong and cold but welcome west wind sprung up. Ten miles over good ground, but mostly uphill, brought us to the trail of the trading party, where it had fallen into many well-worn paths, which made quite a road which led to the water and the mountain pass. I found a fine place to encamp, but, unfortunately, the water hole turned out to be scarcely a spring at all, and in rocks instead of sand, as I had been led to believe. The mountain was fruitlessly searched, and the hole enlarged before the wagons came up, which was after twelve o'clock. There was not enough of water for the men to drink, as it leaked slowly into the little crevices of rock and stones. They eagerly watched, and dipped it up by spoons! Many had had none, nor coffee, that morning. The assistant quartermaster had failed – so it was reported to me – to furnish two of the companies with kegs at Santa Fé.

Charbonneau had been running over the mountain searching the trail and best passage for the wagons. He had seen the distant sand bar beyond, where the Mexicans had reported a small supply of water; but, as to distance, they, as usual, had been able to convey no definite idea. I sounded the advance, and the poor animals dragged the wagons up the rocky defile of the mountain. Six miles on this side I met a guide sent back by Leroux, who reported an abundance of water at three leagues. We came in sight of a river, apparently, but we believed it sand. For hours I rode on, approaching it obliquely; but it *seemed* not at all. At last I struck it and found it the most extraordinary ground that had ever been seen. The dry bottom of a vast shallow lake, of indurated very light-colored clay, it was nearly as smooth and hard as polished marble! I sent back the sergeant major to direct the wagons to turn out of the trail to this strange plain, which was as easy as a railroad. It came in very obliquely from the right. I found it two miles to pass it. It gave no track, and with the sight a little averted, I could hardly realize that it was not ice. I arrived at dark at the shore, where it is a great bed of springs and swamp. The wagons arrived from half past seven to eight o'clock, having come forty miles without water for thirty-six hours, and having been thirteen hours in motion that day! Two wagons with ox teams and two other wagons of one of the companies did not come at all; the latter stopped four miles back and sent on the mules; they have just come up at ten o'clock.

Here were Leroux and Weaver, who had found the other Mexican party who attempted to get away, believing us enemies. They have twenty mules, which I have directed the assistant quartermaster to obtain by trade for ours that are utterly poor and worn down. The news by the Mexicans was very encouraging. They report good ground for a road to San Bernardino, with plenty of water, at four days' journey – my guides thought it about a day off!! And they say that one of them can go with some of my people and bring the Apache there, and that they have plenty of mules, just stolen (captured) at Oposura. The grass here, however, is poor and distant. This "Dry Lake," [168] which I shall call it for want of other name, is at least thirty miles in extent and averages perhaps a mile wide. Mr. Hall

[168] The present Playas Lake, Hidalgo county, New Mexico.

came round the mountain we crossed, and it is nearer from the last camp but one, if travelers could forego the watering place in the mountain; thus, too, in dry weather great advantage could be taken of the Dry Lake. That hole of water, it is thought, would answer for a party with fifty animals. As I have often had occasion to observe, this Dry Lake seemed providential to us; without it we could not have reached water for twelve hours longer; and if, as was to be expected, it had been sand, what an obstacle it would have presented!

Twelve o'clock. Twenty of the mules have been purchased for $666.66, and another for $50. The party would not trade, but the Apache probably will. The two ox teams did not pass the spring last night and are not yet up. I have engaged the Mexican as a guide to San Bernardino and an assistant in opening communication with the Apache. We pay him thirty dollars for his services, he using his own mule. Leroux and he and four others are going immediately to San Bernardino to examine the road and send back when necessary, and thence to find the Apache and bring them to meet me there. The whole surface of the ground about here is whitish with salts, probably of different sorts. The ox wagons have come in since dark. The Mexicans say that a month ago a military expedition from Chihuahua was near this spot and returned.

Very near here ten years ago occurred a very extraordinary and treacherous massacre. An American named Johnson, with seventeen persons of many different nations (with, also, a Mexican captain and four soldiers who withdrew from fear, it is said, before the occurrence), had come from Sonora, probably to plunder from the Apache; the captain and soldiers ran off the night before, when there was much difference in the party, and six opposed the horrible deed. Johnson engaged the village of probably a hundred and fifty warriors (beside women and children) in trade, and they were gathered around closely and unsuspectingly. He had hidden a swivel on a bag of flour, with another on top of it; it was loaded to the muzzle with balls and a chain. A man sat pretending to smoke, and at a signal uncovered the breech and fired; and this was followed by two volleys of small arms. At this explosion, seemingly from the ground and as unexpected as an earthquake, the Indians not killed or mangled fled in consternation. Johnson's party, so few in number, soon retired likewise and were pursued or waylaid by a small party of Indians who had rallied; they were fired on at a short distance with only the loss of a mule. Johnson's party then killed seven of them but reached Janos in a rapid retreat in a day and a half. Three women are said to have been killed by the balls and chain. This fruitless, as well as base and treacherous, attack on so large a force is very strange. Even those of the party who opposed the deed were overruled and had for self-preservation to go through with it. They took from the body of the chief, Juan José, who was an educated man, some orders which President Santa Anna had sent to his generals then invading Texas; the Indians had captured them. Johnson still lives in Sonora, conscience stricken, it must be believed, with the horrors of this base and fiendish deed.[169]

NOVEMBER 25. It was exceedingly cold last night, although there was no wind; it is believed the thermometer would have indicated between ten and fifteen

169 For Benjamin D. Wilson's account of this affair, see Robert Glass Cleland, *Pathfinders* (Los Angeles, 1929), 372-375.

degrees. About seven miles brought us to the defile of the mountain; it is very long and quite rocky.[170] It took the wagons about two hours and a half, and was probably three miles over.[171] Charbonneau, who had killed an antelope before the column reached the mountain, I found near the summit (whilst the baggage was slowly crawling up) in pursuit of grizzly bears. I saw three of them far up among the rocks, standing conspicuously and looking quite white in the sun, whilst the bold hunter was gradually approaching them. Soon after, he fired and in ten seconds again; then there was a confused action, and we could see one fall and the others rushing about with loud and fierce cries that made the mountains ring. The firing having ceased whilst the young bears were close by, I was much alarmed for the guide's safety; and then we heard him crying out in Spanish, but it was for more *balls;* and so the cubs escaped. The bear was rolled down and butchered before the wagons had passed. From the last hill on this side the guides showed me a gap through which we will pass the second march from this; it bore S. 40° W. We then had a fine plain to cross, generally descending.

We met today, first, the plant called nopal, like the Spanish bayonet; it seems a variety of the palm, as the cabbage tree is said to be. It has a cabbagelike head, just above ground, eighteen inches in diameter; this sends out immense green leaves, forming a sphere of points which would probably transfix a man. The edges of the leaves, curved up nearly into cylinders, are jagged as the saw of a mill. The second year, probably, it sends up a stem. We find them twenty-five feet high, and five inches in diameter at the base. This "cabbage" is a good

170 The present Whitmire pass, Hidalgo county, New Mexico.

171 The battalion had now crossed the continental divide.

article of food, but it takes vast quantities of wood and a day or two to cook it by roasting it in the ground; it is then very palatable and called "mescal." Brandy is also distilled from this plant.

Our course brought us to a stream, the Las Animas,[172] where it was dry, though sufficiently wooded, chiefly with sycamore. Charbonneau found running water three-fourths of a mile above, near the mountain; but just as I turned, it was found that it again made its appearance lower down and more in the course. Making the same right angle that I had, in spite of sounds and signals, the baggage got into camp about sundown. A hard day of nine hours and about seventeen miles. The loss of several mules and oxen from breaking down has been reported this evening; and there is more complaint than ever before of insufficiency of transportation; this, after a purchase yesterday of twenty-one mules! The forty miles without water, and the cold, and [the] bad grass of the last camp have told, I fear, very seriously. Here there is, as usual, grama grass and close by, and plenty of fuel. The soil today was more barren than usual. We passed close under a bare peak of the mountain, of granite I think. We cross, as usual of late, many trails of Indians and the cattle, etc., they constantly drive off from Sonora. We have now a high wind from the southeast. To complete my account of wild animals, I would mention that there have been seen in this same mountain a dozen black-tailed deer. Today we passed a prairie dog village and saw a wolf skulking around its suburbs. We also saw some large hares, the same as on the Platte and Arkansas rivers.

There is much that is strange on this vast table-land, studded with peaks and mountains of every shape; but

172 The present Animas creek, Hidalgo county, New Mexico.

this afternoon all must have been struck with the quiet beauty of the scene before us. The mountain passed, before us was a smooth plain, inclined always to the right but unbounded in front. Waving with the south wind, the tall grama and buffalo grass received from the slant sunshine a golden sheen; and the whole had a rich blue and purple setting of long mountain ranges on either side. The light, the shadow, and the varying distances gave variety and beauty of hue: the near heights dotted with cedar, the silvered granite peaks, and the distant lofty summits of the Gila mountains. The sun, with its pencil of rays, touched all with the bright effect of the skillful painter, whilst the tree tops of the Las Animas gave the promise, which the bracing air welcomed, of the well-warmed bivouac and the hours of rest.

NOVEMBER 26. It was not so cold last night and today, though we always find ice at the watering places in the evening. The road this morning bore to the right to enter a narrow flat valley, but it was for some six miles stony and over many spurs from the high ground at the foot of the mountain to the left; so that it would have been better to have turned more to the right at starting and gone farther round. After that we fell into a well-worn trail which led over hard gravel or smooth clay soil, an excellent road though slightly ascending. This evening it turns the shoulder of the mountain to our left and bends to the south. It seems inevitable that wind among the mountains as we will, or can, and the south is ever before us. The camp is on a stream that runs down into the Las Animas a little below our last night's camp, and this is the first water found in it. Just below us is a short canyon of rugged rocks covered with the new species of oaks with the diminutive leaf; it seems an evergreen. The march is about twelve miles. The soil today is pretty good; the high mountain range to our right is remarkably well wooded. A guide has come in and reports it five or six leagues to the next water; and the next day, he says, we fall into the Janos and San Bernardino road, which last place we will reach that night. The wind is high and from the south.

NOVEMBER 27. Very cold last night; and a bright frosty morning and calm. I marched at eight o'clock, following the same trail due south; ground good. Three or four miles from camp I came to water and swampy ground, which finally compelled me to pass a low but sharp point of the hill. This is one of the headsprings of the same creek we followed up yesterday. Then turning 20° to the west, we came five miles over a smooth low table-land, and then turned southwest towards a gap among some rather broken mountains, when we found water running a few hundred yards before it sinks. Here I have encamped. At the last angle, round a rocky spur of the mountains, there were appearances of iron ore, and I found the needle to vary 20°. The soil seemed rich and a dark brown, but in large spaces of it no grass grew. We passed very extensive prairie dog villages; in fact they lined the road nearly all day; and I never remarked them before in apparently rich ground. The buffalo grass of late disputes predominance with the grama. The oaks, first descending from the mountains to the hills, are now beginning to be found even dotting the valleys, and we saw a very extensive grove to our left on the verge of the valley; there is also cherry. A very high wind from the southwest has rendered it very disagreeable since midday. Black-tailed deer and antelopes are plenty; a number were killed.

NOVEMBER 28. Marched through an easy pass to the west of the little mountain and the open valley to the left. A direct road would have kept it, but we turned up last evening about two miles out of the way for the water. After following then a southern course a mile or two, we fell into a trail running W. 20° S., and said to be an old road from Janos to San Bernardino. Thus ascending for a mile, and having made about five miles in all, we came to the verge of a great descent which led as far as the eye could reach, into moutains and rocks, rough and confused beyond description. I had the wagons stopped below, whilst Manuel, an assistant to the guides, as well as myself, was searching the country. Having heard of water in the edge of the valley back and to our left, I proceeded there and encamped about eleven o'clock. The range of mountains running six or eight miles to our left and about 20° west of south seems to have some little open country on this side of it which may afford an outlet. I have sent Manuel to examine down in that direction. Charbonneau I have not seen since eight o'clock; he is either examining the country or hunting. Leroux was, at the least, to have sent a man to meet me today; he went two days ago with the new guide into the mountains to the left to seek the Apache; Weaver, Tesson, and two others are with him. I have some apprehensions for their safety. This San Bernardino seems to elude us like a phantom. There is very little water here, but I have discovered more about a mile off. There are some small oaks for fuel; we have seen them today, quite large trees. Deer and antelopes are plenty; the former are very beautiful and of a dark iron-gray color. It is overcast, warm, and promises rain.

Leroux came in with his party at seven o'clock this evening; he reports that the trail we followed to the brink of the table-land is *the* trail, or road, and there is no other. What seemed impracticable, now becomes practicable. I have directed Mr. Stoneman to take a large pioneer party, with all the tools we have, to go to work very early in the morning. Leroux says it is about eighteen miles to San Bernardino, that the three first miles from here are the worst, and that there is water halfway and some much nearer. I have directed Mr. Hall to go early and find the distance to it, and whether the wagons, being lightened, can be taken with two or four mules. I have determined to pack the whole of the mules to the first water tomorrow and then bring them back. Leroux brought with him a chief of the Apache; that is the best of his mission. He thinks that if he had not managed to get within a fourth of a mile of their village, undiscovered, that he would not have succeeded; and I am told the chief would probably not have come, but that he was drunk when he set out, and that he had showed signs of a strong inclination to return. The Apache promised to meet me at San Bernardino and to trade mules; they said, however, that they had not many. They have lately returned from an inroad to Oposura; they were warmly pursued and lost a part of their spoil and speared many of the mules.

A young Apache told Leroux he had come from beyond the Gila, and that it was a good prairie between it and San Bernardino, with springs. Doctor Foster assures me that there is no other pass practicable for wagons for fifteen hundred miles to the south (a little west), the edge of the great table-land of Mexico. He passed down a similar place to this at Carretas,[173] near Bavispe,[174] only passable for mules, and describes the

173 The town of Carretas is in the northwestern part of the state of Chihuahua.

174 The town of Bavispe, located on the Río Huachinera, is in the north-

change of climate and vegetable productions as very great and sudden. San Bernardino is on the Yaqui,[175] one of the largest rivers of Mexico, and which runs into the Gulf of California. Manuel came back and reported that he was in view of the stream, which seemed a thousand yards below and in a chasm. Leroux speaks of all the country he has seen in his last reconnaissance (and he was on the lofty range to the south called the "Long mountain") as being very much more broken and impassable than the pass we turned back from! Charbonneau has not come in tonight.

NOVEMBER 29. Same camp. 4 P.M. It rained gently most of the night. It is warm today and nearly clear. I sent Mr. Stoneman at sunrise with twenty-one men to make or improve the road. About nine o'clock I got off one hundred and forty mules, well packed, for the first water.[176] One company went, leaving its wagons. At one o'clock I sent a note to Mr. Stoneman to keep on and sleep with his party at the canyon camp. At half past three I received an answer that he had worked only a mile and thought he would be nearer this camp, and that empty wagons might with much difficulty be got through; he thinks rather the worst is passed. I shook hands with Manuelita,[177] the Apache chief, this morning. I told him we were friends and that I was glad to see him; that my great chief had gone on to California with a few men to meet a great many who came by the

eastern part of the state of Sonora, about twenty miles southwest of Carretas. Today it has a population of about 800.

175 This is an error. San Bernardino is on the Río San Bernardino.

176 The battalion was starting to cross the mountains near the Guadalupe pass, which is close to the junction point of the present states of Chihuahua, Sonora, Arizona, and New Mexico.

177 "A good Indian," according to Davis. W. W. H. Davis, *El Gringo* (New York, 1857), 409.

sea; that he would take the country from the Mexicans; that I was going to join him; that my mules were tired and I wished to trade with his people for others; that this same chief and myself had met Apache last year beyond the Arkansas and treated them as friends; that the men he called Americans, and who led the Mexicans to war against the Apache, were men who had run off from their country and become Mexicans; that we did not own them; that the true Americans had now conquered New Mexico and would treat the Apache as friends. We, too, are at war with Mexico, and if any of their war parties came (as they apprehended) soon, while I was with them, our cause would be the same.

Leroux represents the bad road as ten or twelve miles, and that it is then prairie again. He thinks, from the accounts of the Indians, that it is less than a hundred miles to the San Pedro. He said today, in answer to me, that Carson told him, in presence of the general, not to attempt to strike the Gila nearer than the Pedro. Charbonneau came in this afternoon; he had been a great circuit looking for game, at the country, and finally for my camp; that is, he was lost. He thinks the country impassable for wagons. Game is very plenty; he killed two deer close together and saw wild cattle. One of the wagons has hounds so broken as to be spoiled for a mule wagon; two others have tires very loose. The hospital wagon is large and heavy; so Major Cloud, who has a small light wagon, will pack from here; it is his choice. Doctor Sanderson takes the little wagon. The doctor's wagon I have directed broken up for repairs to the others which need them. The pack mules got back about sundown. Lieutenant Stoneman came in with his party soon after. He had made rather more than two miles of road, and thinks that by returning at daylight with a new party he can get on fast enough to enable me to take the wagons, etc., to the first water of the creek.

I send Leroux forward to San Bernardino early to meet the Indians, explain our delay, etc., and examine the road; he will send back Charbonneau to be our guide. Weaver will go to the last water in the canyon, return and report distances, and serve as a guide so far. The reports are so confused that I cannot tell the relative distances, nor whether it will take two or three days to San Bernardino. The wagons will be very nearly empty; and Lieutenant Stoneman thinks it necessary, and that there will be great difficulty. He has found the crowbar invaluable. It is a portage. Mr. Hall went some fifteen miles, he thinks, and returned this evening; his report is rather favorable. He is very willing, active, and enterprising. The sick report is increasing fast; in fact the men are not sufficiently clothed – no greatcoats. But the weather has been much more moderate for two days, and the descent we now make is perhaps one or two thousand feet. The soil here is soft and dark, and seems rich. We would have moved today with great disadvantage under ordinary circumstances; the tents wet, and the ground accumulated so on our shoes in walking as to make it a matter of difficulty.

NOVEMBER 30. I got off the empty wagons and packs by nine o'clock this morning. It was a mile and a half to the verge of the plain; the first three-fourths of a mile was very bad. In one place, particularly, the descent was steeper than I have ever known wagons to make (ropes, of course, were used); one was very near turning over, the hind part over the fore part.[178] The rest of

[178] Henry W. Bigler, a private in company B, recorded: "I think no other man but Cook would even attempted to cross such a place but he seemed to

the road, six miles to this camp, where one company came yesterday, is only exceedingly rough. I had at times two, and at times four, mules in a wagon. One wagon had its hounds snapped in two, and I ordered it left (one company, much smaller than the rest, can do very well with two wagons); another was slightly broken. Weaver came back and reports that it is about seven miles to the last water, where the trail leaves the mountain stream we are on, and that the road is much better, for road *it is*. Above and below this are indications and even tracks of a wagon. But I am mortified to find that there was much better ground for two or three of the first miles, when our track was so bad, and the road, in fact, formerly passed over by wagons. Doctor Foster followed back a ravine putting in on our left (as we came), and found the road (and a practicable one for loaded wagons) to the plain we came from.

My guides are ignorant of the country. Being led to believe two mornings since that it was a good road by the trail, Charbonneau went off hunting. Leroux had been on a mission to seek the Apache as much as to look for a road, and came in late and tired the night before last. Yesterday morning I sent for him and told him I thought I had seen from a high elevation a valley to our left which promised well, and wished him to go and examine it. He assured me he had examined, he believed, the same one, and that there was no outlet to it; and remarked that from the information of the Indians, and from the fact of the old trail (which undoubtedly passes over the best ground in so difficult a pass) it certainly was the only one; and then spoke of the extreme roughness everywhere else. And he had passed all

have the spirit and energy of a Bonypart." Golder, Bailey, and Smith, *op. cit.*, 189.

round, I may say, and had been on high mountains which he pointed out. As Lieutenant Stoneman was then hard at work two miles off, I did not insist, but rather doubtingly. Then Charbonneau came in with no better information, reporting that the country was impassable for wagons. I am glad to record that there is a better road, varying from mine for three or four miles and a very practicable one for loaded wagons.

The scenery today was grand and picturesque. At one spot there is a pass not thirty yards wide on one side. A vast rock overhangs the road. Just opposite, on a vertical base of solid rock forty feet high, rests another rock of a rounded cubical form of about twenty-five feet dimension. On its top rests still another of spherical form about twelve or fifteen feet in diameter. The mountains and sharp ravines were well covered with the new species of oak of large size, cedar, sycamore, etc.; Spanish bayonet, mesquite, and other shrubs, all of a bright green. The march about eight miles. We have descended about one thousand feet. A man named Allen, it is believed, has deserted.

I have no doubt now but that I saw the upper part of the valley of the proper road the day before yesterday. Described it to Mr. Leroux and requested him to go and examine it next day, and he replied that he had. The direction for it is this: To leave the plain we came from about a mile to the south from our road, and a mile and a half from the old trail; in returning, to keep the dry branch where our road turns to the left to go over high hills; it passes just there, between two high rocks, with a pass less than twenty feet between; and just at this spot is a very large oak with a cross cut in its bark. This is called the pass of Guadalupe. I have no evidence that the same difficulty of a break of the great table-land and mountainous descent will not be found to extend to the Gila, and I believe that this is the only wagon pass to the Pacific for a thousand miles to the south. It is the road from Janos to Fronteras, although this is forty miles north of Fronteras. Doctor Foster states an instance of a large carriage coming from the City of Mexico to Oposura by this spot as the only practicable road.[179]

DECEMBER I. Made six or seven miles winding down the dry mountain torrent; the road exceedingly hard pulling, as much from immense tufts of grass and sod as the sand and the rocks in the bed of the stream and at its many crossings. I encamped here, where the water appears for the last time, about one o'clock, no guide having returned, and the distance to San Bernardino believed to be at least eight miles. The pioneers went

[179] Cooke blamed his guides, especially Leroux, for the failure to find the Guadalupe pass. He wrote: "November 28th, a faint road was struck, believed to be from Yanos; it very soon led to a very precipitous and rocky descent of perhaps a thousand feet into the heart of a wild confusion of mountains, which extended as far as could be seen. It was soon discovered that the trail could not, at its first descent, at least, be made passable for the wagons; water within a mile was fortunately discovered, and the battalion camped. Leroux and all but one of the guides were still absent. Some exploration was then made; all pronounced the first descent impassable for wagons; but immediately a large party was sent to work a passage-way. That night Leroux arrived, bringing an Apache chief, whom he had managed with difficulty and much address. Next morning it was owing to Leroux's positive assertions and arguments, that there could be, and was no other pass but the horse trail, that I did not insist upon his thorough examination. He even asserted, but was mistaken, that he *had* examined an opening I had seen from an eminence, and believed might be a wagon road. . . About this time [November 30], Doctor Foster, interpreter, accidentally found the intersection of an old wagon road with mine, and said he followed it back, and that it led to the verge of the plain about a mile from our point of descent. He says this is called the pass of Guadalope, and that it is the only one for many hundred miles to the south, by which the broken descent from the great table-land of Mexico can be made by wagons, and rarely by pack mules." Cooke, *Conquest of New Mexico and California,* 135-137. See also *House Ex. Docs.,* 30 cong., 1 sess., no. 41, pp. 554-555.

on a mile or two to the verge of the prairie and returned. Weaver, a little beyond, spoke to an Indian, whom he, with great difficulty, persuaded to approach him, although then alone; he would not come in. It is not surprising, after the murderous treachery of Kirker and Johnson. The weather is rather warm, a little cloudy, wind west. We passed today beautiful scenery – the broken mountains about, the precipices, and confusion of rocks. Amongst them, mescal and Spanish bayonet now become true palm trees – the evergreen oaks, the cottonwoods, and sycamores brilliantly colored by the frost.

Messrs. Smith, Hall, and myself have ascended a mountain near-by, some eight hundred feet high. Our view was very extensive. A few miles to the south we saw the Yaqui, which, becoming a large river, empties far down into the Gulf of California. To the northwest we saw a prairie for thirty or forty miles, narrowed by the mountains seen everywhere else to a narrow gaplike outlet. We supposed that to be our course. San Bernardino was nowhere visible. We could see toward the Yaqui, the mouth of a break in the prairie, in which we believe runs a creek, on which, to the northwest, we saw what may be mesquite wood and the foundation of an old mud house. The top of the mountain was about thirty yards by fifteen. I suggested what a world's wonder it would be, set like a gem in the grounds of the Capital. The rocks, like all on this mountain, glittered with crystals of silex of white and pink, and even purple. There grew a giant mescal thirty feet high, and others of this year, [with] bristling spheres of green bayonets three feet long; several plants or shrubs without a name; cacti, from a little pink ball at your feet to the size of trees; a nondescript, said to be of the family, sending out rods fourteen feet long, with rosin for bark and two-inch spikes for leaves, which I named "devil rod," etc.

DECEMBER 2. It was a cold night, ice forming thick in my tent. The loads were restored to the wagons (with their usual team of eight mules) this morning. For a mile and a half, perhaps, we followed the dry creek, frequently crossing and laboring over the great lumps of sod, but we leave a tolerable road. Then we turned to the right and wound up a long ascent to the bluff edge of the high prairie. Generally descending, we then passed over good firm ground toward the west and saw, miles off, the ruins of the ranch of San Bernardino. We descended into the broad flat bottom to the east of it, crossed, and encamped near the old houses and a remarkably fine spring fifteen paces in diameter. As we approached, Charbonneau came to meet us and said no Indians had arrived. But soon we saw them coming in, and as we crossed the bottom, old Manuelita, with a superior chief and several others, rode out to meet us. There are some dozens of them in camp, but none of them came from the village where Leroux found Manuelita, who was a visitor.

I invited the two chiefs to my tent and told them that we were the *true* Americans who had just conquered New Mexico; [that we] were friends to the Apache; that my great chief had gone on, and that he and my government would expect them to assist us with guides and mules to go on, to drive the Mexicans from California; that I was making a road to that country, one which my countrymen would pass; and that it would be the duty of the Apache to treat them as friends and help them on; that so long as they conducted [themselves] thus, we would be their friends; that our traders would supply their wants; and that our government gave annual presents to the tribes who were thus friendly. I asked them to send to the other village for a guide (we know of), for mules, etc. The chief replied that if the sun and the moon fell, still they would be friends to the Americans. They made a difficulty about sending and said the others were afraid to come in. One of them then promised to guide us; and they say it is about seventy miles only to the Pedro, that a man can ride a fine horse there in a day, that our wagons can go in five days. They are poor, dirty Indians, but are generally dressed in cotton shirts and many in trousers. They have fine moccasins, which have boot tops. They ride fine horses, which they prefer much to mules, and are armed with very formidable-looking lances [and] with guns and bows. They are ugly and squalid, [and] wear their hair generally long and in various fashions. They wear a kind of leather skullcap, now and then ornamented with feathers and with chinpieces. They seem to understand Spanish. Their own tongue is by far the most brutal grunt that I have ever heard. Their lips scarcely move, and the words come out a stuttering, jerking guttural. They have but two or three indifferent mules here.

The soil of this great bottom is pronounced very good, but the grass is now very poor, and the rising ground is a "chaparral" of mesquite wood. The ox, in a perfectly wild state, abounds here; the guides have shot three or four. As we descended from the high ground, an immense red bull rushed by in front at full speed; it was more novel and exciting to me than the sight of buffalo. No doubt there are many Indians about, who, seeing the safety of those here, will come in tomorrow or next day. I would stay several days if the grass were good enough, with advantage; particularly as there is a prospect of subsisting ourselves on wild bulls. There is no fuel but mesquite. The march was nine miles. I presented each of the chiefs with a knife and three or four yards of domestic cotton. They will only trade for blankets, or they must have a blanket in each trade. We have but one in the small pack of Indian goods, and I have directed Mr. Stoneman to purchase of Chacon as many as he needs. He is taking several mule loads to California; they can be bought at a very fair price. One mule has been bought this evening.

DECEMBER 3. Allen,[180] the volunteer, who was absent five days, and was at one time thought to have deserted, returned to camp yesterday evening. He was very badly off. He had come forward the morning we followed the trail to the brink of the pass, and he came down the trail; and his whole misfortune turned upon his taking it for granted that we could not and would not come that way, but turn to an apparent opening toward the south. He finally struck our road near the Dry Lake. He describes minutely his having been robbed by a small party of Indians of his musket, knife, and canteen. He ate of the carcass of a dead horse we left near there, and having no knife, had to use his teeth!

The village of Apache first visited by Leroux have not come in today. One man came late and gave us to understand that they were afraid. But two mules have been purchased, or bartered for, and at high prices. The guide engaged, and who went to a village, has not yet returned, but Leroux has confidence that he will not fail us. The hunters have reported the killing of per-

---

[180] John Allen, a private in company E, was the only member of the battalion who was not a Mormon. Golder, Bailey, and Smith, *op. cit.*, 190, 287; Cooke, *Conquest of New Mexico and California*, 140-141.

haps a dozen wild cattle today, and many pack mules have been a long time out but have not yet brought any in (7 P.M.). I have had the provisions which were issued to the companies at Santa Fé weighed, and find that there is a deficiency in pork and flour both, of six or seven days. It has arisen, in part, from wastage, and the weighing out of flour by small quantities. I have but fifty-one days' rations, at 10 ounces flour, 1¾ pounds fresh meat, and 10 ounces of pork. No meat has been issued today. I sent this morning a pioneer party on the old Fronteras trail, which will be ours for seven or eight miles through a gap in [the] mountains to the west. They worked as far as water and a camping place – six miles.

This old ranch [181] was abandoned, I suppose, on account of Indian depredations. The owner, Señor Elias, of Arizpe, is said to have been proprietor of above two hundred miles square extending to the Gila, and eighty thousand cattle. Several rooms of the adobe houses are

---

181 San Bernardino is near the northern boundary of Sonora. On May 21, 1851, John Russell Bartlett described it as follows: "San Bernardino is a collection of adobe buildings in a ruined state, of which nothing but the walls remain. One of these buildings was about one hundred feet square, with a court in the centre; and adjoining it were others with small apartments. The latter were doubtless the dwellings of the peons and herdsmen. The whole extending over a space of about two acres, was inclosed with a high wall of adobe, with regular bastions for defence. Being elevated some twenty or thirty feet above the valley, this hacienda commands a fine view of the country around. Vast herds of cattle were formerly raised here, but the frequent attacks of the Apaches led to the abandonment of the place. Some cattle which had strayed away and were not recovered at the time, have greatly multiplied since, and now roam over the plains and in the valleys, as wild and more fierce than the buffalo. . . This establishment was abandoned about twenty years ago; since which time, no attempt has been made to reoccupy it. Such seems to be the case with all deserted places here; a fatality or superstitious dread hangs over them, and when they have been left two or three years, they are not again inhabited." John Russell Bartlett, *Personal Narrative of Explorations & Incidents in Texas, New Mexico, California, Sonora, and Chihuahua* (London, 1854), I, 255-256.

still nearly habitable. They were very extensive, and the quadrangle of about one hundred and fifty yards still has two regular bastions in good preservation. In front and joining was an enclosure equally large, but is now in ruins. The wild cattle we will find ranging as far as the San Pedro; they support the Indians, just as buffalo on the plains to the east of the Rocky mountains. Fires would have been disagreeable today from 9 A.M. until near sundown. It may be worthy of mention that the First dragoons are now serving in four states, or departments, of Mexico, of vast extent, *viz:* Chihuahua, New Mexico, Sonora, and California. My camp is about seventy miles from a town of three thousand inhabitants – Arizpe.[182]

DECEMBER 4. Five days' rations of fresh meat was brought in last night. It is near ten o'clock, and the guide engaged has not come, nor the first village of Indians. There is one here who will go as far as the second water or camp. My guides will go on by noon, and I have ordered the battalion to be in readiness to march at one o'clock. The first water is but six miles.

Evening. I have marched eight miles to the west into a pass of a low range of mountains. There is a remarkable mound of bare rock one hundred feet high just back of the camp, and in front a hill peak with a façade of rocks apparently painted green, yellow, and brown; it is moss and the color of the rocks. There is a rocky basin of water between. There is some good grass. Apparently hundreds of wild cattle water here daily. The road which we cut is much uphill and generally through thickets of mesquite, generally stony, and producing little else than thorns or thorny bushes. Leroux, with

182 The town of Arizpe, Sonora, situated on the east bank of the Río de Sonora, has a population of about 1,500 at the present time.

four others beside the Indian, came on at eleven o'clock. He thinks this Indian can be induced to go as far as necessary. He is to send a man to meet me early tomorrow. The other Indian who promised me to go through did not make his appearance; nor did any others. This camp I believe to be under twenty miles from Fronteras.[183] A quarter of an hour before marching, I sent round instructions to have the camp fires secured, and directed that the rear guard should complete it before leaving the ground; notwithstanding, the prairie caught and was left burning. Three of the Indians went from our camp yesterday and returned in the evening with about two hundred pounds of delicious fat meat, better than the buffalo bull ever is.

DECEMBER 5. The defile, though not steep, was long and rough. The tongue of a wagon was broken soon after marching. The wagon had but about 1,200 pounds of load, and I had contemplated leaving it and another belonging to two of the smaller companies. I therefore directed it to be left, bringing some of the useful parts. Of course, the wagons are not worth their transportation to California, even if I had mules to transport them. I contemplate leaving one from each company before the march is accomplished, as a matter of necessity in fact – first or last. The condition of many of the mules may be judged from the fact that two died last night, the warmest for a month, and after several days' rest and a march of eight miles. After two or three miles we met Manuel, one of the guides sent back. There was a valley in front eighteen or twenty miles wide. We followed, as I think, a wagon road, and I was much discontented that it turned to the southwest, and I believe it is the road to Fronteras. It crossed some hilly ground

[183] Fronteras, on the west bank of the Río Sta. Barbara, was about thirty miles from Cooke's camp. Today it has a population of approximately 900.

in doing so, but the road, always hard, has been generally good, the mesquite being the greatest obstacle.

Fourteen miles brought me to a large spring, which, as usual, loses itself after running a hundred yards. I met the Indian passing back rapidly on his gray horse, bow in hand, and giving the column a wide berth. I, however, brought him to and had a little talk with him in barbarous Spanish. He was very uneasy. I thought, at first, he had run off from Leroux. The wild cattle are very numerous. Three were killed today on the road and several others by officers. Around this spring is a perfect cattle yard in appearance; and, I suppose, I myself have seen fifty. One died (that I saw) only after twenty wounds, half [a] dozen fired at ten paces – quite as hard as the buffalo. Mr. Hall, with Doctor Sanderson, was chased by one and put in some danger by his obstinate mule. The guide points to a gap due west as our course tomorrow. Through it we see a lofty peak apparently sixty miles off, which the Indian stated is beyond the San Pedro. The position of Fronteras is pointed out and believed to be about twelve miles to the south, a little west. It has been cloudy all day, with a cold south wind. There is tolerable grama grass. It was found after reaching camp that the axletree of another wagon was damaged past service and none other would fit; so that I have broken up another. This leaves three companies with two each, and the two largest with three, beside three for the quartermaster's department, field and staff. It is thought that as many as five thousand cattle water at this spring. They are much like the buffalo in their habits, etc.; are rather wilder and more apt to attack individuals. I measured the spinal process (hump rib) of one that was eleven inches in length.

DECEMBER 6. It blew very hard last night and also

rained. This morning it was clear. But there is snow on the lofty mountains, particularly the one in front, seen through the gap of the next ridge. One of the three shepherds deserted last night; he never has been paid. Marched at half past eight o'clock. A half mile or more from camp, where we struck the creek, water was found. Then ascending five or six miles somewhat north of west, it was necessary to cut our way through mesquite. The pioneers left an hour and a quarter in advance, but the wagons were upon their heels in three or four miles. A guide was met early in the day and conducted us to a hole in the hills and mountains where water appears above ground. Here is a fine grove of ash and walnut, and, to make it still more comfortable, an old cattle pen of dry wood. We were thankful, for this afternoon it rained and snowed, with a very cold wind. Leroux only left here this morning. He sent word that if he found water he would send back here, but if not, he would go on to the San Pedro to ascertain the distance. This rain may prove a favorable circumstance. The mules are now grazing at will over about a half mile square of valleys, surrounded by eight pickets stationed on ridges and hills. The wild cattle were again numerous, and quite a number very fat were killed. The meat becomes quite an encumbrance. It may be well, if the guide comes not, to stay a day here, if only to dry it. The animal thus wild seems to grow physically like the buffalo in several respects, and they certainly die quite as hard. The cows and calves keep separate; very few of these have been seen and none killed. A black-tailed deer was killed yesterday – a doe. A buck was wounded. If one is obtained, I shall preserve the skin for mounting. The mules, etc., were so much confined by the neglect of the guard last night that I have ordered the whole of them (officer of the day included) to be put on again to-morrow. The march perhaps of twelve miles. The pioneers were seven and a half hours coming.

The Apache trade to New Mexico the spoil of Sonora; they have done so for years. I have met two or three parties of New Mexicans among the Apache trading. I have found them in what is considered Sonora trading for mules just taken with bloodshed from Oposura![184] Thus a central government permits or suffers one state or territory to abet – to ally itself *de facto* with the enemies of another – with savages their common enemy. Mexico has utterly forfeited all claim to the allegiance of Sonora. Sonora has not for years acknowledged the control of the supreme government. Its present governor holds office independently of, and is not acknowledged by, the supreme government. The last troops sent to Sonora were sent to put down a party which defied the general government. They were bought up by this party, who thus in civil war triumphed. When Sonora was called on to contribute its contingent in money to the present war of Mexico with our country, they refused and answered that the government who gave them no protection had no claim on them, and that all their public and individual resources were inadequate to their protection against the savages who incessantly attacked them. Sonora would do well, and is not ill-disposed, to claim the protection of the United States.

DECEMBER 7. It is clear again today. All our rains have accompanied a wind from south to west. I sent out pioneers this morning. They went about three miles westward, following the tracks of the guides, which

184 Now called Moctezuma. It has a population of about 2,200 at the present time.

are in a large old trail. As the country looked open, with very little mesquite, they returned according to instructions. I await the return of the guides. Meanwhile, much beef is smoking. For the last three miles yesterday there was a comparative intermission of mesquite and a reappearance of Spanish bayonet. I don't know that I have mentioned that the pounded root of this plant is used as a substitute for soap in New Mexico. A party I had at La Joya several weeks tell me they use nothing else in that village. I saw yesterday a new bush, or tree; it resembles cedar at a distance. It has a gnarled stalk resembling artemisia. It bears a small red berry and has thorns.

Night. The guides came in this afternoon, having gone only twelve or fifteen miles to the west, without finding water, but report the grass remarkably green and the San Pedro scarcely as far beyond. I have directed water to be taken in the few kegs the companies have, and [have made] other preparations for encamping without water tomorrow night. The meat of several bulls killed and slaughtered yesterday afternoon was sent for and brought very early this morning, and others have been killed today near-by. The command have been busy all day smoking the meat. The Indian gave very accurate information and directions of the whole route from San Bernardino to the San Pedro. Weaver recognized points on the San Pedro. I have questioned him very closely. He says we shall strike it about the old ranch of San Pedro, about 60 miles above the Tres Álamos. From this point it is about 185 miles by the mouth of the San Pedro to the Pima village, and it is a very bad road – rough, much mesquite, and very little grass. From this same point – Tres Álamos – it is about 105 or 110 miles to the Pima village by Tucson, a good beaten trail and much descending to Tucson, about 30 miles. In the other 75 or 80 miles there is generally but one water, and, he has been told, about halfway.

DECEMBER 8. I marched a few minutes after nine o'clock. The night had been so cold, with so much frost on the grass, that the mules would scarcely drink. The morning was rather warm, but a southwest wind rose very high and cold. The road this morning was over very hilly ground and was therefore quite crooked. The ground was barren and hard, and good for a road except in places covered with loose stones. Near the base of a lofty mountain to our left we struck smooth prairie and were then troubled with mesquite. The snow lay on the mountain nearly to the foot and within a mile of us. We could then see a great valley running toward the north, but no other sign of the San Pedro. The guides saw the wood of it, they say, from a peak of the mountain. We have come about seventeen miles, three farther than they. Finding good grass and mesquite brush in the little valley of a dry branch, I encamped when the sun was more than a half hour high. The bottom of the valley – that is, the San Pedro – seemed so near that I first asked the guides if they thought that I could not reach it this evening; there is no water here. We saw, not distant, a gang of wild horses with colts. No wild cattle were killed; some were fired at far from the route by officers. The course this afternoon was west northwest (see map).

DECEMBER 9. I marched this morning soon after sunrise. As we approached the broken ground with a long black streak of mesquite, etc., where we imagined we should find the San Pedro, we were much disappointed. We fell into the smooth valley of the dry branch of the night's camp, which wound round in one northwestern course, and I finally concluded we had passed too far south for the river, or that this was the head of it; the guides had all become doubtful themselves. Troops of wild horses, and cattle, and antelopes seemed to invite attention, little of which was given. Leaving the great valley of the dry branch, we passed all appearances of broken ground, mesquite, or timber. Beyond, toward the mountain towering before us white with snow, from which a northwester cut us to the bone, we had seen only a smooth slope of prairie. My anxiety became very great and I pushed on at a fast gait to the guides, and after ascending a hill saw a valley indeed, but no other appearance of a stream than a few ash trees in the midst; but they, with the numerous cattle paths, gave every promise of water. On we pushed, and finally, when twenty paces off, saw a fine bold stream! There was the San Pedro we had so long and anxiously pursued.

The western mountains being more distant than the eastern and the ground smoother, I crossed the stream without difficulty and at twelve o'clock moved on down it. Then Leroux, Weaver, Doctor Foster, Chacon, and Tesson went on ahead with instructions to strike off at a certain point, perhaps fifty or sixty miles below, for Tucson, examine the ground so far, and obtain information of the road beyond to the Pima village – particularly what water may be found on it at this season. If I go by the mouth of the Pedro, I go round an angle slightly acute and pass a difficult country, passing through a canyon of the Gila, where it will be necessary for my infantry to cross the river repeatedly, the mesquite very bad and the grass poor. Thus, by Tucson, with a good road, is eighty miles shorter. On the other hand Weaver thinks it is eighty miles from Tucson to the Pima, with but one permanent watering place; and it is a town, perhaps garrisoned, which it is remote from my object to attack. But it is too much in my way and would put the command to too severe a trial to go round, and I certainly shall pass through if possible.

I make it twenty-seven miles without water to the San Pedro. I came on six miles farther and encamped on its bank. Those who have been at the fork of several ranges of mountains in the vicinity represent the grass as luxuriant. My animals obtain the grama grass every night on hills; it is of a straw color and looks dead, but the mules have lately improved on it with short marches, and the thousands of wild cattle and horses are fat. To our south is a lofty mountain, perhaps forty or fifty miles. There is Santa Cruz, and there heads a stream running south into the Sonora and another north to Tucson. This is lost, like the Sonora, in the plains. This vicinity is said to be the coldest part of Sonora without exception. We are then, probably, now at the coldest part of our march. This stream runs north. A bull was killed on the road today and one at our camp last night. I should have mentioned that a man servant[185] of Captain Davis died very suddenly yesterday morning. The wind having died away since noon, it is now quite moderate. It was the first northwest wind I remember since the second day from the Río Grande. March sixteen miles. The San Pedro was frozen over in places this morning. Somewhere near here is a deserted ranch named San Pedro. It belonged to the proprietor of San Bernardino and like that was broken up by the Indians. From it the wild cattle are derived, and they are the thickest at their old haunts. There are numerous traces of them, as of buffalo in their range; and the

[185] Elisha Smith. Golder, Bailey, and Smith, *op. cit.*, 191.

same, even to wallows. Their numbers are concealed by the vast thickets of mesquite. This seems a fertile valley; the low grounds about a mile wide. The highlands evidently fatten numerous herds in winter.

DECEMBER 10. It was exceedingly cold last night. This morning I believe Fahrenheit's thermometer would have stood below ten degrees. There being no wind, it has been warm today. After marching seven or eight miles, the hills approaching the river, we had to pass over a low bluff, and afterwards to wind much over and among the hills, as the ground is exceedingly hilly and mountainous, forming a canyon. Just there, on the eastern bank, stands a deserted ranch, or possibly only an adobe cattle pen. At two o'clock I turned to the right a fourth of a mile and encamped on the point of a spur of the bluff; the grass fine and the river three or four hundred yards off. Two dry creeks put in opposite each other at right angles to the river, just below. That on this side has walnut timber on it; the nuts are the size of a pignut. The pioneers, etc., had gone on a mile and a half and stopped; so I preferred an inconvenient camp after marching six hours, to the risk of not being able to touch the river in season. Just as the mules were unharnessed I received a message that there was a fine camping ground on the river within two miles. Marched about fifteen miles. Fish are abundant in this pretty stream. Salmon trout are caught by the men in great numbers; I have seen them eighteen inches long. There is not on the open prairies of Clay county, Missouri, so many traces of the passage of cattle and horses as we see every day.

DECEMBER 11. Marched very early.[186] The road to-

[186] The battalion was now marching in the southern part of the present Cochise county, Arizona.

day was quite crooked and rather difficult to open, the bottoms having very high grass and being lumpy. At two o'clock I again came to a canyon, and several men having been wounded and much meat killed, I encamped, sending Charbonneau to examine the country. He came immediately in view of a deserted village, which I presume is the true San Pedro. There was quite an engagement with bulls, as I had to direct the men to load their muskets to defend themselves. They attacked in some instances without provocation. One ran on a man, caught him in the thigh, and threw him clear over his body lengthwise; then it charged on a team, ran his head under the first mule, tore out the entrails of the one beyond, and threw them both over. Another ran against a sergeant, who escaped with severe bruises, as the horns went each side of him. A third ran at a horse tied to a wagon, and, as it escaped, its great momentum forced the hind part of the wagon from the road. I saw one rush at some pack mules and gore one so that its entrails came out broken. I also saw an immense coal-black bull charge on Corporal Frost of company A. He stood his ground while the animal rushed right on for one hundred yards. I was close by and believed the man in great danger to his life and spoke to him. He aimed his musket very deliberately and only fired when the beast was within ten paces; and it fell headlong, almost at his feet. One man, when charged on, threw himself flat on the ground, and the bull jumped over him and passed on. I have seen the heart of a bull with two balls through it, that ran on a man with those wounds, and two others through the lungs! Lieutenant Stoneman was accidentally wounded in the thumb.[187]

[187] Standage wrote: "The brethren had quite a battle with the bulls today, killing 9 at one time and the bulls killing 2 mules while in harness, several

An abundance of fine fish are caught, some that are three feet long; they are said to be salmon trout. It was exceedingly cold again last night, but there being no wind, it was disagreeably warm today. Our course is very little west of north, and I fear it is much farther than was supposed to the Tres Álamos. The march today about eleven miles. We crossed a pretty stream which I have called "Bull Run." About ten bulls were killed and butchered. I have directed that not more than rations for two days be carried away in the morning.

DECEMBER 12. Passing around the canyon and the ruined *rancho,* which is probably the true San Pedro,

hurt. . . Our Lieut. Quartermaster Stoneman of 1st. Dragoons shot himself in the hand by his 5 shooter going off accidentally." Golder, Bailey, and Smith, *op. cit.,* 192. On December 11, 1846, Guy M. Keysor, a private in company B, recorded in his journal: "Those in the Mormon Battalion who had yaugers [Jaeger?] were permitted to go a hunting this morning. Shortly after we started, two wounded bulls came jumping into our marching column. One of them knocked down and run over Sergeant Albert Smith, bruising him severely; as soon as they passed the column, they received a volley which brought them to the ground. The Sergeant was put into a wagon and the command marched on; soon descending to the river bottom we halted to water our teams, where another couple of bulls raging and foaming with madness, charged upon us. One of them tossed Amos Cox of Company D into the air, and knocked down a span of mules, goring one of them till his entrails hung out, which soon died; Cox's wound was four inches long and three deep. While these two bulls were performing thus, others stood a few rods off seemingly unable to determine whether they should charge or await the issue; they chose the latter course; meantime, the two bulls retreated, closely pursued. Then our attention was turned to the bulls that were looking on. Some officers shouted 'shoot them,' others cried, 'let them alone'; amid this confusion the wagons and part of the command moved on. The battle was renewed on our side and in a few minutes the enemy lay weltering in their blood. After advancing about half a mile another bull came rushing out of the muskeet thicket, and charged upon the hind end of a wagon, lifting it partly around, and knocking down a mule, but his career was short for all the command now had their muskets loaded, and soon greeted our fierce opponent with a shower of bullets. These bulls were very hard to kill; they would run off with half a dozen balls in them unless they were shot in the heart. The Indians apparently had killed off the cows." *Ibid.,* 193-194.

three miles brought us to the bottom again. The country is broken and rough, and we at times pass behind isolated hills. The bottom grass is very tall and sometimes difficult to pass through. These bottoms average above a mile and are good land. The hills are stony and barren. The mesquite here becomes a small tree, and with others this afternoon gave quite a wooded appearance to much of the bottom. I reluctantly crossed the stream today and back immediately; a deep, steep gully, or dry creek, and hilly ground seemed to make it advisable; no doubt it might be avoided. After coming twelve miles, the trail of the guides sent to Tucson seemed to lead off from the river and toward a gap. Other appearances indicated the spot which Weaver had described. We saw, too, on the verge of the bluff, in the gap, a tall post. Manuel was sent on the trail; the stick was, I believe, a Spanish bayonet, and the trail led I cannot find out where. Charbonneau still thinks the gap the one we are to pass, and that it is only accessible for wagons some ten miles lower down; so I have determined to send early in the morning to have the trail followed. It is probable that it was taken as a near cut to the river below. This camp is at a very good grama grass, the first good spot seen today in a march of fifteen miles. There is plenty of mesquite wood.

Eight P.M. Leroux has returned alone. This is the pass opposite, and truly we must go down some ten miles before turning off. The party reached an old ranch about fifteen miles from the river and found a considerable party – perhaps twenty-five Apache with their families, and some Mexicans who were there making mescal whiskey. They are a portion of the Apache friendly to the Sonoranians. Leroux passed his party for trappers who had sold out to this command, which had been seen coming a day or two since, etc. They said Tucson was close by, probably twelve or fifteen miles, that the garrisons of all the little frontier posts had been collected there but did not exceed two hundred in number, that the general had passed by the Pima only twenty days before and had evidently had some communication with Tucson; in fact three of his people were said to be there, but who I cannot imagine. They spoke of some treaty by which the Americans could pass anywhere, but were to prevent the Coyotero Apache who live north of the Gila from attacking them. Doctor Foster proposed to go on to Tucson; it was necessary, to keep up their assumed character, that some such course should be taken, as the mules of the party being tired down, they anticipated being pursued and taken if they revealed their true business by returning unceremoniously. So Weaver, Tesson, and Chacon also set out for Tucson, but a little later, and were instructed by Leroux to turn off and return by the hills or mountains. Leroux managed to hire a horse to return, leaving his mule. He got an excellent account of the road beyond Tucson – two roads in fact; one with two camping places, or "waters," [and] the other [with] three; that it was a two and a half days' journey for pack horses. So it must be about one hundred miles nearer and a far better road. The Apache he saw were the people who pursued those we met and recaptured the horses and mules. These had left the *rancho* in charge of a few soldiers half an hour before Leroux arrived.

DECEMBER 13. Marched early down the river bottom. This is a mile or two wide and a plain on either side, inclined both to the river and down stream, the mesquite in places taking the exact resemblance of orchards; the road was smooth. We came about seven miles and encamped, where, unfortunately, grass and water were both distant; this was necessary, or otherwise to leave very much our direction for tomorrow. The march tomorrow is represented to be eighteen or twenty miles. At three o'clock I had an inspection of arms and a long drill, drilling myself, first a company in front of the others, and then the battalion, principally at loading and firing, and in forming column from line and line from column. Then the following order was read to the battalion, *viz:*

Order Number 19

Headquarters Mormon Battalion,
Camp on the San Pedro, December 13, 1846

Thus far on our course to California we have followed the guides furnished by the general. These guides now point to Tucson, a garrisoned town, as our road, and they assert that any other course is a hundred miles out of the way, and over a trackless wilderness of mountains and river hills. We will march then to Tucson. We came not to make war against Sonora, and less still to destroy an unimportant outpost of defense against Indians. But we will take the straight course before us and overcome all resistance. But shall I remind you that the American soldier ever shows justice and kindness to the unarmed and unresisting? The property of individuals you will hold sacred. The people of Sonora are not our enemies.

By order of Lieutenant-colonel Cooke,
(Signed) P. C. MERRILL, Adjutant

Weaver and his two companions came in this afternoon; they had nothing material to add to Leroux's report. Doctor Foster has not come. I march on the Tucson trail at seven o'clock in the morning. The weather is fine and has much moderated. There was much good grass on the route today, though unluckily none convenient to this camp; and there has also been extreme difficulty in getting the animals down to water.

DECEMBER 14. With reveille before five o'clock I essayed to march at seven, but the distance of water, etc., and some neglect of the guard made it near eight o'clock. We wound up the bluffs without difficulty, but ascending ground lasted nine miles, the first two giving severe work to the pioneers, cutting palmetto and mesquite principally; the ground [was] sandy but firm, and well covered with grass. We then struck the trail to Tucson. I sent Leroux and three others ahead to renew his intercourse with the few people at the stillhouse and prevent them from running off. We struck a hollow at this same point, which was followed eleven miles to the first water, at this camp. About six miles back Tesson met me with a message from Leroux that he had fallen in with two soldiers, and that there were a sergeant and six men at the stillhouse, and that he would await my coming and orders (so the message was delivered). It was late and the wagons like[ly] to reach a camp after dark. I left word for an officer and fifty men to come on in advance of them, and pushed on with my suite and passed the advance guard and pioneers.

On this ground, among the mesquite trees, I rode in among four or five soldiers in uniform, with horses, and arms to their saddles. They were cutting grass and made not the least motion indicating alarm or preparation! A quarter of an hour after, Leroux returned from the stillhouse near a mile farther on and told me that the sergeant had a message for me. The camp was established on good ground, with water, grass, and fuel, at dark. Soon after, the sergeant and his whole party came to me. They had met Doctor Foster late two days ago with his mule tired out (with a drunken Indian guide), and he had said he would not come back. The sergeant said that an Apache had spread reports that had greatly alarmed the people, who were about to fly, that the commandant requested me not to pass through the town, that he had orders to prevent it but was not able, that I could pass on either side. I told the sergeant if the garrison was very weak I should probably not molest it, and to hasten back and assure the people that we were not their enemies but friends, who wanted to purchase flour, etc., of them. He left soon after dark.

I could not learn if Chihuahua had been taken. They report that a portion of California has been retaken by the Mexicans; I do not credit [it] at all. They say that General Kearny left with a Pima chief ten mules, a pack of Indian goods, and some papers (a letter?). The mules, I presume, [were] broken down. The sergeant says the general left there twenty-five or twenty-six days ago.[188] As near as I can learn, Tucson is as far, or farther, than I came today. The mules came in tonight very much tired. There is water four miles on the road. I have ordered that with a later march than usual the animals will be watered there, giving notice that camp tomorrow evening will be without water – that we enter Tucson early the next day and spend the afternoon there. There are now said to be three roads to the Pima from Tucson, varying from three to five marches. Per-

188 November 12, 1846. On that date Lieutenant Emory noted in his diary: "The general gave a letter to Governor Llunas [chief of the Pima], stating he was a good man, and directing all United States troops that might pass in his rear, to respect his excellency, his people, and their property. Several broken down mules were left with him to recruit, for the benefit of Cook's battalion as it passed along." *House Ex. Docs.*, 30 cong., 1 sess., no. 41, pp. 84-85.

sons are expected there today from the Gila. March today twenty miles. Weather very moderate.

DECEMBER 15. Marched at nine o'clock and watered at eleven at the last water. Then for a half mile was exceedingly difficult ground. After about six miles I left the valley, Leroux and Charbonneau following a trail down the creek (one road, but a bad one), and we saw no more of them until I encamped near sundown. The hill road was then pretty good, although we were much troubled by prickly pears, of which we encountered a new variety. At the stillhouse we saw a dozen or two Indians and Mexicans – men, women, and children. They had huts or wigwams of dry grass or reeds, beside a small adobe house. The process of distillation of whiskey from mescal was going on. It was altogether the most muddy, filthy, wretched-looking place I ever saw in my life. I fell in with four other soldiers this morning, who had brought rations, they said, to the sergeant's party; they acted in the same singular, confiding, friendly manner as the others. It occurred to me that Doctor Foster's stay was becoming extraordinary, and I determined to send him a note by one of the Mexican dragoons directing him to come to my camp this evening, stating that I held the other three, prisoners and hostages. It is now near nine o'clock P.M. and Foster has not come. I have questioned one of the prisoners; he says that Doctor F. was guarded, but that the commander, on receiving a message from the sergeant, had begged him to come with them last night, and that he refused. He states the force at Tucson to be about one hundred and that they have two cannon. He states that the commander sent a man with a letter to me yesterday, since which he has not seen him; but it is supposed he met the sergeant and party and returned.

We also saw today another extraordinary variety of the cactus, a green fluted pillar thirty feet high and near two feet in diameter, very straight but sending out (some of them), about midway up, several similar columns, something like the branches of a candelabra. The ridges of the flutes are thickly set with thorns. In the dry creek bottom were small willows perfectly green, and cottonwoods only turning yellow. Water did not freeze last night, but we see snow on the mountains. We are without water tonight. The guard is somewhat increased – to forty-two. The march twelve miles. But two days' rations of meat have been issued in the last two weeks from my commissary provisions.

DECEMBER 16. A little after midnight I was awoke by the arrival of Doctor Foster; he had been detained under guard until the arrival of my messenger with the note. With him came two officers with an escort. One was a "commissioner" to treat on terms; he was bound by written instructions, which he read to me but retained. They amounted to a special armistice, but restricted my passage to roads and limits to be marked by the commandant. Our conference lasted nearly two hours, and he finally departed with propositions contained in two articles, which they wrote in Spanish at my dictation but in their own form and style. Of this I did not make and retain a copy. They were substantially that he should bind his force not to serve against the United States during the present war, and in token of submission should surrender two cavalry carbines and three lances; and secondly, that my officers and men should freely enter the town for the purposes of trade and refreshment.

With reveille at five o'clock I had marched before sunrise, but [discovered] that quite a number of mules had strayed. Their disposition to search for water and the cover of mesquite bushes in a dark night led to the misfortune. I, however, marched at eight o'clock, about which time the mules were all recovered. I came on with the battalion, leaving only a sufficient guard with the baggage. The road lay over a plain of hard white gravel and sand covered with mesquite and prickly pears of every variety; and it seemed interminable. I had been led to believe the distance eight or ten miles; it proved sixteen. About six miles from town I met a fine-looking soldier mounted and armed with carbine and lance, who delivered me a letter from the commandant. It stated that as a man of honor he could not submit to my terms. The man was politely dismissed without an answer. I then gave orders for the battalion to load their muskets, but before it was executed two Mexicans rode up and gave information that the post had been evacuated; so I countermanded it. One of these two had been discharged by the general at the Pima; the other [was] a citizen (he said) of the town. They also gave information that the town was nearly deserted of inhabitants, forced off by the military; these had carried off their two brass cannon and all public property but wheat and tobacco. I formed line in the suburbs and addressed the battalion respecting my order and warning to respect private rights. I should mention that about a dozen well-mounted men met the column near town and accompanied it. Some of them are said to be soldiers. They were unarmed and in plain clothes.

I encamped half a mile below town, with a canal of water very convenient, but of grass none. Various directions were pointed out where it was said to be "close by"; in one I rode a mile over white sand through thick mesquite without finding a blade. I then ordered wheat taken from the public granary and fed two quarts to every animal. By dark I found a field nearly enclosed by a brush fence, where there was some grass, willows, and other herbage, and directed the mules put there. Although I gave repeated and exact orders for their safe movement in the dark, they were so far misunderstood that thirty or forty went astray. I found perhaps a hundred inhabitants here. They are fine-looking people and seemed rather glad to see us. They came freely into camp with articles for sale.[189] I could obtain but two or three bushels of salt and at a very high price; the command was out of it. We saw, as we marched over the plains, far to the left, a very large stone church [190] built by Jesuits; it is at a large Indian pueblo about ten miles above. At that point it is believed the military halted. There are several pueblos in the close vicinity. I learned that twenty-five soldiers had been sent to the Gila to observe and harrass our march, and that these passed this forenoon to join the others. They were met and conducted on a path around a small mountain.

DECEMBER 17. I had the guides out at daybreak looking for grass; they could only find more of the poor description mentioned, in the creek bottom. After a feed of wheat the mules were taken there in the brush, with a strong guard. Thirty or forty were reported missing this morning, and I sent off ten small parties to hunt them. There being much covert, I reflected that it would be a proper precaution to push a small party toward the enemy, if only for the protection of the mule hunters; and I was seized with a desire of making a strong

189 Standage wrote: "We were kindly treated by the people of Touson who brought Flour, Meal, Tobacco, Quinces to the camp for sale and many of them giving such things to the Soldiers." Golder, Bailey, and Smith, *op. cit.*, 195-196.

190 San Xavier del Bac, built in 1700.

reconnaissance, to be turned under favorable circumstances into a real attack. But a forced march was before us to the Gila, and the men were weary and nearly barefooted. With many doubts of the military propriety of my detaching myself on a venturesome expedition, I called for mounted volunteers and about fifty infantry.

At half past nine I marched at the head of twelve officers and all sorts of people, mounted nearly all on mules, and about forty volunteer footmen of the battalion, and took the path through the Tucson to the pueblo. A mile from town we saw two Mexicans beyond the bottom, galloping in the same direction. We succeeded in taking up one of them; he said he was going to warn his family or prevent them from being alarmed. I took him for a guide. The thicket soon became a dense forest of mesquite trees two feet in diameter. After marching four or five miles, we came to water; and while waiting some time for the footmen to come up, I for the first time spoke freely to the officers and asked their opinion of the prudence of continuing farther in the dense covert which we had found, and which the guide stated became worse all the way to the pueblo. The four gentlemen I spoke to gave each his decided opinion against proceeding any farther. My object then being accomplished, as far as the unfavorable circumstances admitted, I marched back to camp. Before we got back, signal smokes were rolling up in the direction of the enemy. They were signals of our approach and very probably caused a further retreat of the enemy.

I have issued two quarts of wheat to every three men, and have directed about twenty-five bushels taken for the mules tomorrow night and the morning following, having information that there is very little grass between this and the Gila. I found here only about five

Church of San Xavier del Bac about 1854

thousand paper cigars of public property, beside the wheat; of this there is about 1,500 bushels. There are some Pima Indians here who will accompany us to their village. After a thousand inquiries, my best information of the road is this – that it is hard, smooth, and level; that at about thirty miles, at the point of a mountain, there is probably enough water in rocks for the use of the men; that ten or fifteen miles farther there are some pools from recent rains, sufficient for mules and men; that at about fifteen miles farther there is plenty of water and grass, this being five or six miles from the Gila. There is also water four miles from here. I have ordered the march about ten o'clock tomorrow, to water at the four-mile point and lay [by] at night after marching until nine o'clock without water. This night marching is after the repeated advice of Leroux and other guides of much experience in the country. I learned that after the departure of the detachment nearly all the families left the town.

There is an extraordinary similarity between the mountains around, their direction, the cultivated creek valley, and, above all, an identity of the barren, sandy, hard soil of the hills, with the corresponding features of Santa Fé and its vicinity. Approached from the same direction, the southwest, like Santa Fé, Tucson is not seen until very close by. Of course, its adobe houses are the same in appearance but inferior. There is a wall with abutments and battlements in bad repair, which surrounds the barracks; it is on the highest ground. The town is not on the bottom. It is a more populous village than I had supposed, containing about five hundred; and there are pueblos. Beside the very large stone church above and an adobe one here, there is another, very large, at a small Indian village close by. There are no priests at the *presidio.* The New Mexicans discharged from the general's expedition have been placed under surveillance at this place. After having been once released and having departed for Fronteras, they were brought back. They are in destitute and perilous circumstances. One has been hired by the guides as a servant, and I have directed the others to be employed – one in place of the deserted shepherd, the other as a mule-herder. Now, at night, it is reported that the Mexican forces have dispersed; those belonging to the posts of Fronteras, Santa Cruz, and Tubac returned, and the rest broken up. I have, however, beside a mule guard of nine sentinels half a mile off, a camp guard of six sentinels, and a picket of ten men in a commanding part of town. Different from the sandy soil of Santa Fé creek, this seems of a dark rich soil and is in fine cultivation; the fields are now slightly green with young wheat. This stream, which here supplies the irrigation ever necessary in Mexico, heads to the south; in its course to the north, where it is lost in the plain, it appears above ground in only a few spots. The only fruits I have seen here are quinces and pomegranates. I shall leave in the morning for the commandant (who, of course, will return) the following note (in Spanish):

Battalion Headquarters
Camp at Tucson, Sonora, December 18, 1846

Sir: Having received no orders, or entertained an intention to make war upon Sonora, I regret that circumstances have compelled me to break up your quarters at this post. Making forced marches for the want of watering places, and finding no grass or other forage here, I have found it necessary to use about thirty *fanegas* of wheat from the public granary. None has been wasted or destroyed, and no other public property has been seized. Herewith you will receive a letter for his excellency, the governor of Sonora, on the subject of my involuntary invasion of the state. I respectfully request that you send it to him with your own dispatches. With high respect, your obedient servant,

P. ST. GEO. COOKE, Lieutenant-colonel
commanding battalion U.S. volunteers

To Don Antonio Comaduran,
Comandante, Presidio of Tucson

The following is a copy of the letter I have thought proper, under all the circumstances, to address to the governor, said to be a popular one, of the state of Sonora, which is considered very favorably disposed to the United States, *viz:*

Camp at Tucson, Sonora, December 18, 1846

Your Excellency: The undersigned, marching in command of a battalion of United States infantry from New Mexico to California, has found it convenient for the passage of his wagon train to cross the frontier of Sonora. Having passed within fifteen miles of Fronteras, I have found it necessary to take this *presidio* in my route to the Gila. Be assured that I did not come as an enemy of the people whom you govern; they have received only kindness at my hands. Sonora refused to contribute to the support of the present war against my country, alleging the excellent reasons that all her resources were necessary to her defense from the incessant attacks of savages, [and] that the central government gave her no protection and was therefore entitled to no support. To this might have been added that Mexico supports a war upon Sonora. For I have seen New Mexicans within her boundary trading for the spoil of her people, taken by murderous, cowardly Indians who attack only to lay waste, rob, and fly to the mountains; and I have certain information that this is the practice of many years. Thus one part of Mexico allies itself against another. The unity of Sonora with the states of the north, now her neighbors, is necessary effectually to subdue these Parthian Apache. Meanwhile I make a wagon road from the streams of the Atlantic to the Pacific ocean, through the valuable plains and mountains (rich with minerals) of Sonora. This, I trust, will prove useful to the citizens of either republic, who, if not more closely, may unite in the pursuits of a highly beneficial commerce. With sentiments of esteem and respect, I am,

Your Excellency's most obedient servant,
P. St. Geo. Cooke,
Lieutenant-colonel of United States forces

To his Excellency Señor Don Manuel Gandara,
Governor of Sonora, Ures, Sonora

December 18. 10:30 p.m. At 12 p.m. last night I was awoke from a sound sleep by one of the picket guard, who, all out of breath, assured me that a large Mexican army was coming from the town. Such a high-sounding announcement only aroused dreamy thoughts of events of historical importance; but instantly the officer of the day announced that the picket had fired upon some body of men coming into the village. My trumpets instantly rang with the assembly, and the battalion was promptly under arms upon the ground designated for the assembly. I immediately sent the right company to the town, with a reconnoitering party in advance under Lieutenant Stoneman. The other companies were then disposed principally upon the flank toward the suburbs, with a platoon in reserve; and a sergeant and nine men were instantly sent to reënforce the mule guard in the opposite quarter, half a mile off. The company returned in a half hour, having patrolled the town and made no discovery; and so the battalion was dismissed and the camp guard increased.

I marched twenty minutes to ten o'clock. Some Mexicans had previously informed me that a man just arrived had informed them of the retreat of the Mexican forces toward Ures about the time of my detachment marching. The column was soon involved in a labyrinth of wood roads or paths, and Weaver, the only guide present, told me he was uncertain which was right. Leroux and Charbonneau, instead of being ahead with one or more Pima Indians, did not leave town for an hour and a half, and the Indians have not come at all. To my surprise I found water seven miles from town and a plenty of it, instead of an insufficiency four miles out as reported by Weaver, whom I sent yesterday to examine (he took a different path). The mules were then carefully watered about one o'clock. The next three miles down the dry creek of Tucson were excessively difficult, with deep sand and other obstacles. Then our beautiful level prairie road was much obstructed by mesquite. About fourteen miles out, at the base of a low mountain a mile off, we saw the dust of a party of horses at speed, and their tracks were discovered (the mesquite concealed them). I was at a loss what to attribute it to, wild horses, Indians, or Mexican cavalry. Three company mules were reported missing this morning, and it seems that a private one, and two public ones in Charbonneau's care and use, were also lost. I believe they were not put in charge of the guard. Just at dusk more deep sand was encountered; and then, from 5:45 to 8:45 [o'clock], I marched on rapidly (as mules travel well after dark) over baked clay ground obstructed occasionally by mesquite thickets, and encamped on similar ground with a very little grass in spots. I have surrounded camp and animals with sentinels, and ordered that every animal be tied, and fed, under the superintendence of company commanders, with their half-gallon allowance of wheat; and I brought as much more for morning. There is no water, of course, and appearances indicate that it may be very far. The march is ordered before sunrise. There is no moon. March about twenty-four miles.

DECEMBER 20. Marched at sunrise, finding the mountain much more distant than expected. About fourteen miles brought us to the foot of a singular-looking mountain on our left; the other mountain foot was several miles to our right. Leroux had informed me that the hole of water was at the point of the latter; he and several others had been sent on from camp to find it. I expected to halt there an hour or two while the men drank and then push on to the other holes in the ground, which the guides made from eight to fifteen miles distant. After passing entirely through the gap, I found a note in the road to the effect that they had searched both mountains for two hours without finding water. It was then near four o'clock. The road was good – a baked clay plain, with now and then sand mixed. Just before sundown a small hole of rain water was found in the clay near the road, which, by requiring the men to lie down and drink and take none off, gave a drink for nearly the whole of them. At seven o'clock, an hour after dark, and after a twelve hours' march without halt, I had a fire built and directed all who wished to stop as long as they pleased, provided it was not over six hours. I was exceedingly anxious as to the discovery of the hoped-for water in the rain holes. I feared the guides would be in the night before finding them; and I was induced to believe that the mules would still go on better than in the morning, resting without grass or water.

I heard now that men in the rear of the long column had found the rock holes in the left-hand mountain, and the interpreter says the Indians designated that one. Leroux had not got a description of the place certainly. It was reported, however, that there was little there. At 8:30 [P.M.] we arrived at a fire and found the advance guard, etc., and Mr. Stoneman, who had been with the guides all day. Here they had arrived in the twilight and found water, but far from enough, as he reported – not enough for the men. The loose mules and packs had been sent on by me and had rushed into the ponds. I had ordered the camp to be established, when, a minute after, I was informed that the signal of another fire ahead had been made, as agreed upon by Lieutenant Stoneman and Leroux, that there was a sufficiency of water. Soon after, I heard a gun, which was another signal to the same effect. I ordered the march resumed. It was very dark (no moon) and cloudy. In doubt, I discharged two pistols for a renewal of the concerted signal, and they were answered. After advancing with difficulty a mile or two (for the ground was frequently bad – a deep, crooked trail through soft clay in lumps, with artemisia and mesquite bushes), I learned that although the arrangement had been loudly and carefully made, some of the stupid, worthless guides had made the signals without reason; that is, the fire. The first gun I could get no information of. There the ground was very uneven and growing worse, and I ordered the camp established; the mules could not do more.

Some drops of rain fell just at this time; and, to increase my discontent, I then learned that more water had been found at the first stopping place. I sent back, however, the commander of one of the companies whose wagons had lagged very much, and they encamped at that spot. The battalion had now marched twenty-six hours out of thirty-six. The mules had come forty-seven miles without water, and still there was none for them, and no grass – nothing but artemisia and a few mesquites. But I ordered about a bushel and a half of wheat, which I had given to each company to eat like hominy and for coffee (as a substitute), to be all divided to the mules which were tied up. At twelve o'clock I sent for Leroux, who knew nothing of the signals. I directed the gullies searched for two miles above and one below at daylight, and for him to send or go on to the first sufficient water and return with information of it to the head of each company.

Notwithstanding their fatigues a number of men walked back two miles for their chance of getting water where I first stopped! They are almost barefooted, carry their muskets, knapsacks, etc., and do not grumble. I then slept from one to five o'clock this morning, when another effort was to be made. I called the company commanders together and directed them to send on all the mules they could dispense with, and to act according to their condition when they received the report of water; that the wagons should be left, and the mules driven on to water where it was found necessary, etc. The road was now very bad, as described last night. At seven o'clock the march recommenced, men, wagons, beeves, sheep, families, children, all getting on the best they could. After coming thus [for] three or four hours, Leroux returned with information of some holes of water two or three miles on. I immediately sent him off to look for more. About eleven o'clock I arrived there with many of the battalion. Sentinels were posted to prevent even the men dipping it up with canteens, so scarce was it still. One hole was given to the beeves – the foremost were shoved right through by those in rear.

I had calculated, on Leroux's and my own information received of Mexicans and Indians, that last night we were between seven and fifteen miles of a watering place six miles this side of the Gila. Weaver now told me that he was pretty sure it was eighteen miles to the river; a mountain which he knew, we saw between, and intermediate water was uncertain. The weather was very warm – almost hot. As I waited for the wagons, perplexing myself how it was possible to give a taste to so many animals out of a few inches of water resting on mud, our prospects were exceedingly gloomy. But again I saw Leroux and then believed in a saving fortune; he came and announced a sufficiency a mile or two lower! On we came, and after marching nine miles the second day without water, came to the rain ponds between twelve and one o'clock. Here, too, is mesquite for the mules to browse. After Leroux's report, before I reached here, I sent on Mr. Stoneman, Weaver, and two others with directions to send me word if water and tolerable grazing was to be found within eight miles ahead, so that I might go on this evening; to go on, and to send me word from the river an account of the grazing there; at daylight tomorrow to go on, and if he believed the grass would not do for our circumstances, to purchase at the Indian village five miles lower thirty-seven bushels of corn to be sent to me immediately; to engage as much to be delivered in the middle of the village (it is too long a march through in one day and contains no grass by Weaver's account) and two days' rations at the lower end; one to be carried in the wagons half over the forty miles' *jornada* there commencing, which is without grass (Weaver). The company which encamped in rear has come up two or three hours later. They did well, having a sufficiency of water (and there was little more).

Of this road which I have made from Tucson I will say more when the river is reached, but thus far I will pronounce it the most extensive desert I have seen: clay, sand, gravel, artemisias, mesquites, and a few other bushes. Far away to the west, as far as the eye could follow, it was the same. And I am told for a hundred miles south of the Gila there is still no water; and there is no wood, no animals. But everywhere in the dim distance, fantastically shaped mountains appeared. It is a gold district, said to be the most extensive, if not richest, in the world, but can scarcely be worked for its barrenness. But every two or three miles was seen a little grass (a sort I had never seen) of a silky, light, straw color, with a head like a plume; also a very little grama. Between the two mountains there was much grass, and trees, too – a new species of mesquite, or perhaps locust, large and pretty, the wood light and porous. It is pronounced a better road than the *jornada* so celebrated below Santa Fé, and is shorter, but I think it problematical whether it could be used much for commerce. But the other known roads from Tucson, a little longer but with more water, may be found better. Badly off as we were, it would have been worse, vastly, before the late rain; but on the other hand it is said to have been an extraordinary drought here for several years. A Mr. Jackson once lost many of a small drove of mules he took through in an imprudent manner in July.

A Mexican who reached my rear guard last night on foot has just come in. He seems to be a mine hunter and has specimens of ores. He is a strange-looking but intelligent character and is nearly naked. He brought me a letter from Captain Comaduran dated at the Indian pueblo [ ].[191] It is short and dry, acknowledges the receipt of mine explaining the invasion of Sonora, and promises to forward my letter to the governor. His messenger gave it to this man and returned. The latter states that Comaduran asseverated he would pursue me if only with twenty men. He had not returned to Tucson the evening or afternoon after I marched, and the troops did abandon the pueblo when I advanced toward it with fifty or sixty men and got entangled in the forest. I have been mounted thirty-two of the last fifty-two hours, and what with midnight conferences, alarms, and marches have had little rest for five days. The battalion has marched sixty-two miles from Tucson in about fifty-one hours. No ration of meat was issued yesterday.

DECEMBER 21. Marched at sunrise. The road very good. Came between two small mountains. Here the columnar cactus was very thick. A decayed one showed an extraordinary structure; it was a cylindric arch of wooden poles that would answer for lances. This singular vegetable production, like none other, bears a delicious fruit. It tapers from the middle, alike to the top and root. Near the ground it has a bark like the cottonwood. We were in view of the cottonwoods of the long-sought Gila. The path bent more to the westward and approached obliquely. The water and grass spoken of, six miles from the river, Leroux told me was near the small mountain of stone. I did not see it near the road. A ten miles' march brought me to the river,[192] when I

191 A blank in the manuscript.

192 The battalion reached the Gila river a short distance west of the present Florence, Pinal county, Arizona.

crossed the general's trail and encamped at one o'clock in tolerably good grass – it is said the last until we pass the villages.

Before we arrived here, although eight miles above the village, there were many Indians on the ground, and they have flocked in, mounted on horses, ever since, bringing small sacks of corn, flour, beans, etc. A one-eyed chief brought me the general's letter, and another from Major Swords telling me of eleven broken-down mules and two bales of Indian goods having been left for me. On this was indorsed a note for Lieutenant Stoneman. He thought it would be difficult to get enough corn and advises me to buy all that is brought here. I directed the guides to open the few Indian goods I have and begin. They report to me that such prices are asked that they can do nothing, and I have ordered that no individuals shall trade for corn or wheat until further orders. Charbonneau came back, and from his account there is no grass for at least thirty-three miles. Many of these Indians, I was somewhat surprised to see, are nearly naked. They manufacture blankets and show every desire to be clothed. They are good-looking and very lively, [and] know nothing of the value of money or of weights and measures. Their language is rather a pleasant one. The first words I heard, I took for "gold watch." Some speak the Spanish. And I was surprised to perceive one who spoke it well have recourse to his fingers as necessary to explain the subtraction of five mules that had died and been drowned, from the eleven left for me. It seemed he could only do it by bending down the fingers and counting those left straight. Two good mules were found by the Maricopa, as I had learned in Tucson; and they have told me the Apache have stolen them, which I do not credit, as the Apache do not often trouble them, being afraid.

The weather now is like that in New Mexico early in October – warm days and cold nights. It has frozen slightly towards morning for the two last. The cottonwoods are only partially turned by frost. I have estimated the route from Tucson seventy-three miles and believe there is generally water on it for six months of the year; and those are the only months it could be traveled (probably) on account of the heat. The mules, I thought, would nearly starve last night, but they looked very well and full this morning. But the food may not agree with them. There is a kind of seed on some of the dry-looking weeds or bushes which they ate. I have succeeded in getting a feed of corn for them. The principal chief I have conversed with, and he and another have supped with me. He said the commander of Tucson sent to demand the mules and Indian goods of him, that he refused and declared he would resist force with force; he liked us better, who brought useful articles to them – clothing, etc. He said I would see that they were poor and naked, but they were content to live here by hard work on the spot which God had given them, and not like others, to rob and steal; that they did not fear us and run like the Apache, because they made it a rule to injure no one in any way and therefore believed that no one could injure them. They have the reputation of escaping molestation from Apache, on principles of resistance.

But one mule has been lost on the march over from Tucson; it died in camp, probably of fatigue and thirst. I have spoken to the two senior captains on the subject of their settling near here; they seem to look favorably upon it. Captain Hunt has asked me permission to talk to the chief on the subject. I have approved of it. The Pima are large and fine-looking, seem well fed, ride good horses, and are variously clothed, though many have only the center cloth. They have an extraordinary length and luxuriance of hair. With their large white cotton blankets and streaming hair, they present, when mounted, quite a fine figure. But innocence and cheerfulness are their most distinctive characteristics. I am told that Mexican officers used every persuasion and promise of plunder to excite their hostility toward us.[193]

DECEMBER 22. I marched at eight o'clock. I, however, bought a few bushels of sweet corn, which was issued as rations. A guide was sent on to look for grass, etc. After three or four miles of tolerably good road, I was surprised to find it became excellent. Here, in advance, I rode up to a group of women, men, and girls. These last, naked above the hips, were of every age and pretty. It was a gladdening sight, of so much cheerfulness and happiness. One little girl particularly, by a fancied resemblance, excited much interest with me. She was so joyous that she seemed very innocent and pretty. I could not resist tying a red silk handkerchief on her head for a turban; then, if perfect happiness ever momentarily dwells on earth, it seemed that it was with her. I was met, after marching about nine miles, by Leroux, who stated that here was the only place where there was anything like pasture, and I learned that I should be able to pass the village and find grass tomorrow, about fourteen miles; and so I came here to the first irrigating ditch and encamped.

Mr. Stoneman has bought seventy or eighty bushels of corn two miles farther, and I have sent pack mules for a portion. The other I will take as I pass and endeavor to have other brought to me below. I have directed exchanges of mules made, two for one, and about

[193] For descriptions of the Pima and Maricopa Indians by Captain Johnston and Lieutenant Emory, who marched with Kearny, see *House Ex. Docs.*, 30 cong., 1 sess., no. 41, pp. 82-87, 598-602.

six hundred pounds of flour bought, about three days' half rations. I have now about thirty-one days' on hand at that rate. By estimate I have forty-five days of meat, and have directed that the ration of fresh meat be raised to two pounds. The animals are falling off and will fall off rapidly. The camp is full of Indians of all sorts, and a great many have flour, corn, beans, or some eatable to trade; and they seem only to want clothing, or cotton cloth, and beads. I am sorry that they will be disappointed. It resembles a crowded New Orleans market in numbers and sounds, with the addition of the crying of children. They have watermelons for sale. For the last hundred miles all vegetation is green. There are at least two thousand people in camp, all enjoying themselves very much. Very many go in pairs, encircling each other with their arms. They are of admirable form and very graceful. Their language certainly resembles in sound the English. I have said much of this isolated, primitive race, because their characteristics are more striking than those of any other (and they are very many) that I ever saw.

I find I make it seven hundred and one miles from Santa Fé to this village, and four hundred and seventy-four miles from the point of the Río Grande where the general left it and our paths diverged. Thus if he had come by the road I marched, about eighteen miles a day would have brought him here in twenty-six days, which I believe was his time; and it cannot be doubted his mules would have been in far better condition than they were. I have found good grass and my mules have improved. Beside this, I know of some improvements in the road by cutting off distance. And if water can be found through or skirting the prairie, which Leroux says extends from the Ojo de Vaca (about twenty-six miles south of the Copper Mines) to the point of San Pedro river where I left it, then perhaps above eighty miles would be struck off and probably a much better road gained. Will not this prove the best emigrant's route from Independence to California, by the road I came?[194] Leaving there the middle of July, and refreshing themselves cheaply at Santa Fé and below, at Tucson and here, they would arrive at San Diego or Los Angeles by the end of the year. And then if a road, as I believe, can be made to cross the Río Grande about the middle of the Jornada del Muerto, it would cut off all the worst of this road. But to emigrants from Van Buren, Arkansas, might there not be a connection made of Gregg's route with this, that would make it all a very direct one? Emigrants could very cheaply supply themselves with cattle, mules, and sheep in New Mexico. If their destination was Southern California, there could be no question as to the best route.

DECEMBER 23. I marched at 8 A.M. At the chief's I stopped a few minutes. I told him I had traveled much and seen many different nations, and that the Pima were the happiest I had ever seen; that as long as they adhered to their present principles of honesty, industry, and peace, and cheerful content, they would continue so; that while they never injured their neighbors, their true safety lay in uniting vigorously to resist the first aggression; that wishing them well, I desired to add to their comfort and welfare by introducing sheep amongst them, and to give him, for the ultimate use of his people, three ewes with young, which I did. Between the villages, I met, to my delight, Francisco and two others with letters from the general and Cap-

194 Cooke's road was used by many California gold seekers in 1849 and during the fifties.

tain Turner dated at Warner's, sixty miles from San Diego.[195] The news indicates that the general's arrival is very important not only to the welfare of California but to its conquest. This party [196] have picked up seven mules, which I have not yet seen. At the house of the Maricopa chief, Antonio, I stopped and spoke to him. Said "I was glad to see him; I had heard he was a great friend of the Americans; that now I wished him to show it; that I had good information that his people had taken up two good mules lost by the general above and many more below this; that I required him to have them delivered up; then I should know he was a friend and should reward him, and also give the people something for their trouble; that I also wanted corn, fat beeves, and mules; that I should remain until midday tomorrow in my camp near him."

I came on here, where there are some holes of water and grass, far from the river, and encamped. Instead of twelve miles of good road, I found it fifteen of some very bad road. Consequently on account of the grass here and the hard marches lately made, and the trade, etc., for corn, I determined to rest a day. I now think it will, in the long run, advance my march. I learn tonight the name of a Maricopa that has taken up the mules, and I shall thus be able, I think, to recover them. I have determined to trade off or throw away all the pack-saddles, above twelve to a company, and also to take

[195] Turner's letter to Cooke, dated near Warner's Ranch, December 3, 1846, was as follows: "The bearer of this (Francisco) is a Mexican sent back by Gen'l to meet you & to serve you in the capacity of Guide from the Pimo Village to the settlements of California. This man has accompanied our command from New Mexico – is familiar with the Route over which you will march & will be able to do you good service in pointing out the places at which you will find it necessary to encamp, in order to obtain grass & water." Turner to Cooke, Dec. 3, 1846, Kearny Letter Book, MS., M.H.S.

[196] "They said we were a month ahead of the Gen's expectations," recorded Standage on December 23. Golder, Bailey, and Smith, *op. cit.*, 199.

ten or twelve quarts of corn to each animal, to be fed by little when there is no grass. I have called for another report of the amount of pork on hand. One company which should have, without wastage, twenty-six days', has eight! What can a commander do with a people who act and manage thus? If they starve, they will be useless or steal and rob. Another had only seventeen days'. I wish to exchange some of my poorest cattle for fat ones. I have examined them this afternoon and find there are many in good order. There are about two or three of the oxen left; and it must be considered that they were much reduced when I left Santa Fé, some falling motionless in the road the first twenty-five miles. I have made a map, or sketch, of the route and country from the point where I left the general's trail to this village. My compass has lately become out of order and nearly useless, and as the topographical engineer officers have passed the route I shall now follow, I shall discontinue it. The camp is on very disagreeable ground, a light dusty efflorescence of salt and clay combined. I have lately seen much of the samphire plant.

DECEMBER 24. Although remaining in camp, it has been a very busy day and full of vexations for me. Two companies had twenty-five days' rations of pork at half a pound, and I was forced so far to equalize as to raise the lowest to sixteen by reducing the two highest to twenty-two. The plan of issuing the sixty days' to the companies has not answered quite so well as with regulars. The sheep are poor; they have not done so well lately as I expected. Taking the sheep and cattle as they are, I have left, on an average, near forty days' rations of meat. I have about thirty days' rations of flour (at ten ounces) of the old issue, and I have bought full three days' of corn meal, making thirty-three, which I think will take us to San Diego. I have reserved twelve pack-saddles to a company and twenty-four sheepskins. The rest, about a hundred and twenty or more, and above two hundred skins, I have got rid of, trading the skins and throwing away the rude saddles (as they were not salable). This reduces weight of baggage considerably. I ordered that the private provisions bought by persons drawing rations shall not be transported in the wagons; they have a number of private animals. I only succeeded in trading for two mules, giving for them three and a blanket, and for one beef for a worthless mule; but it was so wild that I had to kill it today. After much delay and difficulty I succeeded in extracting from the Maricopa eight mules, which they have picked up from the general's road; some of them are in pretty good order. With the rest today and the corn, I have great hopes of getting on well. Last night there was a report that an American was following me with a letter. This morning we had repeated accounts of many Americans having arrived in the vicinity of the upper village; it was even said they were very hungry. I sent an Indian on his horse with a note, for information; he returned this evening with my note and told me it was all a false report.

Weaver has always reported the cut-off from here (without water) to be forty miles of a good road; that the road he came last time, which the general took, and [which was] followed each time by Francisco, is fifty miles, with some part bad for wagons; but that it cuts off ten miles more than the upper one. He thought there was a nearer way for this latter by going through a certain gap. I sent him this morning to examine it. He reports unfavorably – that it takes us through four miles of bad sand. Leroux, Weaver, and Francisco cannot agree as to the road. Leroux tells me, however, that I can depend upon this – that I can find grass tomorrow at sixteen miles and have not more than twenty next day, of a better road to the river and following the dragoon trail. This, considering the grass, and the extra water to be taken, and bad, uphill road, will be the best division of it. I shall march about eleven o'clock tomorrow. Francisco reports that the general did not stop the second day on reaching the river, although there was grass.

These Indians can have but very few cattle. Meat is a great variety with them – so much so, that I am even told they ate today a poor mule or two of ours that died in camp! They thrive, however, on their vegetable diet [and] are large and fat. They have the simplicity of nature and none of the fancied dignified reserve attributed as a universal characteristic of Indians. At the killing of a beef, at the sound of a trumpet, at the playing of a violin, etc., I have repeatedly seen them rush in a dense crowd to see and hear, with astonishment, curiosity, and delight all strongly exhibited. I entered one of their wigwams, rather above the average in size and goodness. It was eighteen or twenty feet across, dug slightly below the ground, only about five feet pitch inside, made of rank grass or reeds, resting on props and cross poles, and partially covered with earth; the door, a simple hole about three feet high; the fire in the middle; the hole above very small. They are thus smoky and uncomfortable, and seemingly very ill suited to so warm a climate. I found there pottery and various baskets of their manufacture; in these were stored corn and wheat. They have a *pinole,* or parched meal, of the mesquite bean. They parch corn, wheat, etc., in a basket by throwing in live coals, and keep it in motion by throwing it up in the air. They raise cotton, and spin and weave excellent blankets. Their looms are rude and slow to work. They make good pumpkin molasses. They have plenty of horses, which are in good order, and live on – what I cannot imagine, except dry-looking brush. I have seen only a bow or two, and one or two guns, amongst them all.

DECEMBER 25. This morning I obtained about six bushels more of corn by trading old wagon covers, *jerga,* etc. I gave a written paper for the chief, or "general," commendatory, and authorizing him to collect any mules that might be left on the route and keep them until called for by some authorized person or persons in employ of [the] government. The subchief and [the] interpreter Turo said they would prefer to be under the government of the United States to that of Mexico. Twenty minutes before eleven o'clock I marched, with about twelve quarts of shelled corn for each mule and four bushels for the oxen, twenty-four in number. I found the road bad, sandy, and uphill. Half an hour before sundown, having long seen Leroux's smoke, which I directed him to come on and make after finding the grass, I pushed on to examine the ground before dark. I reached here before it was very dark and fixed the sentinels so that the mules could be turned loose in the mesquite without much danger of their thirst leading them off between the sentinels. The wagons did not arrive until eight o'clock. I have had two quarts of corn fed to the team mules; the others had been an hour feeding on grass in the bushes. Determining to march soon after daylight, I believed the mules could not be collected and fed in time. The march eighteen miles; and it is now said to be twenty-four to the river, but a far better road and downhill. It has been hot weather for several days. Fortunately it was cloudy part of today. The road is over a desert of white sand, etc., with only a few bushes.

DECEMBER 26. With reveille at 4:30 o'clock, I could only get off fifteen minutes before seven. We found the gap in the mountain difficult ground, which consumed much time. I struck the Gila about sundown. The guides had gone on, and following their path (the wrong one), it led me through a wretched, uneven, and entangled bottom; and I found them taking their ease at the water's edge at some miserably dry grass. I marked out the camp by fires made by the packmen who had arrived. The wagons arrived about half past seven o'clock. We find the river brackish, and larger and more timbered than I had expected. Salt river, the larger of the two, comes in between this and the Pima village. The march twenty-three miles.

DECEMBER 27. This is certainly the most desert, uncouth, impracticable country and river of our knowledge. It took about three hours to advance four miles, winding about through mesquite trees and other bushes, and gullies of very soft clay, and some sand, The guides who had been sent ahead to find the very best ground in a strip of grass of about four miles were again at fault, and showed me a brushy spot more than half a mile from the river. I sent them on and proceeded, and then found a much more convenient camp, and the grass better at the lower end. What is called good grass in this country as to appearances, would never by any chance obtain the name of grass in the western states. It took an hour this morning to find the mules in the entangled, brushy bottom, and two were found several miles above. Understanding that there will be no more stony road, I had the mule shoes cached at this camp to be relieved of their weight. There are about one hundred and fifty pairs and some sixty pounds of nails. The spot may be thus designated. Ascending the river after leaving the bluff termination of a cut-off about sixty miles below Pima village and opposite Rock Island, [and] after leaving this bluff eight or nine miles, the road goes close by a low bluff bank of the river, and a few hundred yards below descends a bank into the bottom. Above, eight steps from the edge of the bank, the cache is in the middle of the road.

Last night a New Mexican who had been employed in the dragoon camp and a Chilean rode into camp. They had some news of the capture of a small place above San Diego by a party of dragoons, with a loss of one killed and three wounded. They also describe the failure of an attack several months ago by Commodore Stockton on the pueblo. They say several hundred Indians are stationed at Warner's to prevent the passage of people, etc., from the country, and that General Kearny has about two hundred animals half a day's travel from Warner's. They represent that Mr. Money and another, with women and children, are following them, whom they had sent for provisions, living on horseflesh; that Mrs. M. was about being delivered of a child. Terrible situation! March about seven miles. I fed no corn here.[197]

DECEMBER 28. I sent Leroux, Charbonneau, and three other guides express this morning.[198] Mr. Hall

197 On December 27, Standage wrote: "Started late, roads bad, Mules worn out." *Ibid.*

198 Cooke reported to Kearny: "On the 27th December (after making the forced march, without water, across the bend of the Gila), in consequence of the information received in your letter, I determined to send my useless guides express, to give you information of my approach, &c; hoping thus, as I said, to meet orders at Warner's ranche on the 21st of January, and to be of service to your active operations. I also sent for assistance in mules, under-

went with them. Their instructions were to proceed with caution when there was any reason to expect to meet Mexican troops or important parties with droves; to observe any discovered, until they passed the southern Sonora road from the crossing of the Colorado; otherwise, to endeavor to inform me of their approach; if strong enough, to seize any drove of mules or horses coming out of California without passport and bring them to me (one or two to go on, if possible); to bear my letter to General Kearny, wherever to be found; and, if necessary, one or two of them to examine the road from Warner's to San Diego and meet me there to guide me, etc., by [the] twenty-first of January; [and] to endeavor to bring me from twenty to seventy fresh mules from the vicinity of Warner's to the Colorado (a part of them assisted by hired hands), and also eight or ten fat beeves. I marched at eight o'clock. I found the road a level plain of bare clay, with bushes and rather soft. The guides, as usual, misunderstood or neglected their duty, and there was some confusion and delay in getting my camp ground. It is half a mile from the river, and quite as far from grass in the opposite direction and also from the direct road. This leads from here, a cut-off, across a bend of twelve or fourteen miles, which it is necessary to commence a day with. The grass seems as rank, dry, and even brittle as possible, but it is a rare article here. I sent the mules to water at 1:30 [o'clock] and thence a mile or more to the grass, where they will remain with the guard until daylight tomorrow, when I have directed them driven to water and thence here, when I shall give them two or three pints of corn. March eight miles. A bright day and not very

standing that you had placed a number of them in that vicinity." *House Ex. Docs.*, 30 cong., 1 sess., no. 41, p. 558.

warm day. Last night ice made quite thick, the first time for many days.

I considered maturely this morning the idea of taking on by hard marches two hundred of the best men with a few pack mules to reënforce the general, leaving the rest to follow with the wagons. But when I considered the probabilities that even then the crisis would be over; that between the general's name and management, and the force he took with him, and Captain Turner's letter to me that Colonel Frémont was daily expected with a large force, and the navy; and when I considered the great difficulty now about to be encountered, of this river with its sands and deficiency of food for animals, and the *tierra caliente,* or ninety-five miles desert, then to be encountered, and how crippled the part left would be in the loss of my constant watchfulness and in the best men – I concluded reluctantly, I hope wisely, that it should not be done. I do not mention here half the difficulties; for instance, one is that the men are afoot and could not push on so far. In fact, I am not within what is called "striking distance." The bluff before us tomorrow has been examined, and much work is to be done on it tomorrow morning to make it practicable.

I feel as if every day here was to be an experiment or venture – a great difficulty to be overcome – and to be then rejoiced as one day less of such. Now this camp – it is on a dusty clay bank half a mile of bad ground from water, and three quarters in an opposite direction from some miserable, dry, brittle stuff called grass. The large drove of mules, difficult to move, has to work backwards and forwards between the two, and is now risked, perhaps a mile from camp, for the night. And this is one of the good camps, where there is grass; others have none, etc. The cattle, already poor, of course are starving, and they are my dependence. The sheep are very poor and are left behind now daily. Many of the men have private mules and horses; they use public corn, or transport their own in public wagons. Great trouble I have to correct such fatal abuses and guard against their improvidence in consuming the subsistence stores beyond the allowance, as they must have done. To march with knapsack, blanket, musket, etc., gives enormous appetites.

DECEMBER 29. With a very early reveille, by my arrangements the mules were driven a mile and three-quarters from grass to water and back, fed a quart of corn each, and the march begun before eight o'clock. The pioneers under Lieutenant Stoneman went very early, and by the time we reached the bluff (about two miles) a good road had been made up it with much labor. I found the head of the dry branch we then struck very rough. The road was, however, better than I hoped for some ten miles to the river, when a lofty bluff of coal-black trap rock forced us into the sands of the river bed (when high). This was hard work for two miles, when I regained the bank and encamped. The mules were turned into the flags, or cane, and willows of the sand beach until I could get a report of the grass or mesquite said to be at the foot of a bluff near a mile off. I sent there, however, principally to examine if the wagons could ascend it and to have a road made, Weaver reporting that if so, ten miles of a hard road could be found – if not, very bad bottoms and the river to be often crossed. Meanwhile many of the mules came away from the river to pick about for a very little dead black grass under the bushes! Reports were favorable, and between 3 and 4 P.M. I sent the guard with all the mules, [with orders] to keep them out until daylight; also the sheep. The beeves kept at the river. The grass is the white, light, apparently dead kind we have had before, and mesquite. The pioneers have made a road. The river is quite salty. The weather was very cold this morning. It was cloudy and threatened snow. Twelve miles today; and the mules seem to stand it famously.

DECEMBER 30. I encountered a very difficult hill – in fact, two of them – soon after marching. Besides being a cut-off of four or five miles, the bluff must be crossed, or the river six times. Just after leaving the bluff of black rocks between twelve and one o'clock, I found some grass, and grazed the mules for an hour with their harness on. Proceeding over the soft clay and sand, about three o'clock I overtook the pioneers and guides, who stated the river was far off and inaccessible; that Francisco, whom I had sent forward early in the morning to look, had found grass three or four miles below. The wagons were then much behind, but I determined to go. After much difficulty I found the place by sundown – a soft beach with green cane or flag, willows, and some grass. The wagons did not come up for an hour after dark; the mules much fagged and many given out.[199] The day was very cold with a high west wind. The march thirteen or fourteen miles – too far, if avoidable, considering the heavy pulls at the hills and over some of the soft road.

DECEMBER 31. I mustered and inspected the battalion this morning, commencing before sunrise. Meanwhile the mules were eating a feed of corn. I marched between eight and nine o'clock. I found the road today pretty good. There has been a rain here a week or two

---

199 Standage wrote: "Pushed wagons to day through the sand till after dark." Golder, Bailey, and Smith, *op. cit.*, 200.

ago, which evidently improved the ground; the path, in places, was of hard beaten clay, where mules scarcely made a track. The absence of grass on a river bottom, with our limited information, is difficult to be accounted for, but I think it must be owing to a want of rain. The river does not habitually overflow; it did not last year; and, but for its old reputation for barrenness, it might be supposed that some late great flood had made a deposit so deep as to destroy the grass. Weaver proposed this morning to burn the bottom to be rid of dense brush, but I told him it served me as a pavement to the soft clay, which is very loosely deposited from mechanical suspension in water. A few mules following each other, in many places step regularly in the same deep holes, as footmen do in deep snow. There is much large mesquite wood; the leaves are now falling and are said to be tolerably good food for mules. The beeves are fond of them. The river bottom seems to expand today to many miles. For ten or fifteen miles there seems a very flat country at least. The vicinity of the river is ever marked by cottonwoods. But it is a great difficulty of the road that it is so far to the water; also, that it is impossible to more than guess the distance; and, again, that it is so inaccessible, for thorny brush, sand, and gullies.

Francisco met me with information that he had found several ponds with good grass at them. I found them near the road. And the first thing I did was to send a man down the high bluff bank to taste if it was not too salty and bitter for use; and, accordingly, it was utterly undrinkable, for salt, etc. This had never occurred to Francisco, who had passed them perhaps often! I had now come twelve miles, and it was reported very far to get to the river ahead, or to the right, where it is sandy. Mr. Stoneman went to it while I marked the time, by the watch, for his arrival there, to be signaled by a pistol shot. It took twenty-two minutes. As the grass was remarkably good (for the country) in the old slough, I encamped here between two and three o'clock, determining to send the mules to water near sundown. But several mules that were taken to the river did not drink. The food was green, and a little of the water here they will drink. A drove, too, of two hundred mules is conducted very slowly and with much dust; so I have not sent them, but will water in the morning within eight miles, making an early march.

The beef, although some of the beeves do not look very poor, has some extraordinary appearances at least, and is scarcely fit to be eaten. One was left today (a second time). The sheep are frequently left; they seem taken sick from eating some herbs, perhaps poisonous. There are many bushes or shrubs here which I am convinced are not known to science. There is very much of a sort which has dry, black, twisted stems three inches in diameter but can be broken off by a kick. I saw three spots of grass today but too far from water for a convenient camp. Near a point of rocky bluff called "Painted Rock" I saw a long pile of earth and cinders, which seemed to be thrown up [by] an eruption. The day was cold. The mules traveled unusually fast. The march twelve miles. I determined this morning to embark one of my ponton wagon bodies (with a load) on the river, to descend in company at night. Thus an experiment will be made, and I shall save the transportation of not only a wagon but a wagonload. I cannot try it tomorrow because I am not on the river, but I shall the first opportunity. Two days ago two men came the day's travel on a raft and report that there are no snags.

JANUARY 1, 1847. Marched at half past seven o'clock.

I soon found that instead of getting soon to a watering place, the road passed over an extensive upland; and thus the mules were not watered until I struck the river and encamped here at one o'clock. The day, too, was unusually warm, although last night was exceedingly cold. The road was pretty good. Some bad sand and some bad clay, but much of pebbles. Wherever there is a bed where water sometimes runs, we find more or less grass; this favors the belief that want of rain prevents its growth. But the bottoms are covered frequently with efflorescences of salt; this, on the Río Grande, is said to make the land unproductive. Also, much of it seems of pure clay, and that, I think, will not produce vegetation. The river here runs against a vertical bluff, but the guides have found a road. There is very little grass indeed, but it is a bottom of green weeds and willows and young cottonwoods. I gave the mules a pint of corn and turned them out. We found here the party described by the two Mexicans we met. Mrs. M. was happily delivered of a fine child two days ago. She traveled yesterday ten miles on horseback! They tell us it is under seventy miles to the crossing and report favorably of grass and mesquite, but say the wells, or holes of water, the general wrote me of are dried up; but it is more probable that they have filled up with sand. Their account of news varies from the former story, and we only know that the general had a sharp engagement in which an Indian reported some killed on both sides.

I have several wagons that are worth very little, and their transportation, considering the future, may be fatal to many mules, and more or less cripple my movements. I am now preparing a boat of two ponton wagon bodies lashed together end to end between two dry cottonwood logs. In this I shall put all the baggage that I can risk, and, after a trial, probably much more.[200] The Gila is a rapid stream of clear water, in places three or four feet deep, and here about one hundred and fifty yards wide. The water is decidedly salty; in fact, Salt river is said to be the larger. I asked one of this party we met if there was late news in California of the progress of the war, etc. He said that half the people did not believe that there *was* a war. Speaking of Mr. Money, he said: "He is just like a Spaniard and would rather believe a lie than the truth." I have determined to send Lieutenant Stoneman[201] at first in charge of the boats. They have been fresh pitched, but one of them still leaks tonight; perhaps in the morning it will not. It is owing to the shrinking of the wood in this dry climate; even old gunstocks show it plainly. I shall take with me the running gear of one of them; that of the other, and an entire wagon of company A which it no longer needs, some men will take down on a raft.[202] It appears that the most authentic information leaves General Kearny engaged with a superior force, strongly posted in a fortified defile defended by one or more twelve-pounders. This gives me much anxiety. I do not doubt our success; but what valuable lives may have paid for it, who can tell? March ten miles.

200 Cooke gave the following reasons for attempting to navigate the Gila: "Sixty or seventy miles above the mouth of the Gila, having more wagons than necessary, and scarcely able to get them on, I tried the experiment, with very flattering assurances of success, of boating with two ponton wagon beds, and a raft for the running gear. I embarked a portion of the rations, some road tools, and corn." *House Ex. Docs.*, 30 cong., 1 sess., no. 41, p. 558.

201 Cooke stated: "He professes to have had similar experience, and is desirous to undertake it." Cooke, *Conquest of New Mexico and California*, 169.

202 Standage was not in sympathy with Cooke's experiment to navigate the Gila: "This plan will certainly lighten the loads for the mules and enable them to travel faster but I am of the opinion it is very risky." Golder, Bailey, and Smith, *op. cit.*, 200.

JANUARY 2. After a very cold night and a hot morning, the day fortunately turned out cloudy and cold. About half the mules had escaped the guard this morning, wandering through the bushes, small cottonwoods, etc., in search of food. I separated about 2,500 pounds of provisions, corn, etc., for Mr. Stoneman's flotilla. It consisted of pork, above thirteen days' rations (to which quantity two of the companies had been before reduced) ; and flour, above eighteen days' rations; and seven or eight bushels of corn; some tools; part of my own baggage, etc. Although I did not sound the advance until 9:30, Mr. Stoneman's men, whom he had sent at daybreak to bring down some cottonwood logs partly prepared the day before, had not come. I did not consider them necessary. I thought two poles would answer, and it was a part of my plan to see a successful commencement, at least, of the experiment.

We ascended immediately a steep bluff, which we followed five or six miles, a part of the ground quite deep with sand; then through a clay bottom, winding round to the foot of a mountain. And at the point very near the river I encamped soon after three o'clock, the guides representing that I could not strike the river again for fourteen or fifteen miles. I saw on the hill small eruptions apparently of mud, but I found it a conglomerate of stony hardness crusted from fusion. I believe that the one seen at the painted rocks yesterday morning was the same. The mountain close by utterly bare and composed of black confused rocks – everything indicates volcanic action, and some of a late date. The Santa María stream of Mitchell's and Tanner's maps of 1846 seems to have no existence; we pass the mouth of no river. The large flat bottom above this is composed of little, confused, long hillocks and flat ground white with efflorescent salts – in places quite thick. There is also a moist appearance, very likely produced by deliquescence. There is here much of beach vegetation called "grass," as some of it is; the mules are turned loose upon it. I habitually post the advance guard as the first relief, surrounding a large space, generally aided by natural barriers. I have ordered the guard of last night put on again tomorrow as a punishment. The moon was at the full. Mr. Money asked permission to return to California with me, alone, I believe; it was granted. It is now after sundown and Mr. Stoneman is not here. I fear much he has failed from the shallowness of the river. Weaver states it is lower than he ever saw it before. The march eleven or twelve miles. I think all the mules were recovered this morning; four died last night. I brought the wheels, etc., of one of the wagons, with some load, four mules drawing it.

JANUARY 3. I ordered an early march, Weaver stating it fourteen miles to the next point of the river. No news from Mr. Stoneman until I had ordered six pack mules left here grazing and a note for him to lighten his load, or, if necessary, abandon much of it, sending me on the mules three days' rations of flour for the command, which I considered the only important part of his cargo; adding [that] I should regret the loss of the corn more, if anything, than the pork, not valuing the ponton bed, which leaked badly. After that one of the raftsmen came in and reported that Mr. Stoneman embarked about noon, and that he saw him come about two miles with difficulty. The raft they could not get a quarter of a mile and abandoned it. I sent him to find Mr. Stoneman (afoot), with another similar note, but directing him to signal for the mules to go to him above if necessary.

I marched over unusually good clay bottom ground

about eleven miles, when we crossed a sandy point, and I saw the guides and Mr. Smith (in charge of pioneers) on a great bluff of impalpable sand. I rode up and found that the trail led there, [and] that it continued the same four or five miles on the high ground. This was the fourteen-mile point and it was only one o'clock. There was here a prospect of some food on a large island close by and none ahead. I encamped and determined that I would not follow that trail. The bottom was considered, and pronounced impassable. Mr. Smith, all the guides, and myself then left camp to examine the whole bottom. I took to the left near the bluff; and forcing my way occasionally through brush and willows, found passable clay ground for a mile, down which was much shorter than the bluff trail, and led up to it by an easier ascent if a little worked on. Mr. Smith and the guides found practicable ground about as far, and then obstacles insuperable to wagons. He returned. Weaver comes in later and reports that farther back from the edge of the sand bluff than the trail, the ground is much better; so I shall cut off, or avoid part, and find better ground for the other. There seems to be little or nothing to eat on the island, though Weaver says there was plenty of good grass at a pond there when he came last fall. I have one more quart of corn for most of the mules (beside that in the boat), which I shall give in the morning. Company D had to be supplied with flour at San Bernardino from the others, and again at the Pima with pork. I found yesterday they had wasted or made way with half their corn, and this evening a balance of nearly half the remnant is missing. I have ordered the company to be issued a pound and a quarter of beef only, until they produce sixty quarts of corn, and directed its commander to establish a quarter guard, under charge of the officer of the day.

My messenger to Mr. Stoneman came in at sundown. He went five or six miles back to him, through almost impenetrable thickets. Mr. S. told him he would manage to get to the mules or get them to him, and after lightening, he was determined to get the boat down to the mouth or until he overtook me. He has not a single cooking article, and nothing but the pork and flour of his load. Mr. Money has not come; his wife was sick. I learn that her father lives at a mining town called "Sonia," about sixty miles south of the Pima village. The town has been built in the last ten years. We found here the petrifaction of a bone, which Doctor Sanderson pronounces much larger than the corresponding bone of an elephant. If this river was frequented by mammoths, their extinction seems to have been followed by that of every other living thing. One may travel a day without seeing an animal, a reptile, creeping thing, an insect. Fortunately, this is the third camp I have formed without losing anything by turning off the road for water or grass.

I find that my marches on this river average quite as long as those on the Río Grande. Soon after I left that river, I commenced my present plan of the companies leading in succession every hour and a quarter, the staff teams taking their turn. Each also commences the day's march in turn. Thus, generally, each set of wagons has a daily average of breaking the way and following a pretty good road. A corporal and three butchers drive the cattle every day and butcher nearly every night. The guard take charge of the beeves as soon as they arrive in camp; the corporal is mounted. A corporal and two assistants drive daily the loose mules; two of them are mounted. These, with the other droves, leave daily last, with the rear guard. The two shepherds take charge of the sheep day and night. There are twelve packsaddles to each company, which are mostly used to lighten the wagons. These follow the advance guard and pioneers, and are generally unpacked and grazing before the wagons and companies come up. The corporal with the pack mules has just arrived. He thinks Mr. Stoneman passed the camp ground while he was absent above (trying to get to the river), deceived by a signal of my messenger, [which was] made to discover Mr. Stoneman's whereabouts; and that Mr. Stoneman is a few miles above, where, after dark, he saw a fire at a distance. Of course, the attempt to lighten the boats has failed thus far.

JANUARY 4. I again left a party with seven pack mules for Lieutenant Stoneman. I marched at eight o'clock and passed over the bottom ground I had examined for about a mile, and then ascending the bluff at a more gentle hill; then at places, by winding a little, the soft sand was changed for soft clay and sand, covered slightly with pebbles. After more than three hours of hard pulling I got into the bottom again. Here the guide met me with information that the river bore far off (he had ascended the mountain partly, to look), and that it was twelve miles before we could strike it again without losing very much, and that there was a good camp and grass at the twelve-mile point. The mules are [at] that stage when too hard a push will make them give out by teams, and I could not risk it without a necessity. So at twelve o'clock, much against my will, I encamped near-by an island, with the usual mixture of flag grass, young cottonwoods, etc. There is much thorny brush, in forcing my way through which to examine the ground I half tore my clothes off. Mr. Stoneman's being behind was some consideration; it will give him an opportunity to overtake us. Francisco says it took the general until eight o'clock at night to get a little below the point for tomorrow's camp, marching from our last night's camp, five miles above; and, if the guides are to be depended on, it was impossible to go on today, the river being two to three miles from the trail.

Night. The pack mule party came in about sundown without hearing anything of Lieutenant Stoneman. The camp is at the foot of a volcanic peak of rocks some five hundred feet high. The adjutant ascended it before sundown and believed he could see the river for twenty miles; and again, since dark, I sent him up with Mr. Foster. They could see the appearance of a small fire opposite the camp of the night before last, sixteen or seventeen miles above, opposite a similar mountain point. I have reason to be exceedingly uneasy, Mr. Stoneman's answer to my messenger giving him to understand that I placed no important value on nearly all his cargo. That he "would stick to it until he got to the mouth or overtook me," together with my knowledge of his indomitable perseverance, has allayed anxiety until now. I know this river is visited by the Tonto Indians, who are only formidable to sleeping men. Mr. S. has two armed men with him, but is himself without arms. Inexperienced, and greatly fatigued at night, they may have been found asleep by a fire. Doctor Foster having volunteered, I have directed him and Appolonius, a guide, to return early tomorrow morning to our last camp five miles above, and then take the river and ascend it by the beaches (crossing when necessary) until the matter is discovered. He takes an order for Mr. Stoneman to abandon everything but five hundred pounds flour and the best ponton, and those if necessary.

But I send also to the last camp a party with six pack mules, to remain there three hours (until twelve o'clock), [and] then to start to rejoin me. The mules this evening (for the first time) crossed the river, where there is better food; and I had to increase the guard to forty-two privates, and sent over twenty-four of them, and still fear that they will escape (some of them) into the dense thickets. Starve or risk their loss are the only alternatives.

JANUARY 5. The officer of the day reported at daylight that the mules had been passing down the river during the night, following some islands; and, accordingly, when they were driven up, but little more than half were present. Nevertheless, by sending some mounted parties, they were found, and I marched at 8:30. Soon after, I heard some shots and was led to believe that Mr. Stoneman had arrived in the vicinity. About noon Doctor Foster came back to me and reported that he had seen him a few miles above camp, and he had left all his load some twenty miles above the last camp. Foster wrote a note to the corporal with pack mules telling him where the flour was, and leaving it to him to go or not. When I received the report, the flour was at least twenty-eight miles in the rear, and I determined at once not to send then, there being a chance that the corporal had gone. Thus two feeds of corn, which I had brought so far, is lost! And when most needed! The loss of the flour straightens me a little, as I have but fourteen days more, not allowing for wastage. I have reduced the rations to nine ounces again.

I departed from the general's trail some five or six miles back, where it takes to the sand bluff, and have cut one through the bottom; much brush but pretty good ground. After marching about twelve miles, I encamped at a poor place for grass; but the guides had become so entangled in this immense flat bottom that they required time to look out the direction. The march was above six hours. This bottom is called rich ground, and I believe it could easily be irrigated. The river has been a long way off all day. Mr. Stoneman is boating. Mr. Smith works hard with the pioneers all day. Mr. Merrill, the adjutant, always marches at the head of the column of wagons (and men), directing them on the best road, and relieving regularly the leading wagons. Every night I have a long, laborious ride, frequently above my head in dense brush, looking for a camp ground, for water, and for grass. If Mr. Stoneman had done as I particularly wished and urged, *viz.*, have got off before I did (we were twenty-one hours in that camp), my corn and flour would have been saved; for the experiment would have shown itself a failure at once. I had put in but three days' rations of flour, until in the last hour his assurances induced me to add three more. Mr. S. spoke of his experience in rafting or boating.

JANUARY 6. The mules, which had a square mile to ramble over last night, and which I think fared pretty well, were very early got into camp by my arrangements, and the advance was sounded [at] 7:50. A mile or two brought us back to the dragoon trail. There was much heavy road. After passing some sand hills, the road descended to a river beach, where I had the mules watered. Then for three or four miles we passed a constant succession of dry beds of mountain torrents, first of sand, then all of stone. I was anxious to reach the point of the mountain where the guide had spoken much of a very bad place. But here, Francisco insisted, we were leaving the river and the last chance for pasture; and so, after coming twelve miles in a little above six hours, I encamped. I fear the mules will do badly, although there is mesquite and some cane. I have two guards above and below, however, and they have free range over a large extent. The ponton boats are here. The corporal with the pack mules has not returned and of course has gone up after a part of the flour. Mr. Stoneman represents that in many places there are but three or four inches of water to be found in the river.[203] The weather is like the finest October weather in Missouri. Last evening Weaver brought me some large cakes half an inch thick, of pure salt. This camp in the dust is wretchedly uncomfortable, owing to a high wind. We have seldom had any wind on this river.

JANUARY 7. I send Doctor Foster and Francisco this morning to the crossing, believed to be twenty-five miles. They were directed to observe if any troops had come from Sonora, or if troops or droves of mules were approaching from California; also, to find the best ground for grass and a camp, as near as they could to the mouth of the Gila, for tomorrow night. All the mules, I believe, were recovered this morning. Weaver was sent on very early to examine thoroughly the difficult spot where the volcanic mountains come into the river. Mr. Smith followed very early, with a party to work there; and Mr. Stoneman with another, advanced as usual to work upon the road. I found, after passing many of the stony ridge points and clay gullies, that the work was very badly done, and caused the last party to

[203] Cooke reported to Kearny: "The experiment signally failed, owing to the shallowness of the water on the bars; the river was very low. In consequence of the difficulty of approaching the river, orders mistaken, &c., the flour only was saved from the loading, and the pontons were floated empty to the crossing of the Río Colorado, where they were used as a ferry boat." *House Ex. Docs.*, 30 cong., 1 sess., no. 41, p. 558.

work back to the wagons. I then forced my way through a dense thicket in the bottom, round some points, and sent back directions as to the ground and an order for the party to be increased by ten men. I then came on until I overtook Mr. Smith, and a road was cut through a dense growth of willow, cottonwood, etc., round the last point, and we again ascended to the usual open bottom. Here Weaver represented that it was the best place for forage he knew, that I could easily go to the mouth from it, and [that I] could not go farther, as the road was entirely off from the river from that point to the crossing. So I encamped and directed the mules all sent across the river, where only there was pasture – flag grass, young cottonwoods, etc.

Having dug a road down the bank, the river was found to be swimming. I then had them sent back through the thicket road, and they crossed over, many of them swimming. It has given me much uneasiness. The river, where I have wanted it as a barrier to the mules, has always been but a few inches deep; here, where I must cross it, it is swimming. The pasture, I fear, is very poor. The ponton boats came down in time for the rear guard to cross in. The corporal and party after flour, whom I certainly expected this evening, has not come back. A pair of hounds were broken short off and another damaged considerably. Having none to remedy it, I have directed the wagon abandoned. In fact, there are four others which are not only not necessary but a great expenditure of force to drag along. But I shall not leave them until necessary, or at a point where I can easily send for them from Warner's. It was very cold this forenoon. The march was about seven miles. The general's party crossed the river here.

JANUARY 8. Mouth of Gila. I got the mules over

safely and early; they had icicles on them! Marched [at] 7:45. There were still some hills of the Devil's point to pass; then we had a very good road. There is a vast bottom here, extending up from the river's mouth, which seems good land; and, for the first time, there is something like a soil and much dry grass. I stopped about eleven o'clock for three-quarters of an hour to graze the mules, but I must doubt that there was any beneficial substance in it, although the mules ate freely. Nine or ten miles from camp I found Foster and Francisco with the pioneers. There was no appearance below of any party since Leroux's. They reported there was no grass short of the river mouth, [and] that there was some bunch grass there but inconvenient to water.

I encamped here about four o'clock, and went about half a mile through mesquite thickets and stationed the advance guard so as to surround (scantily) a large space with bunch grass thinly scattered. The river is close by; to go nearer the grass, I would have had to return in the morning. The mules hold out astonishingly, but great pains is taken; the guard duty very hard; and, apparently, much risk is run of losing some of them, at least, every night. There are very many of the new kind of partridge or quail here. Some have been shot. They have a yellow head, with a beautiful drooping plume on the top, rising slenderly a couple of inches and then expanding and curving forward. It is composed of five or six feathers but looks like one. They are slate-colored. The march was about sixteen miles. The country around the two rivers is a picture of desolation; nothing like vegetation beyond the bottoms of the rivers. Black mountains with wild-looking peaks and stony hills and plains fill the view. We are encamped in the midst of hemp.

JANUARY 9. Marched very early. The wagons were six hours reaching to the crossing. The road was very bad for sand and soft clay – perhaps half of it. The pioneers did much work and straightened the trail much. The mules are weak, and their failing, flagging today, at ten miles, is very unpromising at this stage, with the dry, barren stretch of a hundred miles before them. The grass, too, last night, I considered plenty and pretty good. I found grass in the great thicket of small willows, but sapless and brittle to the very roots. I endeavored to have cottonwoods cut and brought to them, but it could not be done tonight. I, however, sent out forty men to gather the fruit called "tornillo," of a variety of the mesquite.[204] They brought in perhaps twelve or fifteen bushels, which was spread out on a hard part of the sand bar for them. I have heard later of some grass a mile or two lower down and have directed the drove sent there early in the morning. The boats have not arrived; neither has the corporal sent after flour. If I have to make double marches at the 24, 32, and 20 miles' distances, without water between here and the Carrizo, my rations will not last to Warner's, unless the corporal brings up some of that left. Of the last-mentioned twenty miles, the half is sand, and it will make two days – the one a hard one. There has been quite a gale of wind down the river. Francisco was sent across and set fire to the thickets beyond, which thus made a great conflagration. This Weaver highly recommended, as promising great assistance to the pioneer party which I shall send over in the morning to

204 Standage wrote that the mesquite which was gathered was "a kind of sweet seed that grows on the tree resembling the honey locust." He added: "The mules and men being very fond of this. The brethren use this in various ways some grinding it and mixing it in bread with the flour, others making pudding, while some roast it or eat it raw." Golder, Bailey, and Smith, *op. cit.,* 201-202.

cut a road through the bottom thickets. Francisco says the river is deeper than when he passed before.

The Río Colorado here resembles the Missouri in size and color of the water. It has immense bottoms difficult to pass; they are of rich soil. I believe it to be the most useless of rivers to man; so barren, so desolate and difficult, that it has never been explored; running through volcanic mountains and sand deserts, at places through chasms of vertical rock perhaps five thousand feet deep. The hapless wanderer, to its verge, is famished for even a cup of its water, which is more tantalizing to his sight than was ever the mirage of eastern deserts. The rocks of these chasms, I am told, would fit together if restored to the union which has apparently once existed. It cannot be navigable far. This point is about sixty miles to tide and about a hundred above its mouth. At the first fountain of this river, in Oregon, the First dragoons encamped eighteen months ago.

JANUARY 10. The mules were driven at daylight to tolerable grass in the river below. At 9:30 the ponton boats arrived, and at ten o'clock three of the pack mule party with four hundred and twenty pounds of flour. To this I added every pound I could spare of my own and the dragoons, which all makes fifteen or sixteen days at half a pound a day. The corporal and two other men were represented as remaining to hunt for the other deposits of provisions, and that they would not be up for two days – a singular notion. I immediately ordered the companies to cross as soon as possible, leaving only their empty wagons, mules, teamsters, and mule and cattle details, the empty wagons to be drawn over as early as possible in the morning.[205] The wind blows

[205] Cooke gave Kearny a brief description of the crossing of the Colorado: "I passed that river on the 10th and 11th of January. On the first day and

again and slow work is made at crossing. The ford leads far down. I sent Francisco (and several of the teamsters followed him afoot half across) to observe the route; it took his mule in places well up on the side. The weather is said to be colder than known in many years. It seems, by Weaver's account, that I have done injustice to this river's uses, etc. He says it will admit of navigation by steamboats for three hundred and fifty miles from its mouth from April to September, and that the rich bottoms extend that high. It is probable that sugar cane would flourish here. He says the Cochano have rich fields as high up as I have named, where the canyons commence. He speaks of a very rich extensive bottom below, that does not overflow. The sick report now numbers ten.

Night. The boat has made exceedingly slow work; but the battalion is crossing and will continue at it, if necessary, all night. The moon will not rise before two o'clock. I have directed the sheep taken over at five o'clock in the morning, when the reveille will be sounded. Then one load over, after daylight, will probably complete it.[206] I have directed a man to ride each mule in the teams; the water will take them above half side. The sheep, of which a hundred and thirty are still remaining, have done better of late than I expected a

night, the loading of the wagons, and many men, were boated over. On the morning of the 11th, the mules were driven two miles, from grass; then drew the wagons through the long ford of a mile, nearly swimming. The wagons were then loaded in the willow thicket, and I marched 15 miles over the sandy road, to the first well, the same day; a great effort and labor." *House Ex. Docs.*, 30 cong., 1 sess., no. 41, p. 558.

206 Cooke crossed the Colorado river about twelve miles below the mouth of the Gila, near the present Mexican settlement of Algodones, Baja California. Kearny's detachment, guided by Kit Carson, had passed over the Colorado at the same place on November 25, 1846. Cooke's Mexican guide, Francisco, had accompanied Kearny. *Ibid.*, pp. 97-100, 610; Bartlett, *op. cit.*, II, 150.

week or two ago, when a few were left every day. The cattle are very poor; there are ten left to us. Talking with Doctor Foster the interpreter, this evening, I for the first time became aware that I had all the time been laboring under a mistake as to the number of Mexican troops at Tucson – that they were about a hundred and thirty, instead of two hundred and thirty as mentioned in a late official letter to Captain Turner.

JANUARY 11. 9 P.M. With my mind full of anxiety, I force myself to the task of recording the deeds of the day. I am in camp at the well, fifteen miles from the river. I made a firm resolve that here the battalion *should* come today, and for these reasons. I had not rations or time, under the probable state of affairs in California, to spend another day beyond the river; and as the mules must graze on the other side, and they must pull the wagons over when they came, there would be but little less to do in a day – tomorrow than today.

The battalion were crossing, I believe, all night. I heard them until 2:30. But the matter, very difficult indeed in the wide, swift river with two wagon beds, was slowly and very badly managed. The first difficulty I encountered this morning was that instead of the "boat" being in readiness to cross the sheep at reveille at five o'clock as ordered, it was not over from before that hour until a quarter before seven. Then I had all the baggage of the field and staff taken down in ten minutes time, and it was taken over and ten men beside. I was told then by the adjutant that many loads of company property had still to be taken over. The trips had averaged an hour and a half, and on all sides the idea of the impossibility of making the set day's journey was conveyed to me. I told the adjutant that no more of the company property should come in the boat – that the sheep only should be brought. The baggage was then put in wagons. The mules had been driven up at daylight, and I got the wagons started at eight o'clock. The river was a mile over in the course of the ford, and in several channels hundreds of yards across. It runs swiftly at least four feet deep; in fact, occasionally it swam a small mule.

About nine I got up to the bank opposite the old camp. Here, in high willows which concealed everything, I found everything doubly confused: tents standing; every man doing what suited him – some eating, some cooking! [Since] the time was passing fast, I hurried all. I then saw a wagon, the only one of company C, standing in the water halfway across, with the mules taken out and nothing apparently doing. Half an hour after, a lieutenant of the company reached me with a report that they were stuck, etc., and could not get out.[207] I told him they were not trying; that they had had the same opportunities as the other companies to get baggage over (the boat had been used turn about), and that I saw the other wagons get over easily, and even with men in them (that was an abuse that vexed me exceedingly); that I should march immediately and could not help them. Meanwhile, the boat came half loaded with men and baggage, contrary to my order, and with less than a third of the sheep; and instantly the crew disappeared, and no one claimed or unloaded the baggage. My orderly threw it out, and I almost forced two men into the boat to take it back. They spent half an hour in water deeper than they could reach with their ten-foot poles. So bad seemed the chance of getting over more than one more load that I

207 The wagon was stuck in a hole in the middle of the Colorado, according to Cooke's report to Kearny. *House Ex. Docs.*, 30 cong., 1 sess., no. 41, p. 558.

sent word by them to Mr. Smith that he should bring over the boat full of the best sheep, and that the rest might be abandoned if they could not swim. The river had an inch of ice in calm places, and quite a number of mules fell and were drowned (owing to weakness) as we came over.

Then at ten o'clock I forced off the command to march fifteen miles of a bad road, leaving a company in the river and two-thirds of the sheep on the other side. I knew these last were in good hands, and also that the company would then be excited to do their best. The first mile was ascending and through deep sand, the mules pinched with cold and sullen, the tar on the wheels stiff with cold. The prospect of getting to this camp was almost desperate. I gave orders that when mules failed, the company commanders should first take all the private animals belonging to individuals (excepting those having wives), and then, if necessary (that is, highly advisable), to anticipate the same thing I had determined on to be done here – to leave one of their wagons on the road. Two were thus left. I rode on, and stopped all pack and loose animals at a fine quantity of mesquite and tornillo which had fallen to the ground, until all the wagons had passed. The fires which Francisco had made the day before yesterday and Weaver yesterday (with the pioneer party), raged around us and within a few feet. I sent ahead twenty men to collect mesquite beans, believing that the wagons would arrive after dark. I knew there was no grass.

I arrived here at four o'clock and was met a few hundred yards off by a man who told me "there was not a drop of water." Instantly the twenty-four miles to the next water hole, where the prospect was worse, and the thirty-two (still farther) to the Salt Lake, were in my mind to fright me for the three hundred and sixty persons who go confidingly where I point the way. I found Lieutenant Oman digging most energetically with his pioneers as I had directed, not only at the old well [208] but they had commenced another. Soon, in the first, they struck damp sand and so on to water. When the quicksands were entered, it caved in, so as to render it impossible to make the hole more than two or three inches deep. Many expedients were discussed. It was concluded that our only hope was in a washtub belonging to a captain who has a wife. The new well progressed slowly through hard clay. The first wagons came at sunset; at dusk the tub arrived. Lieutenant Oman reported to me, to my utter astonishment, that they were unwilling to give up that valuable article, almost our lives depending on it, it seemed to me. I had it taken. The well, after a long time, seemed to work pretty well and promisingly. Then it failed again. And then I had the tub taken up, and the bottom, which had been bored, knocked out; then it worked better. It was late, however, and anxious expectants for cooking and drinking water thronged the hole. I was seated in my tent consulting with the guides, when Lieutenant Oman suddenly reported that the well had failed worse than ever. My doubts seemed converted to the certainty of evil and disaster. I then learned that the company I had left was encamped six miles back, their team having given out. So much for their wretched management in bringing their wagon loaded, etc.

[208] Kearny camped at the old well on the evening of November 25, when Lieutenant Emory noted: "We halted at a dry arroyo, a few feet to the left of the road, leading to the Colorado, where there was a hole five or six feet deep, which by deepening furnished sufficient water for the men." At the same time Captain Johnston wrote: "Halted at an old Indian well, which we dug out, and found water at about 9 feet below the bottom of the ravine – there was once an Indian village." *Ibid.*, pp. 100, 610.

I sent for Weaver to inquire of the road (long ago anticipated for the command) to follow the river some sixty miles down. He came and so represented the country as to give scarce a hope of its practicability under our circumstances. Once more I went to the well and ordered a fresh detail to be put to the new one. They had found, in ten feet, only muddy clay, and its upper surface was two feet lower than that of the old one, which is about nine or ten feet deep. I then, as I said, with a mind full of trouble, sat down to write. In half an hour Lieutenant Oman came and reported [that] in the new well he had "come to plenty of water that could be dipped with a camp kettle." It threw a radiant glow of light over all the gloom which was settling deeply on every avenue where hope had lingered.[209] I am writing, with only an effort to suppress feeling. It must be remembered that this well[210] failing, what had I to

209 "I viewed this, as in other instances, a Providential deliverance," reported Cooke. "It was the most trying hour of my long military experience." *Ibid.*, p. 558.

210 Thereafter the new well and its immediate vicinity were known as "Cooke's Well" or "Cooke's Wells," although the names "First Well" and "Three Wells" were occasionally used. Bartlett encamped at Cooke's Well on June 8, 1852, when he wrote the following description of it: "The water obtained here was from a hole dug in the earth some ten or twelve feet deep, in a place about twenty feet lower than the general level of the desert. It had to be dipped up in a bucket, and passed to a second person midway towards the top, who emptied it into a basin on the surface, from which the animals drank. There was no grass here, but a thick growth of mezquit trees about twelve feet high, with very wide spreading branches." Bartlett, *op cit.*, II, 148. William P. Blake, geologist and mineralogist, who was a member of Lieutenant R. S. Williamson's Pacific Railroad surveying expedition in 1853, described Cooke's Well as it appeared in that year: "This was dug in the clay under a bank or terrace, about thirty feet high, similar to that at the Álamo and Mezquite well. It was also nothing more than a hole scooped out in the clay, and the water was small in quantity and slightly brackish. It could not be obtained clear, as it was surrounded by fine clay, and held a large amount of it in suspension." *House Ex. Docs.*, 33 cong., 2 sess., no. 91, vol. V, p. 111. Cooke's Well was located a short distance from the present Paredones, Baja California, Mexico.

expect of the next, which I know to be dry now, and not, like this, deriving its supply from a great river, and to be reached after going without water for a night and two days, in addition to this hard day; and the next hope (three almost of our average days' journey) still farther on; and behind, starvation and failure! My faith had not failed, for, at the worst, I gave orders for a beef to be killed at daylight and cooked before ten o'clock, and other preparations for a night without water. The sheep were all got over. I think I shall send Mr. Oman, to whose energetic industry I am much indebted, through to the next well tomorrow, to dig in anticipation of our arrival next day. Many mules gave out today, and, at best, our prospect is bad. There is not only so little water, but so very little for the poor animals to eat. I had about five bushels of the mesquite tornillo collected yesterday by each company and brought here.

I found here, on the high bank above the well, stuck on a pole, "No water, 2nd January. Charbonneau." This fills me with fearfulness not only for the full success of my party, but almost for their safety, for they had rode their tired animals hard so far, were disappointed for water here, and would be for fifty-seven miles farther. It is half past ten o'clock. I have just ordered a party of twelve well-armed picked men under Lieutenant Oman, with a guide, to go through to the Álamo Mocho well tomorrow, to dig and prepare for us; also a picket guard posted up the trail, for here parties are most apt to arrive at a watering place at night. And all the guard tonight, as generally heretofore, is employed in herding the mules. Eighteen hours of unceasing labor has been my lot today – of anxiety enough to turn one gray. I knew the battalion *could* be brought here today in season; and they were brought and encamped before dark, it seemed in spite of themselves.

JANUARY 12. The company came up about ten o'clock. The mules, after being fed with mesquite beans and watered last night, were driven about by the guard to the mesquite groves, where they ate the fallen leaves and browsed. About nine o'clock this morning I commenced watering, intending to march at eleven. The well was replenished rather slowly. And at 11:30, I marched with three companies whose mules had been watered, leaving two (which had commenced) with orders to follow as soon as it was well done. Mr. Smith remained also to water the sheep and beeves. The sheep, he tells me, drank twenty-five buckets of water; there are one hundred and twenty-eight. It has fortunately been cloudy, for the weather yesterday and today, when the sun shone, was a moderate summer heat. The ascent to the bluff, a tolerably long hill of impalpable sand, was very severe, but with the help of the men the wagons were soon up. I left two wagons in the camp. There are now one to each company and two others. One is quite sufficient for all the load of a company. And it is a great risk of losing all to attempt to take through empty wagons; they can easily be sent for with fresh mules.

At four o'clock I came up to the pioneers, guard, and guides. They had stopped where they found Appolonius at the grass, and which he and Francisco both believe to be more than halfway to the Álamo Mocho, or well, which the general wrote me was twenty-four miles. But I thought I had only come ten miles. But, everything considered, I encamped, the foremost wagon nearly an hour to sunset, but the last after. On a wilderness of sand, strewed and mixed with small stones and gravel, we see everywhere, covering a tenth of the surface, little bunches of straw-colored grass. It is a summer grass, produced by a rain and dead enough, but the mules eat it with the eagerness of starvation. This desert, so far, has but one other vegetable production – a tall slim bush called by the Mexicans "stinking wood." There is one other nondescript, a small strange shrub which grows into a pear-shaped basket frame, the stems or branches all uniting as if tied above. About eighty miles to the west is seen a range of mountains which we cross. The bushes furnish a small fire for making tea and frying meat.[211]

JANUARY 13. I marched at sunrise. It is impossible, it seems, to get in motion earlier, as the mules cannot be distinguished and harnessed in darkness. I found a mile and a half of bad sand, and the dry grass thicker there than where I stopped. Thus (to anticipate) Francisco and Appolonius were an injury to me, for, in consequence of their reports, I stopped before sundown and a mile short of half way. The clouds disappeared at ten o'clock, and it turned out the hottest day we have had. I have seen as cold, sunny days at Fort Gibson in June. The road was very sandy, and crooked too. The advance party got here at sundown yesterday, and I found that they had much improved one of the wells and had dug a third.[212] The company wagons reached

211 "Travelled 12 m. and camp'd without water," recorded Standage on January 12. Golder, Bailey, and Smith, *op. cit.*, 202.

212 Kearny reached Álamo Mocho on November 26. Emory noted: "We found in what had been the channel of a stream, now overgrown with a few ill-conditioned mezquite, a large hole where persons had evidently dug for water. It was necessary to halt to rest our animals, and the time was occupied in deepening this hole, which after a long struggle, showed signs of water. An old champagne basket, used by one of the officers as a pannier, was lowered in the hole, to prevent the crumbling of the sand. After many efforts to keep out the caving sand, a basket-work of willow twigs effected the object, and much to the joy of all, the basket, which was now 15 or 20 feet below the surface, filled with water. . . Two buckets for each animal

here at two o'clock, having come the thirteen miles in seven hours. Two staff wagons arrived nearly two hours after, and it was evident that they could not go on through the desert, for here there is nothing for them to eat but a little scattered mesquite which has not borne fruit. The water is very bad and warm, and the supply is scanty and slow. And *now,* after eight hours, the watering is still going on. The poor animals, after drinking, seemed unsatisfied and had to be driven away toward the green bushes, on which they might browse. After consultation and much reflection I have directed two wagons to be left, of the two smallest companies, taking a large part of their team mules to make out the hospital wagon team; and one for the field and staff officers, dragoons, and servants, directing the personal baggage of the six officers of these two companies to be carried in the wagons of the other three companies. I have strong hopes of meeting a relief of mules in a day or two. They should be here, if they were obtained within

were allowed. At 10 a.m. . . Captain Moore had succeeded, by great exertions, in opening another well, and the one already opened began to flow more freely, in consequence of which, we could afford to give each animal as much as he could drink." Johnston wrote: "Probably we took 800 or 1,000 buckets full of water out before morning – some of the horses taking five buckets full without stopping – the buckets holding about four gallons." *House Ex. Docs.,* 30 cong., 1 sess., no. 41, pp. 100-101, 610. Blake, the geologist, described Álamo Mocho as it appeared in 1853: "The name of this place appears to have been suggested by the abundance of cotton-wood trees that grew there several years ago, and that have been cut down. One or two decaying trunks were all that remained. Our camp was on the margin of a steep bank of clay, about thirty feet high. The well is dug at the foot of this bank, in one of the lowest places, and appears to be in the dry bed of a watercourse, or canal, similar to that seen near the lagoons. The desert beyond the well, south and southwest of the camp, appeared lower than the plain on which we were, and was sparsely wooded with low, and partly dead, mezquit bushes. The well was about eighteen feet deep, and lined with boards, and protected by a low curb; but there were no buckets or conveniences for drawing the water." *Ibid.,* 33 cong., 2 sess., no. 91, vol. v, pp. 109-110. Álamo Mocho was located at or near the present El Álamo, Baja California, Mexico.

a day of Warner's. I am relieved of some apprehension for the party by finding water here which they could use, but their not returning begins to be alarming otherwise. We have for a day or two been surrounded by smokes, made, too (some of them), at a small distance. Very fresh tracks of two horses were seen here yesterday. I have consulted Weaver on the subject; he believes that they can only be Indians.

Weaver and Francisco agree that the usual old trail by the Pozo Hondo[213] is the shortest by several miles, that it is the best road, that the water there is better to depend on than the Salt Lake, its sweet quality considered, and that it divides the distance more equally to the Carrizo. Weaver thinks it from five to seven miles nearer than the Salt Lake. So I have determined to take that route, and send Lieutenant Stoneman, Weaver, and twenty-five well-armed men to go through tomorrow and prepare it for our coming. They say there is good mesquite rather more than halfway; so I shall leave here about eleven o'clock tomorrow. I am by no means sure that it would not be the safest plan to abandon all the wagons here. The corporal and two men who acted so foolishly in remaining back to hunt further, after finding and sending to me all the rations I needed, have not come up and possibly never will. He went back at all (more than five miles) on his own responsibility, on receiving the note of information written by the interpreter, Doctor Foster. A man of company A has been missing since we left the river; it is believed he remained to be of assistance to these men, to one or more of whom he was very friendly. I have caused a detail of men to work constantly at the wells, in giving water to all animals that come up, night and day.

213 Deep Well.

January 14. I had the mules driven in at 9:30 and ordered the wagon mules first watered. Mules had been watered, however, as they came up, for the twenty hours. Lieutenant Stoneman sent off his party of twenty-five men before sunrise, following more than half an hour after. Long after that, Francisco reported that he, Weaver, and the advance party had all taken the wrong road, and his own mule was missing; so he went afoot to set them right. Afterward he sent back Appolonius (who went with Weaver and was to have been left in the best mesquite) more than halfway to the well, to guide us by their tracks, Francisco going on to guide them. When the wagons were ready, at eleven o'clock, Appolonius was missing, hunting a mule! I marched then, leaving many mules waiting the slow flow of water into the wells, to be watered. The first mile or two was bad sand; then we descended to a clay flat. I stopped at some mesquite with many fallen leaves, and had the pack animals fed there until many of the company wagons had passed. Then for several miles there was a little sand blown from the hills which were near. Afterward the trail led me over a great flat of baked clay, over which a sheet of water had evidently stood, or gently flowed toward the south. There are miles square of it without a bush or weed. In many places the mules scarcely made a track. I did not overtake the advance guard until six o'clock (dark), when I found them here, on the edge of a mesquite thicket, where one of the advance party had been left to point out the place. A mile back I fell into a vast trail of ten thousand mule or horse tracks – herds driven in the last few months to Sonora. Our trail was lost in them, and I had several fires built to mark its course. The wagons commenced arriving at 7:15. The march was about seventeen miles.

I fear there is very poor food here for the mules.[214] The mesquite leaves seem not to have fallen to much extent. The poor animals are eating dry weeds and sticks. The weather is quite warm, but fortunately there were clouds which nearly all the day veiled the mules from the fiery sunshine. I saw large quantities of sea shells, some perfect. The ground has evidently been the bottom of the gulf, which has now receded a hundred miles. The salt on this plain confirms the idea.

JANUARY 15. I marched before sunrise. The mountains to our left and front were mingled with clouds; the rising sun painted all with bright and varied hues; and then we saw the distinct colors of a rainbow, its extremity an orange red, and violet spot in the midst – an omen of promise, which only before have we seen in the other desert of Tucson! The road was the same flat, clay plain, and much to our surprise seven or eight miles brought us to the Pozo Hondo.[215] As I approached it, Major Cloud met me with letters. Tesson had brought mules and cattle. The pleasure of this great relief was sadly changed to the most sorrowful feelings on hearing of our great loss in action[216] of Captains Moore and Johnston and twenty-one dragoons. Then was genuine grief shown by all that knew them. Our difficult and straightened circumstances were lost sight of for the time. What a loss to my regiment! Ah! who but loved Johnston – the noble, sterling, valued Johnston! And who had warmer friends than poor Moore! Peace to their ashes! Rest their souls! May their country honor the memories of its heroic champions, who,

214 "Camp'd without grass or water," wrote Standage on January 14. Golder, Bailey, and Smith, *op. cit.*, 202.

215 Probably a short distance west of the present El Centro, Imperial county, California.

216 The Battle of San Pascual, December 6, 1846.

serving her, have found their graves in distant and desolate regions! A weight was taken off my mind and that of others on hearing of the general's safety, though twice wounded – slightly, it is reported, and we trust truly.

The first report to me was that there was plenty of water, but I soon discovered that it was a woeful mistake. There was not enough for the men! It was half past ten o'clock. I immediately ordered the water issued by measure, a fat beef killed, food cooked, the wild mules caught and harnessed, the march to be continued at one o'clock as far as the reported grass, and then, after a rest, to be resumed for the Carrizo. The Salt Lake is now dry. Tesson started with fifty-seven mules, thirty-three as wild as tigers. He lost twenty-two. The guide, Leroux, did badly in sending Tesson only, and with mules and cattle together; and we have suffered for it. It took two or three hours hard work to catch and harness these terrible mules. One broke away (and ran off in harness) from three picked men. The first wagons with the new broken mules got here at dark. Now – 8:30 – one company has not arrived. We came eleven miles. I have ordered the mules kept tied up in harness and the bunch grass cut for them (there is very little of it), the pack mules to be kept saddled, and the march to be resumed at two o'clock. Besides being nearly starved, our old mules have had no water since yesterday morning; the men, too, are without [it]. It is necessary to go on in the coolness of the night speedily, to end this terrible state of things. The ten miles of much dreaded sand is before us.

JANUARY 16. The last, worst desert is passed in safety but with great suffering.[217] I marched this morning at

[217] Standage wrote on January 16: "Saw many of the brethren laying by the road side begging water." Golder, Bailey, and Smith, *op. cit.*, 203.

two o'clock exactly, believing it only ten or twelve miles and a much worse road than I found it. I had a large advance guard, and all the guides on duty, telling Weaver to keep the foremost wagon in sight. It was a starlight night. Four miles from our bivouac I halted till all passed, and found that even then a team or two had apparently given out. I gave various orders of relief, transferred mules, etc. Toward daylight it was exceedingly cold, too much so to ride. Then the guides got lost, and, by their not obeying strictly my orders, the wagons lost at least a mile, and over bad road. Here the new teams seemed almost exhausted. Two companies had each lost a set of harness – accidents by the new mules. I managed to procure others. I found the road was about to prove very much longer than I had been led to believe and had great misgivings. About ten o'clock, as usual, it became of summer heat. Finally, near eleven, I reached with the foremost wagon the first water of the Carrizo.[218] A clear, running stream [219] gladdened our eyes after the anxious dependence upon muddy wells for five or six days. One company, which was late in marching and met with an accident, was so much thrown into the heat of the day that the mules entirely failed several miles off, and a new team had to be sent; and it arrived at sunset. I found the march, with the deviation, nineteen miles. Thus, without water for near three days (for the animals) and encamping two nights in succession without water, the battalion

[218] The battalion reached Carrizo creek near the western boundary of the present Imperial county, California.

[219] "The Carmisa [Carrizo]," according to Captain Johnston, "is a place in the pass of the mountain where a stream rises, and sinks again immediately. The water comes out warm, and flows freely in a clear little stream towards the plains, and half a mile down it is lost in the sand; around this water the carissa grows, and a species of salt grass." *House Ex. Docs.*, 30 cong., 1 sess., no. 41, p. 611.

made, in forty-eight hours, four marches of eighteen, eight, eleven, and nineteen miles, suffering from frost and from summer heat!

Fortunately, we found the ground today, ascending the dry creek bed, a tolerably good road. It is now evident that the march from the Álamo Mocho well here, fifty-six miles, could not have been made in any other way – that is, the push of eighteen miles the afternoon and evening of the first day; the rest, refreshment of meat, and drink of water during the heat of the following day; then the evening and night march to grass; and then, after a few hours' rest, the march five hours before sunrise, when the extreme cold braced all and postponed the torture of thirst. The sheep got within a mile of camp last night, and tonight, I fear, are many miles back. I had a ration of two and a half pounds each of fat beef issued today on our arrival. We have contented ourselves today with a solitary meal: breakfast, at one or two o'clock. The dry grass here is as salt as brine. I had all the flag grass cut for the mules (there was very little), and succeeded in finding some bunch grass, where the poor animals are now grazing. The loss of mules appears to be sixteen in the two days. Our greatest assistance, beside the beef, was in twenty-two of the general's old mules which were watered yesterday morning before my arrival, to clear out the well; and it was not replaced. The wild ones would not drink out of buckets; and, indeed, some of our mules went two or three days without water before they would thus drink.

Nine Mexicans have overtaken us here. To two principal ones I gave permission at Tucson to follow me. I believe they are poor men seeking to better themselves by moving to California. They are nearly starved, have been living on our dead mules, etc. I have directed that two sheep be given to them. They met my foolish corporal and two men going up the Gila for rations. At the crossing of the Colorado they were a day behind us and met a large war party of Indians. One of the Mexicans left Tucson eight days after me but brings no news. He says the military did not return for three or four days after my departure. I should rest here tomorrow if there were pasture, considering the hard day the guides represent to be before me – fifteen miles of very sandy road. I have determined to undertake it with a very early start, as they say there is good grass for the next camp. A great number of my men are wholly without shoes, and use every expedient, such as rawhide moccasins and sandals, and even wrapping their feet in pieces of woolen and cotton cloth.[220]

JANUARY 17. With reveille, at five o'clock this morning, I found that, after light, many of the mules, particularly the new, wild ones, had escaped the guard. Thus the march was delayed until nine o'clock. All the mules were believed to be recovered except six, which came forward. I sent the Indians after them and got

220 Corporal Tyler, of the Mormon Battalion, described the hardships of the march across the desert to Carrizo creek: "We here found the heaviest sand, hottest days, and coldest nights, with no water and but little food. At this time the men were nearly bare-footed; some used, instead of shoes, rawhide wrapped around their feet, while others improvised a novel style of boots by stripping the skin from the leg of an ox. To do this, a ring was cut around the hide above and below the gambrel joint, and then the skin taken off without cutting it lengthwise. After this, the lower end was sewed up with sinews, when it was ready for the wearer, the natural crook of the hide adapting it somewhat to the shape of the foot. Others wrapped cast-off clothing around their feet, to shield them from the burning sand during the day and the cold at night. Before we arrived at the Carriso many of the men were so nearly used up from thirst, hunger and fatigue, that they were unable to speak until they reached the water or had it brought to them. Those who were strongest reported, when they arrived, that they had passed many lying exhausted by the way-side." Roberts, *op. cit.*, 45-46.

them during the march. The road was very deep with sand and the forenoon very hot, but the teams reached the Palm springs [221] between twelve and one o'clock; and there being no grass, I determined to continue the march to the Vallecito. The first wagon arrived just at dark, the others much later. The road, not quite so deep with sand, was much more broken, and obstructed with great lumps of mescal. Altogether, it is the worst fifteen miles of road since we left the Río Grande; and that it was accomplished, under all the circumstances, by mules or men, is extraordinary. The men arrived here completely worn down. They staggered as they marched, as they did the day before. Eleven mules, and perhaps a few more, were left on the route. The sheep came up this morning before we marched, but are not up tonight. A half ration of pork has been issued. We have been passing up the winding bed of a dry mountain stream, or rain weather torrent, between mountains utterly barren, looking of the color of ashes. Between them are great mounds of clay and sand, sometimes conglomerated with stone and pebbles. These are

221 Blake, the geologist, described the Palm springs as they appeared on December 15, 1853: "These were situated under a bank of argillaceous, sedimentary beds. The water rises at various places, and seems to saturate the ground so thoroughly for a space two or three hundred feet in diameter, that a hole dug in any part of it soon becomes filled. The water was sulphurous, and gave off a slight quantity of sulphuretted hydrogen gas. A slight efflorescence of nitre was seen on the surface of the ground around the pools. The water, however, was not so strongly charged with these ingredients as to be unpleasant to drink, especially after having used the stagnant and muddy water of the Desert. I found its temperature, under the shade of a palm tree, to be 60°; air, 70°. Three or four palm trees, each about thirty feet high, are standing on the bank from which the springs issue. They are much injured by fire and the persevering attacks of emigrants, who have cut down many of the finest of the group, as if determined that the only trees that grace the sandy avenue to the Desert, and afford a cool shade for the springs, should be destroyed." *House Ex. Docs.*, 33 cong., 2 sess., no. 91, vol. v, pp. 122-123.

utterly bare and water washed. At the Carrizo a fine, clear stream gushes out from steep embankments and runs near half a mile before it disappears in the sand. Seven miles above, the narrow valley has a bank, from which it is soaked with good water and forms a few small springs; and there are twenty or thirty palm trees, the first I ever saw.

Here, at the Vallecito,[222] is a wet, flat valley a mile or more in extent, where grow, besides grass, a few small willows. Thus we are nearly without fuel. The grass, which is plentiful, I fear is very poor, as the mules are straggling on the broken ground around. The night is cloudy, the wind high and cold. We met an Indian below who stated the general had captured the pueblo with considerable loss of men. It is evident that I could not have brought the two other wagons left at the Álamo Mocho wells with the relief received, and equally evident that if the mules had been sent to me by a careful person without delay and loss, that they would have reached me there, and that the two wagons could have been brought. The beef cattle sent separately would have reached in ample time; and, in fact, they were not absolutely necessary. But for the providential clouds and cool wind this afternoon, the mules could not, probably, have performed the day's march. It is astonishing to consider what the wild young mules performed and endured, driven thirty miles to meet me; then next day,

222 Vallecito was in the eastern part of the present San Diego county, California. Captain Johnston, who encamped there on November 29 and 30, 1846, wrote: "It would be considered a poor camp on the Arkansas, but here it is fine." *House Ex. Docs.*, 30 cong., 1 sess., no. 41, p. 612. On December 16, 1853, Blake described this camping place: "Vallecito is the first place where grass and vegetation greet the eyes of the traveller who has crossed the dreary Desert. It is a narrow valley between the granite ridges, and is well supplied with springs that are surrounded with grass and willows." *Ibid.*, 33 cong., 2 sess., no. 91, vol. v, p. 123.

in its heat, to go through the terrible process of being broken to harness; two hours of the most violent possible exertions (I saw one, at least, which, a second time thrown, lay panting and motionless); then to draw wagons two marches; and thus, without food, too, to arrive the third day without water.

JANUARY 18. Same camp at Vallecito. Some of the men did not find strength to reach camp until daylight this morning. The sheep did not come up until after midday. They stopped for the night at the palms. A number were left on the road. I went through the companies this morning. They were eating their last four ounces of flour. I had beeves killed and a double ration issued early. The battalion should have eight days' half rations of flour, by a close account and calculation which I have kept up; and according to the actual quantity on the second of December, to that date there had been an equal loss or wastage of eight days. Of sugar and coffee, there has been none for some weeks. Of pork, there should be six days' (at eight ounces); but there is not much, and I have directed that it be used with the beef at discretion. I have eighty-eight sheep left, and four of the beeves which I brought from the Río Grande. With the new beeves, altogether, I have five days' double rations of fresh meat. I have five public wagons, and there are three private property. One of those came up late today. I sent back this morning early for mules left within six miles; five were brought up. The party of emigrants from Sonora brought up three good mules, which were lost the night before last. These men I keep from starvation. I have given them two more sheep this evening.

The Indian alcalde of San Felipe brought me today a letter written three days ago by Mr. Montgomery, commander of ship "Portsmouth" and governor of San Diego. He writes me that my party arrived the fourteenth instant; welcomes my approach and promises refreshment, etc., for the battalion; states he has had credible reports of the general's establishing his camp on the river of the pueblo after two days' engagement with artillery (whilst constantly advancing) ; and warns me that several leaders of the Californians who, having broken their parole, are expected to attempt to march for Sonora by this route; says the character of the Californians has been underrated as military men, etc. I presented the alcalde with a small looking-glass of my own, having nothing else to give him. He asked me not to let the other Indians know he had brought me the letter, etc. I told him he must look to the Americans hereafter as the rulers of this country and as his friends; and that he should send me speedy information by bypaths of the vicinity or approach of any bodies of the Californians; that he should have them watched from the mountains, etc. He, and his interpreter also, a San Felipe Indian, are fine-looking men, nearly naked, hair long, [and] face painted with red spots. Their language seemed bad, somewhat resembling that of the Apache. I have had a company inspection and a dress parade this evening, and have made arrangements and given orders for a regular march tomorrow, with military precautions. We have yet hopes of striking a blow. The men who this morning were prostrate, worn out, hungry, and heartless, have recovered their spirits tonight [and] are singing and playing the fiddle.

JANUARY 19. Again, this morning, many of the mules were astray. It is almost impossible to keep our new mules from going on whence they came. Owing to this, the march was delayed until nine o'clock. The companies marched in front of the baggage, which was placed under charge of the acting assistant quartermaster. There were pioneers, and an advance guard of twenty privates, with orders not to go more than a half mile in advance. The guides had told me it was a good, firm road, with a very narrow canyon for a short distance, but that a Mr. Ward's wagon from Sonora had passed it, and no doubt we could, etc. After coming three or four miles uphill, and much of it coarse sand, I found that the guides, with the pioneers, etc., had stopped, and seemed to be doing nothing. There was a rugged mountain, with a gap, in our front, some two hundred feet high. Weaver very coolly turned to me and remarked that he believed we were penned up. "Ah," I replied, "then you never saw this mountain before, I suppose. I have heard nothing of it. Find a crossing, or I shall send a company of my men who will soon do it." With much active work I got the wagons over in about an hour and a half.

Then, up a mountain torrent bed, I came to the canyon and found it much worse than I expected – there were many rocks to cross, etc. But the worst was the narrow pass, besides crookedness of hard, high rocks. Setting an example myself, there was much labor done on it before the wagons came; that is, with axes we pounded, broke, split, and hewed the rocks to increase the opening. I thought it was all safe before the wagons came, and went on a short distance and found a hill to be ascended, to avoid a still narrower canyon, with a great rock to be broken to pieces with our axes before it was practicable. Much work was done here. When the trial was made, with the mules all taken out, I found that there was at least a foot of solid rock too much! The wagon was run back, more work was done, the trial repeated, until the wagon was so wedged that it could with difficulty be got either way. The sun was now only an hour high, and it was six or seven miles to the first water. I had the body lifted off and carried forward, the running gear uncoupled, and turned one wheel up, and thus taken through. Meanwhile, we still cut and hewed at the mountain side. The next wagon's body was brought through, and the running gear run through, with difficulty, and by lifting up one side somewhat. Then the hospital wagon, being a small one, came through without mules, but all standing.[223] I then pushed on and saw the wagons up the very steep hill and down to the canyon again, and learn that, with much more persevering labor on the place, the other wagons were brought through with load and mules in! Then we ascended the sandy stream to the mountain top.

At sunset, as I overtook the guide and advance, Francisco met us and pointed to a ridge a mile or so in front and said it was very bad, and he believed we could not see to work and pass it tonight; and, as there was grass here, he had returned to tell me. Weaver called it five or six miles to San Felipe. I sent on the pioneers and advance guard, and told the officer to fire a gun if we could pass it; and I awaited the coming of the wagons. At dusk they came, and hearing no report, I encamped. We are not only without water but are entirely unprepared for it. I believe the grass (dry enough) is better than any we have had since we left the last grama grass one march east of Tucson. I have ordered the wild

[223] Passing this place on June 2, 1852, Bartlett wrote: "This pass had been used only for mules, until Colonel Cooke entered the country with wagons. Not being able to get through, he was obliged to come to a halt, and open a passage with axes and hammers through the solid rock, a work of great labor. This defile consists of perpendicular walls of rock about fifteen feet high, and of a width barely sufficient for wagons to pass." Bartlett, *op cit.*, II, 123.

mules hobbled and the guard to enclose them all, and move at every relief. I had a beef killed for supper; broiled beef creates very little thirst. I have ordered the march to be renewed at reveille, [in order] to breakfast at the watering place. The road from the Colorado is by far the most difficult of all. I sent the advance guard through the defile before commencing work today. The weather last night was exceedingly cold, very thick ice forming. The water at the Vallecito is very disagreeable to the taste. It has probably valuable curative properties, serving to act upon the liver and as a gentle aperient.

JANUARY 20. Another very cold night and very little fuel. Some of the mules again escaped and came forward. I marched before sunrise and was soon at the rocky hill, which was very bad. But, by using ropes, the wagons were got over in about an hour. There was an excellent descending road five or six miles to San Felipe, the site of a deserted, small Indian village. I arrived at about eleven o'clock, turned the mules out to graze, and killed two of the small, poor beeves for breakfast. There is nothing else in camp. Charbonneau met me here. He left San Diego on the seventeenth; no further news; no orders for me had been received. Mr. Hall and Leroux were kept there by the governor of the town, who believed the road unsafe; so there is little or no likelihood of communication being soon opened with the general through messengers. Charbonneau says there is very little flour at San Diego. I sent forward three Indians from the noon halt to Warner, telling him to send eighteen cattle to meet me tomorrow at the creek, some seven miles on the road from Warner's to San Diego; expecting myself to turn and encamp there, not going nearer than within seven miles of Warner's rancho. Charbonneau represents it as above five days (some very hard) to San Diego from this camp by taking that left-hand road. He says the best road is by San Pascual, but he did not go it or come by it.

At 2:15, I marched up the pass seven miles to this ground, where there is good water, but I am disappointed in finding grass very scanty. The camp was made at dark. On the march, in an open prairie, I gave the battalion a short drill whilst the wagons were closing up. During the march I considered the subject of the military propriety of my changing my course from San Diego to the pueblo. These views presented themselves to my mind, considering myself under orders for San Diego. The orders were given at a time when it was impossible to know the wants of the service, the circumstances of the country, etc., and evidently because it was believed that the road would take me there – the most practicable road. The general has been there, and left it for a point higher up. He must have left it pacified, or quiet, as is reported to me, and the place is in our full possession and commanded from the sea. I have information that the enemy's forces are concentrated at the pueblo, which is attacked or menaced by Lieutenant-colonel Frémont from the north and the general from the south. If I march there, I approach from the eastern outlet, thus hemming in – almost surrounding – the enemy; or, at least, menacing him from a third quarter; and I approach on the highway, the only one perhaps, of his escape to Sonora, or by which he might drive off or secure his plunder of horses, etc.

I march through a part of the country not yet passed over by any of our forces, and represented to me as the most disaffected, and possessed by our richest and most influential enemies. And from that district, it is said, come a very large Indian force employed by, and probably forced into the service of, the enemy. I may communicate with them, or, at least, by my presence undermine this prop of the enemy's power and dependence. The general has very few land forces proper with him. Mr. Montgomery said he needed infantry much. The general will evidently need a garrison for the pueblo, which is not commanded from the sea. The sailors and marines are not suitable, and are probably needed in their proper sphere. His few dragoons he will absolutely require for the most active field service. I know that no orders have been left or received at San Diego for me. I have just received a messenger from there. I have others there who are to bring them to me promptly if received. I sent to inform the general that I should be at Warner's tomorrow, that I might receive orders; he has probably not yet received my communication. My messengers, three days ago, were detained at San Diego. I ascertained that there is a wagon road to the pueblo by which I can reach there almost as soon as to San Diego; and, finally, Captain Montgomery writes me, January 15: "It is generally believed that parties of Californians headed by leaders who have violated their paroles, will endeavor to effect a retreat to Sonora rather than submit to our arms," etc.

It thus appears to me that it does not admit of further question. I have ordered Charbonneau and some Indians to go very early and stop the cattle from being sent, as before required, and to collect at Warner's all the mules belonging to the public, including those which have escaped from me, and gone on to Santa Isabel. One of the five adventurers after the lost flour came up this evening; reports all safe but broken down at the Vallecito, nineteen or twenty miles back, with above four hundred pounds of flour. I have directed two of my extra guides to go there on stout mules at three o'clock in the morning and assist them up to Warner's with the flour, which, though little, will be vastly welcome to men entirely without. Captain Hunt now says he believes that the two men who stopped at the Red river to await the others may have misunderstood him as giving them permission. I have directed the acting assistant quartermaster to make arrangements to leave at the Santa Isabel ranch some thirty or forty worn-down mules; also to endeavor to send for the wagons left.

JANUARY 21. A cold cloudy morning, threatening snow. I found the pass over the mountain smooth and not difficult. The path – now a road – winds amid a forest of large evergreen oaks. Cold as it was, the fresh, deep, green grass was springing everywhere from the ground. This mountain divides the waters of the Colorado and the Gulf from those which run directly west to the ocean. The higher ridges are crowned with pines and we saw some snow amongst them. From the top a smooth prairie valley of the San Luis opened to the view, but everywhere closely hemmed by mountains. I descended rapidly to the lower slopes, and there drilled my battalion again whilst the baggage closed up. An Indian, sent by some one, showed me a better wagon road than that of the advance guard and pioneers, which I took, and encamped in the valley a few hundred yards below Mr. Warner's house. Mr. Warner is here, and I have had much conversation with him.[224] He has de-

[224] Jonathan Trumbull Warner, the youngest of a family of nine children, was born in Connecticut, November 20, 1807. He came to St. Louis in 1830 and during the spring of the following year was appointed clerk to Smith, Jackson, and Sublette's trading expedition to Santa Fé. On August 29, 1831, shortly after his arrival in New Mexico, he left Santa Fé with a mule-trading expe-

tailed very much of the course of events before and since the insurrection. My best information places General Kearny in the capital, which the Californians evacuated the night of the ninth instant; that these then marched to attack Frémont, who is said to have been, about the sixth instant, within eighty-five miles of the pueblo; and, finally, that it was the general's intention to pursue from the pueblo on the eleventh. My only conclusion is that the enemy, if successful at least in escaping disaster, may yet be in force and likely to encounter me; or else, if broken, that a portion will yet take this road to escape to Sonora. They may, if they choose, evade me beyond this, except at certain points.

Charbonneau has not returned from Santa Isabel. I find here some thirty or more cattle, cows and calves principally, which the San Luis Indians have driven from the farms of some ten or eleven Californians who were captured by the Indians below and brought here and put to death. It is said that these men were about to make their submission. Mr. Warner says they have several hundreds more, beside wild mares, at a valley fifteen miles distant, and wishes me to have the whole taken and, if not used, put in safety. He also wishes

dition to California, reaching Los Angeles, December 5, 1831. Deciding to remain in that province, he became a Mexican citizen and in 1833 settled in Los Angeles, where he became a successful merchant. Since his name was difficult for the Mexicans to pronounce, and since it had no equivalent in Spanish, he changed it to "Juan José Warner," although he frequently signed himself "J. J. Warner." In 1837 he married Anita Gale. On August 30, 1844, in behalf of his children, he applied to the government for a grant of the Valle de San José, claiming that he needed "a place in which to put a considerable number of cattle and sheep belonging to the children of my marriage with my aforesaid wife." His application having been approved in 1844 and 1845, he moved to the property, built an adobe house on it, and lived there for a number of years. His establishment, known as "Warner's Ranch," was a famous stopping place for emigrants who traveled the southern trails to California. Joseph J. Hill, *The History of Warner's Ranch and its Environs* (Los Angeles, 1927).

much to get rid of these Indians, who, he says, have nearly ruined him. I have told Antonio, a chief, that I wish him to pick twenty of the Indians to accompany me to the pueblo, to assist in cattle guarding, driving, and to act as scouts, etc. He assented. It appears that lately these Indians, attacking a few Californians in the valley of Temécula, were drawn by them into an ambush of Indians of a connected tribe and thirty-eight slain. He said that several hundred of them from here and lower down wished to go with me as far as that valley to bury there their dead. I assented on condition that they drove there the cattle before mentioned. I told him to send out a party of five or six to watch a pass on the road twelve miles from here. He has sent them. I consider it absolutely necessary to rest here tomorrow, not only on account of the weak and exhausted condition of the men, but to carry out my objects of collecting the general's mules (and my strays at Santa Isabel), and also to enable the party with the flour to overtake me. The men are weak for want of food. I have issued two and a half pounds of meat, but it is poor and the proportion of bone is great. I shall commence tomorrow an issue of four pounds and reduce it if they do not eat it, which I shall ascertain.

JANUARY 22. 11 A.M. A fine April morning for Missouri or Virginia; a frost, however, and a very cold night. This is a beautiful little valley, shut in by mountains or high hills on every side. The former are nearly covered with green shrubs, amongst which the rocks show themselves, and are crowned with pine and cedar; the latter with oak and other evergreens, and excellent grass. The grass is just up and the country looks verdant. Some large cottonwoods are leafless, but the mistletoe has lent them a green drapery. The name Agua Caliente comes from a bold spring which issues from fissures in the rock at a temperature of about 170° Fahrenheit. It runs clear and freely, and now sends up clouds of steam for a half mile below. The little oval valley here, a mile or more in length, is a smooth, symmetrical, gently convex surface. In the center is an immemorial evergreen oak, whose boughs reach within five feet of the ground in a circle, forming an arbor of ninety feet diameter.

Charbonneau has not yet returned from Santa Isabel with the mules. I have Indians out with orders to drive up every animal on the ranch. There are four of the general's mules said to be among them. And I have directed Mr. Smith to procure beeves of Warner. He will exchange some sheep for them; we have about eighty, but poor. I shall probably be able to procure two *fanegas* of wheat to issue as rations. Warner, the Connecticut man turned California proprietor, is quite a study. He exhibits traits of either character, which may be considered the opposites, of our northern continent. The Indians have driven up late a number of mules. Charbonneau returned this evening, leaving others to do his business. And they have only brought three of six or seven mules from Santa Isabel. Bill, the overseer, came with him; and Mr. Stoneman has bargained with him to send for five wagons, the two nearest costing twenty dollars each. He also takes charge of twenty-four of my broken-down mules. Mr. Smith has obtained of Warner twenty-two beef cattle in good order. He gave four sheep for one, a small balance in money being due. Corporal Muir has not come with the flour, and it is after night. The Indians here, in cold nights, sleep in the stream, lying with their heads ashore! I bathed today, as most others, in the open air, although it was somewhat cloudy.

JANUARY 23. I marched very early. Before [leaving], however, I saw Baupista, an influential chief of the Cahuillo, a nation of perhaps two thousand men. A somewhat independent band of his nation lately defeated and slew thirty-eight of the San Luis tribe, who were pursuing the Californians. I told him that I regretted that any part of his nation should have taken so unwise a course in favor of the Californians, who would now abandon them; that, if reports were true, the war was nearly over, and I wished him only to stop any attempt to drive horses, mules, and cattle out of the country; that I advised him to settle his people to their usual pursuits for a regular livelihood; that the Americans were pouring in from every quarter and would forever govern the country; that they were his friends, and were accustomed to do much for the improvement and aid of Indians who were well behaved and obedient. Antonio was one of the interpreters. I told him to tell his people to settle down and be more quiet, and to drive in all the captured horses, etc., to Warner, whom I had commanded to take care of them until disposed of by the general.

Antonio then accompanied me with ten Indians. He is guide until I get into the valley of Temécula, Weaver having never followed that part of the cart road. I found the road pretty good; hilly, with some steep places, particularly one we came down. I have attempted to march to the pueblo in six days; so I could not stop at the Indian village twelve miles from Agua Caliente, and came on to this first good ground (with water), six or seven miles farther. I encamped rather before sundown. It commenced raining pretty freely before four o'clock and has continued several hours. The beef for supper is only now getting into the hands of the men at 7:30. Four or five beeves are killed for a ration. Mr. Warner joined me about midday and is now in camp; what his object is, I know not. Just at dark Corporal Muir and party arrived with the flour shipwrecked a third of the way up the Gila. I blamed him for going so far and staying so long, not coming with the first half which he discovered and sent to me. He said he did not dare to come without it, and would have expected to have been sent back if he had. There are many of a large bush or tree which we first observed beyond San Bernardino, with polished, brass-colored limbs, and a small, pale-green leaf. It is now in blossom! It is a pretty bush, called, I believe, in Spanish, the *agre*. There are others new to us. Very little grass to be seen today, and the country here is a mere pass amongst broken mountains and stony hills.

JANUARY 24. 8 P.M. From 4 P.M. yesterday until the same hour today it has rained hard almost incessantly. Last night the rain was accompanied with high winds, which prostrated all of our few tents. In this storm and darkness the poor mules and cattle passed generally the line of sentinels and strayed, and I have found Antonio and his ten mountain Indians of good service. They soon drove them back to camp, except five or six, which may still be missing. Four died. With very scant fuel, the ill-clad battalion must have suffered much. My camp was a bare one, exposed to a great draft of wind between the gap of the mountains. I heard of this better spot of brush and trees for shelter three or four miles on, and at eleven o'clock, when the sun was out a short time, marched. The road was very heavy, but I reached here about one o'clock and encamped. The advance guard and pioneers went nearly a mile farther, and worked at a spot which they reported would have been impassable in the then state of the road, as was, also, this mountain torrent now roaring behind my camp. It continued to rain hard until near sunset, when happily it cleared up. This is comparatively a warm spot, but the grass is very poor, though enough of it. The loads must have been much heavier today; every blanket was saturated. Thus, my good beginning to reach the pueblo in six days from Warner's has been defeated [by] at least one day. I trust the matter may not be worse and that the storm is over, for it is the rainy season.

JANUARY 25. A bright morning. I found the stream still belly deep and afterwards passed through a flooded bottom. The road, also, was very hilly, and a wagon wheel was broken. I left the company with it. The road passes through some high winding valleys in leading from the first stream into the Temécula valley. The scenery has been enchanting; the foliage that of the first of May in the middle states. The mountain sides were, after the rain, of sparkling green, while over to our right, towering above all, we saw the lofty San Jacinto and San Bernardino mountains, which had just received a covering of snow of shining, unmixed white. At twelve o'clock I came to fine grass and halted an hour and a half. Then the company had repaired its damaged wagon and arrived. This upper part of the Temécula valley is very pretty, with green meadows of great extent, and snowy and green mountains to be seen in every direction. I encamped near sundown at the first ranch, which is deserted. Here was the slaughter of the San Luis Indians. The party come to bury the bones arrived this evening a little before me, about a hundred and fifty in number. As I approached the ground, I saw them marching in regular single file and form a line across the road. We could see the glitter of arms, and the galloping of men about the array. A drum was also beating. Few but believed we were about to have an action.

The grass is very scant and indifferent here. Little or no fuel. I used an old corral for that purpose. Soon after encamping, I received a letter from the acting assistant adjutant-general from San Diego, which, as usual, supposes me to be at Warner's or beyond, and takes my march to San Diego for granted. It states that the general is returning there; and the bearer informs me that the pueblo is occupied by Lieutenant-colonel Frémont and a large force. Therefore, I consider it plain enough that I should turn off for San Diego; a road leads there from a point very near me. I have answered to that effect and directed the messenger to return tomorrow. Antonio requested me to remain until noon tomorrow, to protect the Indians whilst they buried the bones of the slain. I reluctantly told him that I could not possibly do so. They fear, he said, an attack from the heathen Indians. The march was about twelve miles. Mr. Warner states he has never known so warm a winter rain. In fact, it was little colder than our summer rains of equal violence and duration.

JANUARY 26. I marched 7:45. In about two miles the road turned up a steep winding ravine. After working on it, the companies that have wagons had to put about half their force upon them to get up; then the road is pretty good. It wound over very high hills, and nothing but such (of great height and steepness), and mountains, were to be seen in any direction – all covered with verdure. I found the San Luis, which is generally nearly dry, quite a river. The first mules fell in crossing. But after the men and pack mules had waded over, the wagons had no difficulty. It was uneven quicksands.

After marching seven hours, I encamped on the San Luis a mile or two above the San Juan ranch. It is a fine place on a meadow of green new grass, with plenty of dry wood between me and the river. It is entirely overcast and just at this moment has commenced to rain a little. I will yet have hard work with the wagons if we have much of it. The mules have been half starved for a week, and this new grass, I fear, is not strengthening. The march about sixteen miles. I have been told that the men eat the head and offal of the beef, and I have ordered five pounds given them tonight. Many sorts of trees and bushes show their new leaves. The mustard is plenty and large enough for greens, but there is no vinegar of course.

JANUARY 27. It rained a little in the night, and was cloudy and foggy this morning, but cleared off. I marched very early. The road led several miles down the beautiful green meadows of San Luis to the ranch house, which, as most others, is covered with tiles. It was deserted. Just below, the regular road crosses the river, and another turns to the left up the bluffs and leads by Buena Vista. This is the best. But Antonio told me falsely that it was new and miry at this season, and that the middle road, which did not cross the river and went much to the left of San Luis, was the best. But I found that it merely led around the bend of the river and to San Luis Rey. This is a fine large church of stuccoed brick, with an immense quadrangle of apartments with a corridor, and pillars and arches on each side within and on one face without. There are all the arrangements and appurtenances of a monastery, not omitting the wine apartments and brewery. I saw furniture and some paintings, but no occupants. The church was closed; it has a steeple with bells. In the center of the court is an oblique sundial, with orange and pepper trees, etc., in four large walled beds. The orange tree was bearing fruit of the size of a walnut. The Indians, too, had disappeared. Some two hundred of them I left in Temécula. Here I was overtaken by an express from the general; he had come by the other road to the intersection and followed me. I installed him as guide and put Antonio at the head of the "irregulars" with the cattle. We were sorry to learn that Lieutenant Emory had already sailed (by the isthmus) for the United States. My march is directed to the mission of San Diego, five miles from the town.

The road wound through smooth green valleys and over very lofty hills equally smooth and green. This afternoon, from the tops of these hills, we had magnificent views of the ocean a mile or two off.[225] The sun was sinking beyond, and so placid was the sea that it shone a vast space of seemingly transparent light, which, by contrast, gave to the clear sky a dusky shade. What a strange spectacle was that! The earth more aërially clear and bright than the cloudless heavens! I encamped, after marching above eight hours and about sixteen miles, at another deserted ranch, named "Agua Hedionda." Last night the wild cattle of my little herd mostly escaped, and, after receiving the general's letter, I directed that it should be increased on the road. My zealous irregulars – the Indians – in consequence drove in here some hundreds of all sorts. I directed a selection

225 Corporal Tyler described the feelings of the Mormons when they first saw the Pacific: "One mile below the mission [San Luis Rey] we ascended a bluff, when the long-long-looked-for great Pacific Ocean appeared plain to our view, only about three miles distant. The joy, the cheer that filled our souls, none but worn-out pilgrims nearing a haven of rest can imagine. Prior to leaving Nauvoo, we had talked about and sung of 'the great Pacific sea,' and we were now upon its very borders, and its beauty far exceeded our most sanguine expectations." Roberts, *op. cit.,* 50.

of them made, and driven at dark into a corral for the night. I issued but two pounds of beef for a ration. We passed, near San Luis, a small herd of very fine jennies belonging to the mission; that is, to the government. The wild oats are six or eight inches high.

JANUARY 28. I marched very early. The dew was so copious as to wet the tents as a rain. On the driest objects there was some frost. The road was very hilly and heavy in places. I reached San Diegetto at two o'clock, all the wagons not getting there before three. Seven and a half hours of travel. I was forced by the state of the mules (not to say of the men) to encamp, as the next ground with water was reported from seven to nine miles. Grass is short here and pools of water at an inconvenient distance. Some Californians were in camp an hour or more. Mr. Foster, etc., just from San Diego. They give a very distressing account of the state of affairs – a decided variance between the high government functionaries, etc. We hear, as last night, the loud roar of the ocean. All of the staff officers have asked and obtained permission to ride to San Diego tomorrow morning. It was reported to me that the general intended sailing for San Francisco the day after tomorrow.

JANUARY 29. Marched at 7:20. Soon got into the valley called "Soledad." Here was water and a luxuriant thick growth of grass. I then followed the guide on a byroad which led to the mission of San Diego, six miles west of the seaport of the same name. It led up a hill about three hundred feet high; after ascending which, finding excellent green bunch grass, I rested and grazed the mules half an hour. Then, on this lofty tableland, the crooked new road was for a mile or two over ground covered with pools of rain water and saturated.

A mule could scarcely be ridden, and in the absence of the guide I had thoughts of returning to extricate the baggage; but the wagons being very lightly loaded, were got through. At one of the bad hills, also, a wagon was upset – the first instance on the march from Santa Fé. I soon after fell into the old road from San Bernardino to the mission, which was firm; and a few miles more brought us to the mission of San Diego.[226] A march of about sixteen miles. The buildings being dilapidated, and full of Indians and dirt, I have encamped the squadron on the flat below. There are around us extensive gardens and vineyards, wells and cisterns, more or less fallen into decay and disorder, but olive and the picturesque date trees flourishing and ornamental. There is no fuel for miles around, and the dependence for water is some rather distant pools in a sandy stream which runs (sometimes) down to the ocean. The grass is very short. This evening I rode down by moonlight and reported to the general in San Diego.

Order Number 1
Headquarters Mormon Battalion,
Mission of San Diego, January 30, 1847

[226] The mission of San Diego, established by Father Junípero Serra in 1769, was the first one founded by the Spaniards in Alta California. Lieutenant Whipple, writing in September, 1849, described it as a "large pile of adobe buildings, now deserted and partly in ruins." He added: "There remains an old Latin library, and the chapel walls are yet covered with oil paintings, some of which possess considerable merit. In front there is a large vineyard, where not only delicious grapes, but olives, figs, and other fruits, are produced abundantly. In the days of their prosperity, for many miles around, the valleys and plains were covered with cattle and horses belonging to this mission; and the padres boasted that their yearly increase was greater than the Indians could possibly steal. But in California the sun of their glory is set forever. Near by stand the thatched huts of the Indians, formerly serfs or peons – now the sole occupants of the mission grounds." *Senate Ex. Docs.*, 31 cong., 2 sess., no. 19, p. 2.

The lieutenant-colonel [227] commanding congratulates the battalion on their safe arrival on the shore of the Pacific ocean, and the conclusion of the march of over two thousand miles. History may be searched in vain for an equal march of infantry. Nine-tenths of it has been through a wilderness where nothing but savages and wild beasts are found, or deserts where, for want of water, there is no living creature. There, with almost hopeless labor, we have dug deep wells which the future traveler will enjoy. Without a guide who had traversed them, we have ventured into trackless prairies where water was not found for several marches. With crowbar and pick and ax in hand we have worked our way over mountains which seemed to defy aught save the wild goat, and hewed a passage through a chasm of living rock more narrow than our wagons. To bring these first wagons to the Pacific, we have preserved the strength of our mules by herding them ever over large tracts, which you have laboriously guarded without loss. The garrisons of four *presidios* of Sonora, concentrated within the walls of Tucson, gave us no pause. We drove them out with their artillery, but our intercourse with the citizens was unmarked by a single act of injustice. Thus, marching half naked and half fed, and living upon wild animals, we have discovered and made a road

227 That Cooke thought highly of the accomplishments of the battalion, and that this attitude was appreciated by the Mormons, is indicated in a statement made at a later time by Elder Wilford Woodruff: "He [Cooke] had a good, generous heart. He entertained great respect for the Mormon Battalion and he always spoke kindly of them before the government and all men. When he went through Salt Lake City with Col. A. S. Johnston, in 1858, he uncovered his head in honor of the Mormon Battalion, that five hundred brave men that he had led two thousand miles over sandy deserts and through rocky canyons, in the midst of thirst, hunger, and fatigue, in the service of their country. May God bless Col. Cooke; and may he bless the Battalion and their posterity after them." Roberts, *op. cit.*, 88.

of great value to our country. Arrived at the first settlement of California after a single day's rest, you cheerfully turned off from the route to this point of promised repose to enter upon a campaign, and meet, as we believed, the approach of the enemy; and this, too, without even salt to season your sole subsistence of fresh meat. Lieutenants A. J. Smith and George Stoneman, of the First dragoons, have shared and given valuable aid in all these labors. Thus, volunteers, you have exhibited some high and essential qualities of veterans. But much remains undone. Soon you will turn your strict attention to the drill, to system and order, to forms also, which are all necessary to the soldier.

By order of Lieutenant-colonel P. St. Geo. Cooke,

P. C. MERRILL, Adjutant [228]

228 The following notation, in Cooke's handwriting, completes the journal: "A true copy of my daily record. P. St. Geo. Cooke, Lt. Colonel Comdg. San Luis Rey, Feby. 22d, 1847."

JOURNAL OF WILLIAM HENRY CHASE WHITING, 1849

JOURNAL OF WILLIAM HENRY CHASE WHITING, 1849

FEBRUARY 21, [1849].[229] At a late hour in the afternoon my party left Fredericksburg,[230] the last settlement it was to see until Presidio del Norte should be reached. This little town is a colony of the Dutch, many of whom have emigrated to Texas and pushed their settlements in every direction. It has a pretty site on Barrons creek, one of the little streams which swell the Pedernales, and some day or other may become a place of importance, but now its people are miserably poor. Without the usual thrift I have seen among them, they undertook to build themselves a fine town before they attended to their fields and their crops, and have been

229 Whiting's journal is published from the manuscript copy in the office of the chief of engineers, Washington, D.C. It is entitled: "Journal of a reconnaissance from San Antonio de Béxar to El Paso del Norte." On September 8, 1849, when Whiting transmitted a part of his journal to the chief of engineers, he wrote: "As my notes were taken chiefly to aid in guiding the troops through an unknown country, courses, distances & the general features of country indicating the position of water holes compose nearly all the matter of them. Occasional observations & descriptions occur as they were suggested. . . . I would respectfully request that the Notes or journal herewith submitted be not made public, everything of any importance connected with the expedition having already been published." Whiting copied his journal from a diary which he kept during the reconnaissance. This diary, which is practically identical with the journal, was published in part (March 7-May 5, 1849) in the *Publications of the Southern History Association,* VI (1902), 283-294, 389-399, X (1906), 1-18, 78-95, 127-140. Whiting's report to J. G. Totten, chief of engineers, dated San Antonio, Texas, June 10, 1849, was a summary of his journal. It was printed in at least two places: *House Ex. Docs.,* 31 cong., 1 sess., no. 5, pp. 281-293; *Daily National Intelligencer* (Washington, D.C.), July 28, 1849.

230 See *Southwest Historical Series,* V, 260.

through two long seasons nearly starved in consequence. Captain Eastman, First infantry, is encamped near this place, and to his polite assistance I am much indebted in increasing my scanty outfit. Here I employed another man, William Howard; he had been out with Hays. We now number sixteen, including Lieutenant Smith,[231] Dick Howard,[232] the two Mexicans, my servant, and myself. We camped on Live Oak creek about five miles from Fredericksburg.

FEBRUARY 22. We started this morning at half past eight with fine clear weather, Dick leading the trail and striking across to the left of a high hill, bearing about west from camp, until in about twenty minutes we fell in with an old path known I believe as the Pinto trail, and in former times and to this day used by the

[231] William Farrar Smith, a native of Vermont, was a classmate of Whiting at West Point. Ranking fourth in a class of thirty-one, he graduated from the military academy on July 1, 1845, when he was promoted in the army to brevet second lieutenant in the topographical engineers. Between November 6, 1846, and August 21, 1848, he was assistant professor of mathematics at the military academy, and from 1848 to 1850 was assistant topographical engineer connected with explorations in Texas. During the early fifties he helped to survey the boundary line between the United States and Mexico. He was president of the International Telegraph Company from 1864 to 1873, and served as president of the board of police commissioners of New York City for a period of years starting in 1875. He died on February 28, 1903. Cullum, *Biographical Register,* II, 114-115, III, 167; Heitman, *Historical Register,* I, 904.

[232] Richard A. Howard, a volunteer guide, had been a guide for the Hays expedition in 1848. Both Whiting and Smith thought highly of him. The former called him "an accomplished guide, whose judgment, whenever at fault, his decision compensated." Smith, in his report to Johnston, referred to "the invaluable services of our able guide and friend, Mr. Howard," and added: "To his accurate knowledge of the portions of the route previously passed over by him, his correct judgment with reference to country with which he was unacquainted, and his advice and address in Indian difficulties, the success of the expedition is mainly indebted." Samuel A. Maverick, Chihuahua Expedition, 1848, MS., University of Texas Library; *Senate Ex. Docs.,* 31 cong., 1 sess., no. 64, p. 7; *House Ex. Docs.,* 31 cong., 1 sess., no. 5, pp. 282, 293.

William Henry Chase Whiting
From a photograph

Indians. Entering a spur of the Pedernales valley, we followed it on a general course of about N. 70°W. by compass for nearly two miles, when we reached its terminating ridge, a rough, stony hill of limestone formation from which, by Dick's advice, I assumed a direction N. 37° W., bearing in a range of blue hills in the distance. These we reached at quarter of 2 P.M., our route lying through a rough tract and the travel quite hard upon the mules. Water was found in abundance, as in a distance of six or seven miles we crossed the creeks of the Pedernales four times, the last one somewhat boggy. From this divide we could see the vicinity of Pecan spring, bearing N. 32° W., and to the left a bluff and notable hill, N. 37° W. Here Dick and myself separated from the party and leaving the trail to the right entered the beautiful valley through which runs Threadgill's creek.[233] Excellent pasturage and abundance of water was found all the way to the spring, which we reached at four, at the same time with the train. They had continued by the old trail, a very rough route. Our march has been twenty-five miles. Pecan spring is a small, clear, pleasant spring, gushing under a spreading pecan tree and affording a delightful resting place. An observation for latitude showed its position 30° 29′ 35″. A road should not pass it, but leaving it to the right should cross Threadgill's creek below and bear directly upon the bluff before noticed.

FEBRUARY 23. We struck for that this morning, and crossing Hickory creek and two prongs of Mesquite creek, passed it. Our route, now without a trail, and led by Dick, continued in a pleasant post oak country, until at eleven we reached a live oak clump upon an emi-

233 Threadgill creek flows into the Llano river in the eastern part of the present Mason county.

nence, itself a good landmark. Here I took some bearings. Bluff hill was S. 18° E.; the bounding ridge to the eastward of Threadgill's valley, S. 53° E.; and far ahead the right-hand point of the divide between the Llano and the San Sabá, N. 15° W. This is notable as a landmark; and a peculiar notch to the left, well known to the old Texan frontiersmen, is plainly visible. Howard now led the train by a course generally north and through a fine valley clothed with a growth of post oak, live oak, and mesquite, and presenting fine traveling. The soil is light and loose. On our left and near to the hills is the head of Willow creek, and still nearer, Pecan spring, at which we arrived at twenty minutes past two. We were delayed nearly an hour by a refractory mule, which for a long time eluded all the efforts of the two Mexicans with their lassos. Pushing on from this spring, we struck into a singular formation of reddish brown rock, appearing in rounded masses and covering the ground to the hill on our left, of which it appeared to form the base and the summit. From a hasty look I supposed it ferruginous sandstone. Here again came in sight of the notch and shaped our course upon that.

From signs in the mesquite bottom we found there were Indians about, and Dick and I left in search of them. We soon fell in with a Delaware encampment of three or four lodges. One of them, Jack Hunter, who had been with Hays, I invited over to our camp. In accordance with instructions from the general, I was to secure the services of some of the Delaware as guides and hunters. Found the party encamped on the left bank of the Llano, where they had arrived at half past three. We have made about eighteen miles. The route selected by Dick Howard has never before been traveled and shows the singular accuracy of his judgment. An unbroken valley may be had to the Pedernales, avoiding the stony tract to the southeast of Pecan spring. The ford at our camp on the Llano is good but requires some grading. We have met John Conner,[234] the well-known Delaware chief, noted for his extensive knowledge of the whole country roundabout and as well for his courage, address, and worthy deportment. I tried to engage his services, but he said the Waco were after him and he could not leave his family. He left us some fine turkeys and also some bear meat and venison.

SATURDAY, FEBRUARY 24. We left camp at nine and proceeded on our course N. 15° W., passing through a pleasant and well-timbered valley for three-quarters of an hour, when, at Dick's suggestion, I altered it to N. 43°W., bearing upon a cluster of three lone hills plainly to be seen against the more elevated San Sabá divide. This morning we met with the cottonwood, the first I had seen – known, I believe, to botanists as the *populus canadensis*. I regretted [the] inability to carry books with me through a country the productions of which are so interesting and generally so little known. About three miles from the Llano crossed a branch of Comanche creek at an old Kickapoo encampment, the site in a fine live oak grove. We crossed and recrossed Comanche creek several times this morning, generally in good places, and part of the forenoon followed a Comanche trail. Indian trails, when running about the course of the traveler, it is well to follow, as they almost always pass by the best ground.

---

[234] John Conner (or Connor) was frequently employed as scout, guide, or interpreter during the forties and fifties. *House Ex. Docs.*, 32 cong., 2 sess., no. 1, p. 433; W. B. Parker, *Notes Taken During the Expedition Commanded by Captain R. B. Marcy* (Philadelphia, 1856), 116-117, 142, 220-221; Rupert Norval Richardson, *The Comanche Barrier to South Plains Settlement* (Glendale, 1933), 118, 121-122, 141.

We came to camp at two in a mesquite flat upon a small branch of Comanche creek, our march having been about fourteen miles. Here we were joined by the Delaware, Jack Hunter, who agreed to accompany me for two dollars per diem, finding his own animal and equipments. Now fairly in the Indian range, sentinels were placed over the animals this evening and through the night. I stood the first tour myself, Lieutenant Smith following, and so on through. The mode of watching in vogue with the old frontiersmen is very different from our practice in the army. Careful not to expose himself in any manner, the sentinel lies down among the animals. Mules and horses, especially the former, almost always perceive the approach of anyone, however stealthy, and by watching them, good guard against the dexterous thieving of the Indians may be kept.

SUNDAY, FEBRUARY 25. Left camp this morning at quarter to nine, crossing Comanche creek about two hundred yards above. Dick led the trail on the course of yesterday, N. 43° W. About half past ten we reached a lone hill on our right, covered with post oak and formed of the same reddish stone before noticed. Here we could plainly see our landmarks and the table ridge, or divide, of the San Sabá. The country became more open, and at quarter past eleven, after traversing an elevated and rolling tract, we reached our three hills. They, like the divide of which they are the spurs, are of the same limestone formation – in distinct tables – so common in this country. Named the left hill "Brady's hill" and bore N. 65° W. up the divide. This we readily ascended by an easy slope and directed our course for the San Sabá about northwest. The elevated plain we were now on extends to the river, there terminating in steep bluffs of considerable height. It is slightly rolling, and small groves or mottes of timber appear here and there. Two notable hills far up the San Sabá and on the other side were now the objects upon which we bore, and at four we came to camp upon a little creek of the river, which we named "Rock creek" from its craggy banks. Our march twenty miles. An observation for latitude gave us 30° 53′.

MONDAY, FEBRUARY 26. Started this morning at half after eight, the same beautiful weather continuing. After crossing the first ridge on our course, we turned to the north, following a valley or ravine to descend to the San Sabá; a half hour's march brought us by a suitable pass under the lofty cedar bluffs of the river, which we crossed just above its junction with Camp creek. Here the fine growth of mesquite grass, the young wild rye, induced me to stop to let the mules graze and recruit, their feed of the night before having been quite scant. The San Sabá is a beautiful stream, heavily timbered with the pecan, the elm, and hackberry, and having fine tracts of land upon its banks. Saddled up and left at three o'clock, and after marching seven miles through a fertile mesquite bottom camped on a little watercourse which I called "Owl creek," due west from the mouth of Camp creek. Latitude 30° 53′ 56″ N.

TUESDAY, FEBRUARY 27. We left at eight this morning, marching a little south of west for the extreme point of a range of hills bounding the San Sabá valley. No natural road can be finer than the route for miles along the banks of this river. About two miles from camp we crossed a creek with clear water and at ten minutes past nine we reached the hill upon which we had been bearing. Three miles and a half farther brought us to the Short Bend, a fine place for encampment about seven miles from Owl creek. Here we see the northward bending of the river and its turning again to the west, tangent to which we now held our course upon a distinct Comanche trail. Our attention was soon taken up with a populous dog town, the first I had seen. These little animals strip the whole plain adjacent to their holes of every green blade of grass, and few features of the prairies have more of the desert in them than the dog towns. At quarter to twelve, after passing a small creek of clear water, we came upon the old summer camping grounds of the Comanche, the first of a series of beautiful plains, sheltered on the north by the range of hills parallel to the river and on the south shaded by the extensive groves of superb pecan which clothe the river banks. The grass, though so early, was green and luxuriant. This bend of the San Sabá I called "Grave Bend," for here we found the grave of a Comanche warrior. Crossing a divide of no great elevation, we came upon Bowie creek, about eight hundred yards above which are situated the ruins of the San Sabá Fort.[235] We found, a short distance above there,

[235] During April and May, 1757, Father Alonso Giraldo de Terreros, under instructions from the Spanish viceroy in Mexico City, established the mission of San Sabá on the south side of the San Sabá river, near the present Menard, Menard county, Texas. Its purpose was to Christianize the Apache Indians. At the same time Colonel Diego Ortiz de Parrilla, in accordance with orders from the viceroy, erected a *presidio* to protect the mission, locating it about two or three miles distant on the north side of the river. Garrisoned by about one hundred men, it was called the *presidio* of San Luis de las Amarillas, in honor of the viceroy, although it was usually known as the *presidio,* or fort, of San Sabá. On March 16, 1758, the Comanche Indians and their allies attacked and burned the mission, killing Father Terreros and nine others. The savages did not make an assault on the *presidio,* which continued to be garrisoned by troops for some years thereafter. The ruins of the fort may still be seen near Menard. However, they are not the remains of the original building but of a stone structure erected at a later time. *Athanase de Mézières and the Louisiana-Texas Frontier, 1768-1780* (Herbert E. Bolton, ed., Cleveland, 1914), 48-49, 64; William Edward Dunn, "The Apache Mission on the San Sabá River; its Founding and Failure," *Southwestern Historical Quarterly,* XVII, 379-414.

a pleasant spot for camp, and stopped at 2 P.M. after a march of eighteen miles. I strolled over the ruins hard by.

The fort is situated directly on the bank of the river, in a position admirably chosen for defense against the Indians and exhibiting all the judgment for which the old Spanish adventurers were noted, the rapid stream flowing directly under its rear wall and accessible by the posterns. It made the central point of a large plain semicircular in form and bounded by a range of low hills some two miles from the work; from its towers the approach of an enemy could easily be descried. Built in the shape of an oblong of about 270 feet by 200, its flanking defenses were four octagon towers, one at each angle. On the main front stood a kind of citadel and the chapel. Constructed of unhewn limestone, its ruined walls and dismantled barracks overgrown with mesquite, moss, and grass, [and] huge cactus preventing access to the dilapidated cells whose tenant is now the rattlesnake, it presents in this wild country, many miles distant from any habitation, a striking spectacle. Still more so it must have been when, more than a century ago, side by side in its long corridors stood the steel-clad soldiers of Europe, the adventurous and grasping miners of the new world, and the equally enterprising disciple of Loyola, surrounded by the warlike Comanche tribes. Of its foundation and its date I am ignorant, and here, without books, can only speculate upon it and listen to the old traditions of somber and mysterious interest which are told by my men of its fall. It is said that a terrible tragedy similar to that of Mackinaw was here enacted by the Comanche, and that but one, a priest, escaped to tell the tale at Béxar.[236]

[236] On February 18, 1847, Doctor Ferdinand Roemer, a German scholar

An alarm was given during the night, at this camp, of Indians attempting to steal some of our mules, and the loud report of the sentinel's rifle roused the sleepers round the camp fires. Whatever the cause – prowling Indians or wolves – the shot had dispersed them. The rest of the night was quiet.

WEDNESDAY, FEBRUARY 28. We left camp at nine, following an old trail of the Comanche, which led us across the river a short distance above the fort and again about ten brought us to the stream at a good ford. Our course, as yesterday's, is still westerly, occasionally half a point south of that. I omitted to mention that the fort is due west from the mouth of Camp creek and its latitude nearly the same with the last recorded. Our path, after crossing the river, wound through a live oak and mesquite growth scattered here and there in groves upon the prairie. At twelve we crossed the so-called Turkey bayou and soon after reached a large, still lagoon. This I called the "Branch." At one, still follow-

and traveler, described the ruins of the fort: "The fort lies close to the river on the left or north bank, which is here about twenty feet high. The ruins consist of remnants of masonry work five to six feet high (in some places from fifteen to twenty feet), and plainly show the design of the whole structure. The outer walls of masonry are an almost square rectangle whose shorter wall, lying near the river, measures 300 feet, while the longer wall measures 360. On to the inner side of this outer wall are built several casemates, or rooms, each eighteen feet deep and opening into the courtyard. The whole number of these surrounding the court is about fifty. In the northwest corner of the plot of ground is a main building with a courtyard and seven rooms, the walls of which are still partially preserved as high as the upper crossbeams. The main entrance to the fort lay on the west side, and besides this there was a little opening towards the water. On three corners of the fort there were projecting towers for defense and on the northwest corner a larger and round tower. The quarry stones of which the walls were constructed were held together with earth only, but in the wall of the main building we observed traces of mortar." Adele B. Looscan, "The Old Fort on the San Sabá River as Seen by Dr. Ferdinand Roemer in 1847," *Quarterly of the Texas State Historical Association*, V, 138.

ing the Comanche trail, we discovered a beautiful sheet of deep, clear water, which I named "Howard lagoon." Having arrived at a bend of the river, along which we traveled until it bore southwardly, and finding good grass and convenient water, we encamped at 2 P.M. Our march of today had been eighteen miles.

THURSDAY, MARCH 1. We started at half after nine this morning and found, after marching about six miles, the so-called headspring and lagoon of San Sabá, bearing about south of west, one-half west, from the fort. The grass here was very fine; and as this is the last water known to any of the party, I judged it prudent to stop and give the train a good rest before venturing out into the great prairie. Numerous signs were discovered during the afternoon by such of the party as had been hunting, of the near neighborhood of Indians, and at night the guard over the animals was doubled. About one at night the mules stampeded with a great snorting. The strength of the new ropes with which they were fastened was all that saved them to us. The night was dark; and pulling back with all its force upon its lariat, every animal appeared with ears pricked, looking in one direction, the quarter whence their fright had come. After some moments of anxious suspense the crack of the sentry's rifle showed he had discovered the cause. The Indians, for such they proved, disappeared incontinently, and the mules resumed their grazing. I was pleased with the conduct of my men at this alarm. Awakened at the least sound, when the startling tramp of the frightened herd came upon the still air, not a man arose from where he lay. Each one quietly turning on his rude bed with head slightly raised from the saddles which served as pillows, and every sense alert, remained with rifle cocked until the disturbance ceased, watching for the slightest motion before them.

FRIDAY, MARCH 2. Left the San Sabá spring at nine. Course west by compass. Soon fell in with a much used trail, the signs upon which convinced us that Indians had passed in the night. I am particular today to mention the times of arriving at all watering places. Three miles from camp we passed, a little to our right, a large hole of water. Were delayed at it twenty-five minutes. Twenty-five minutes' ride from this and still upon the trail, and we reached another fringed with live oak timber. From a hill on our course, about seven miles from San Sabá spring and called "Castle hill" from the turretlike appearance of the rocks at its summit, Dick took the bearing of our course for the next day or so, S. 80° W., being nearly the true west course. Here, directly ahead, we descried a large lagoon. We arrived here about twelve; it is nearly one-fourth of a mile in length and, I should think, is permanent. Twenty minutes after twelve we found another small water hole; all of these are situated in contermination of the San Sabá gully, which still meanders through this beautiful valley. I have never yet seen, so far, a finer natural road. The hills now begin to partake of the great limestone table formation of the prairie. The horizontal tops, limited by perpendicular bluff of lime of no great elevation, commence to be seen. At twenty minutes after one, having marched eleven miles and reached a small water hole, I decided to "noon it," as the Texans have it, and dispatched four men in advance to look for water. The trail hitherto followed, here bends to the northward – I presume it was toward the head of the Concho. The men sent out, shortly returned, reporting sufficient water up the valley for our purposes; and saddling up, we rode four miles on the course S. 80° W. and camped for the night at 4 P.M. Cloudy and no opportunity to make observation.

SATURDAY, MARCH 3. We left camp at nine and, by the advice of Dick Howard, struck a course S. 60° W. At twenty-five minutes after eleven, after traversing the several ridges which bound the head valley of the San Sabá, we emerged upon the arid table prairie. Found it barren and thinly clad with scattering mesquite. Occasional groves or thickets of live oak were seen in the lowest parts. Upon reaching some ravines or gullies, which disappointed us as to water, we changed the course to S. 70° W. at half past two. At ten minutes of four we reached another gully. Still no water; and the course was continued until nearly dark, at twenty minutes past five, when on reaching an extensive burn I determined to camp. This was done in a live oak grove, situated about a mile to the left of our course in one of the hollows or depressions of the prairie and which promised us some shelter from the cold norther which now had sprung up. We here took an observation for latitude and found ourselves in 30° 36′ 9″, our estimated march 22 miles, and longitude about 100° 39′, being nearly 34.4 miles west of the head of the San Sabá. A mist which obtained during the night helped our suffering animals by moistening the scanty grass.

SUNDAY, MARCH 4. Being without water and hence with little to cook, we left camp early and at ten changed our course to due west at the head of a ravine, probably the opening or rise of some river whose water springs are very far below us. Our general march was over alternate prairie and gentle valleys; the same general desolation apparent. At eleven we struck the trail of Highsmith's [237] men, and at one, that of Hays.[238] We

237 Samuel Highsmith was born in Boone county, Kentucky, in 1804. When he was about eight years of age, his parents moved to Missouri, where an older brother, Abijah, engaged in the so-called "Sink-hole fight" with the Indians on May 24, 1815. Some time during the twenties Samuel migrated to Texas with Abijah, fought in the Battle of San Jacinto, April 21, 1836, and afterward enlisted in the Texas Rangers. During the Mexican war he served as a captain in Colonel Hays's command of Rangers. He died about 1849. John S. Ford, Memoirs, MS., University of Texas Library; Dudley G. Wooten, *A Comprehensive History of Texas, 1685-1897* (Dallas, 1898), II, 338-339; Louis Houck, *A History of Missouri* (Chicago, 1908), III, 131.

238 John Coffee Hays, son of Harmon A. Hays and Elizabeth Cage Hays, was born at Little Cedar Lick, Wilson county, Tennessee, January 28, 1817. He was one of a family of eight children. Leaving school at the age of fifteen, he went to Mississippi, where he learned to be a surveyor. He migrated to Texas in 1836, arriving shortly after the Battle of San Jacinto, and immediately enlisted in the military forces of the republic. In 1840 he became captain of a company of Texas Rangers, with whom he was to gain national fame. Meanwhile, he had at times followed his profession of surveyor. During the Mexican war he was chosen colonel of a regiment of Texas mounted volunteers, which consisted principally of Rangers, and saw extensive service throughout the conflict. In 1849, the year following his Chihuahua expedition, he left Texas for California, where he was to live the rest of his life. Shortly after his arrival he was elected sheriff of San Francisco county, and in 1853, President Pierce appointed him surveyor-general of California. During the early fifties he helped to found the town of Oakland. In 1848, before leaving Texas, he had married Susan Calvert, a native of Alabama; they had six children, only two of whom, John and Betty, reached maturity. He died at his home near Piedmont, Alameda county, April 28, 1883. John S. Ford, a Texas Ranger who knew Hays intimately, wrote: "The fame of Colonel Hays rested on a substantial basis; it was acquired by hard fighting, by suffering privations, and by the exhibition of high qualities adorning a citizen and a soldier. His campaigns against the Indians and Mexicans making descents upon Texas, and the success of his operations, rendered him one of the most famous Rangers in the world. . . He was lenient to the erring. . . He was almost idolized by many. He was modest and retiring; an expression of admiration of his acts would cause him to blush like a woman. . . He knew how to conduct marches requiring toilsome endurance, and to prevent his men from becoming despondent. . . He was cool, self-possessed, and brave; a good shot." John S. Ford, Memoirs, MS., University of Texas Library. See also *Jack Hays, the Intrepid Texas Ranger (Frontier Times,* Bandera, Texas, n.d.), 1-63; Elizabeth H. West, "John Coffee Hays," *Dictionary of American Biography,* VIII, 463; Webb, *The Texas Rangers,* 32-34, 67-123.

now began to feel thirsty. Many a hole was passed where Hays's party [239] had camped with water and where we had been assured it would be abundant, but there was none for us. We moved on till half past six and camped in the dry bed of a creek or arroyo. Our animals began to show signs of suffering. Few of them grazed much, and we ourselves felt far from comfortable.

MONDAY, MARCH 5. We moved, breakfastless, at daylight. Our march, now become painful and almost insupportable, was continued until twelve, each place where those who had been with Hays expected water, having none. At one of these, some green grass induced me to stop and give our mules a feed. We traveled generally west, sometimes a little south of that.[240] We left this spot at two, and at half past five again halted in the bed of a dry creek, where some fresh wild rye promised a little help to the train, now nearly broken down. This arroyo is in a large valley surrounded by high hills of the same limestone table formation as the great prairie itself.

The road has been fine but it has the curse of thirst upon it. At twenty minutes past seven we were again *en route*. Judging that we could not be far from the Pecos or its tributaries and knowing that another night without water would set us afoot, it was thought best to push on. How weary were the miles of that last march! Silent, unmurmuring, each man rode on, his weary mule unable to make more than a mile and a half an hour. We took an old trail; and traveling through a canyon, or ravine, about S. 60° W., at half past twelve the grateful sound of rippling water reached our ears,

239 Hays and Highsmith had parted company on November 25, 1848. *Western Texian*, Jan. 12, 1849.

240 They were traveling through the present Crockett county.

and we were soon encamped on the west bank of Live Oak creek, a little tributary of the Pecos.[241] Our day's march has been over forty-two miles, an extraordinary ride, considering our animals. One mule gave out completely and was obliged to be abandoned, the third which has fallen since our departure from Fredericksburg.

This little stream of limpid water, called Live Oak creek from the growth near its mouth, makes its way to the Pecos through a ravine, or canyon, remarkable for its striking formation – a basin enclosed by a general ridge, with detached peaks or spurs resting against its elevation in the form of truncated cones. They are marked by two distinct, horizontal beds of limestone at different heights. These appear at the sides of the hills and look, in their regularity, like walls of masonry, the upper one bounding the top. The summits are level and apparently at the same general elevation with the great table prairie, out of which they seem to have been cut by some great aqueous convulsion.

TUESDAY, MARCH 6. Laid by all day; necessary on account of the exhausted condition of our animals.

WEDNESDAY, MARCH 7. At half past eleven this morning we saddled up, intending to go no farther than the Pecos. Our road lay on the right bank of the creek, following very large and lately traveled Indian trails. The bones of horses and cattle, scraps of cloth, [and] small articles dropped here and there, told of some hapless captive and the late march of a band of the plunderers of Mexico. A ride of five miles brought us to the river. This singular stream is not perceptible at all in the valley in which it flows, until the traveler is right

241 Live Oak creek flows south through the western part of the present Crockett county.

upon the bank. Destitute of timber or trees, except perhaps the stunted mesquite and chaparral which thinly clothe the country, it rolls its discolored and rushing waters in a bed rarely in any place over forty feet in width, and winds from one side of the narrow valley to the other in abrupt turns. It is generally so deep as to be unpassable by fording – a pocket edition of the lower Río Grande. We encamped about two miles above the mouth of Live Oak creek [242] and in a grove of the same kind of trees, which here, from its solitary position (no other timber being seen for miles), is quite a notable landmark. The river is now generally from six to ten feet below its banks, which are steep and composed of red sandstone and clay. From the drift we could see here and there, it has at times been subject to extraordinary rises. Deciding to remain here the rest of the day, I examined the river in the vicinity with a view to a crossing. Found at the Indian trail a good place for the animals to ford. The bottom is here of gravel, but, though only waist deep, I could not keep my feet, such is the rapidity of the current. A little higher up where the river divides, forming three small islands, I determined to make a little footbridge.

THURSDAY, MARCH 8. Our work was commenced after breakfast by carrying upon our shoulders three logs of live oak and a few poles; rather a heavy job, as the grove is about half a mile from the islands. In an hour and a half we threw a little bridge across the stream. By this our packs, etc., were shortly and safely passed and without any accident. The Mexicans forded the mules. The grass at our last camp not having been good, and finding better on this side, I determined to lay by the re-

242 Live Oak creek flows into the Pecos about ten miles southeast of the present Sheffield, Pecos county.

mainder of the day. Our poor animals are hardly recovered from their exhausting march from the San Sabá head. In the course of the afternoon Dick Howard and I ascended a high hill hard by. The climbing was difficult; but bleak and bare and precipitous as were the sides, it was very pleasant to find many varieties of beautiful flowers growing and blooming to the very summit. Near the top and in the face of the limestone cliff is a small cave, in which we found a few small stalactites. The floor is perfectly dry and covered with fine exfoliated limestone. We could see far up the Pecos. A large white bluff, apparently some twenty or twenty-five miles off and on the other side, bore N. 27° W. An observation for latitude gave for this point, called "Solomon's ford," 30° 32′ 27″.

FRIDAY, MARCH 9. We left camp this morning at eight, the weather charming. Marching nearly ten miles up the river in a course about N. 23° W., we spied on the opposite side a fine mare. The Mexican boy Poli swam over and caught her after some trouble and brought her to us. She was recognized as one belonging [to] the unfortunate Wham, one of Hays's late expedition, who, delirious from continued starvation, escaped from his keepers and was lost in the mountains to the southwest.[243] The heat of the day being intense, at half past twelve we stopped to noon. In cool weather the practice which I find most advantageous is to start

---

243 Doctor Wham (or Wahm) escaped from the Hays expedition on the night of October 13, 1848. Samuel A. Maverick, a member of the expedition, recorded the following in his diary: "14th [October] . . . Dr. Wham made off in a fury last night. Suppose he is lost. Send back for same and crazy. 15 Oct. . . Wait for men gone for Wham. . . 16th. . . They found but did not secure and finally lost unhappy crazy man in the black ravines." Samuel A. Maverick, Chihuahua Expedition, MS., University of Texas Library. Doctor Wham was later found by the Indians and returned to his home. Mary A. Maverick, Memoirs, MS., *ibid.*

about eight or nine o'clock and push the day's march through without stopping; but when very warm or in the summer days, it becomes necessary to rest three or four hours in the middle of the day.

Just after dinner, as we were enjoying our pipes under the shade of our blankets stretched upon sticks and bushes, the report of a gun aroused all hands. Looking towards the opposite side of the river, we descried three Indians; they had fired to attract our attention and were now making signs to know if they could safely approach. Upon [our] holding up a white handkerchief, they came nearer but with great hesitation and were pronounced by the men with me to be Lipan. Such they proved – an old chief, Capote by name, and two squaws. They kept, however, out of arms' [range], and requested me to come out and talk with them. This I did. The old fellow was very distrustful. His band, he said, were higher up the river and the tribe was all together. His great chief wished to hold a talk with the Americans, and if we would wait he would go and bring him. This I promised to do and off he went. But very clear was the red gentleman from back; and though suspecting a ruse to get their *caballada* and families out of our way, I waited as I had promised. These Lipan are a brave and well-armed tribe of Indians; but their numbers have been much reduced of late years, the Rangers having severely beaten them in several fights. Their whole number of warriors probably does not pass one hundred. Their dialect is the same with that of the Mescalero or Apache, and in common with them and the Comanche [they] subsist upon unhappy Mexico.

SATURDAY, MARCH 10. We saddled up at eight this morning and moved up the river on a course about

N. 28° W., Dick, Smith, and the Delaware scouting in the advance, for the appearance of the Indians had given rise to suspicion. Pleasant marching for about three miles through the only pretty scenery we had yet seen on the Pecos brought us to the spot where Capote had camped the evening before. Everything indicated a hasty departure on his part. We supposed [that] they imagined us to be a scout of Texas Rangers, whom they very justly hold in great fear.

About two miles farther on we left the river by a westerly direction to cut off one of its bends, leaving the white bluff (a singular vein of white stone) to our right. I should like to have examined the nature of this bluff, which appeared perfectly white and intersecting the gray limestone and sandstone bluff from summit to base. The contrast is so strange that I took it at first glance to be sunlight and shade from a passing cloud. At one, now traveling northwest, we saw it again, and at two reached the river. Here, after a march of some seventeen miles, we were pleased to find excellent grass and a convenient spot for resting. A shower of rain, the first since our leaving Fredericksburg, came up this afternoon and lasted from five till seven.

SUNDAY, MARCH 11. At eight, a beautiful morning, we moved up the Pecos valley, our path winding through the troublesome intricacies of short, thick chaparral. The most tedious of all marching and the slowest, it is particularly severe on the animals. The mountainous character of the landscape begins to disappear, and large notches are seen between the table hills, now making notable landmarks. Few landscapes can be conceived more bleak and utterly desolate, in its monotonous and somber features [and] its destitution of trees and foliage, than the Pecos country affords. Even game seem to shun it, and a few miserable deer were all the animation we could find for the scene. The chaparral was so troublesome that by two we had only made fourteen [?] miles. Here we camped on the river bank. Our course has been west all day.

MONDAY, MARCH 12. Today we have made a fatiguing march of between twenty-five and thirty miles. Starting at twenty minutes to eight, our course was directed nearly west, on the left of a notable elevation, which I called "Lipan hill." It, in common with many others in this vicinity, is isolated and, having the usual horizontal top and showing the same stratification as the great tables, seems to have been cut from them by some great convulsion. The Pecos prairies, at so much less elevation than the dry plains, would naturally seem to have been formed by subsidence from the latter. We made some southing during the morning and our progress was toilsome. There was no trail and we had to wind our way through the thorny chaparral.

At 4 P.M. we struck a large Comanche warpath; it filled us with astonishment. Close together, twenty-five deep worn and much used trails made a great road, which told us that this was a highway by which each year the Comanche of the North desolate Durango and Chihuahua. This trail strikes southwest for a few miles and then by a south course crosses the Río Grande in the Big Bend. It is worthy of attention, as in the country we now enter, certain passes can alone be traveled; and some of the large warpaths, closed upon the marauders, would interfere more than anything else in their operations. Upon this trail we pursued our way S. 20° W. until half past five, when we camped, greatly fatigued, upon a singular spring in the prairie.[244]

244 Probably the Ojo Escondido, or Escondido springs.

TUESDAY, MARCH 13. We left our camp this morning by a course S. 28° W. at twenty-five minutes past eight. Three miles of troublesome chaparral brought us to the western point of a high table ridge, a notable landmark which, from the abundance of brown ironstone about its base, I called "Iron hill." From it we could gain a fine view of the extensive basin lying between a distant range of mountains and the Pecos. The peaks of these mountains and their apparent position correspond with a range designated on Disturnell's map as the Chinati and Diablo mountains. However, as that map is extremely incorrect, little dependence is to be placed upon it. Here I took several bearings. The center peak of the blue mountain to the right bore S. 70° W., the smaller one, S. 50° W., and the one to our left, S. 25°W. Our course was assumed southwest.

At twenty minutes of one, after a march of about twelve miles from camp, we came upon the Awache spring,[245] a clear gush of water which bursts from the plain, unperceived until the traveler is immediately upon it, and soon swells in a clear, running brook abounding in fish and soft-shell turtles. It continues for several miles in a northeast course until it sinks as mysteriously as it rose, again to appear still farther on. Its water is pleasant to the taste, extremely limpid, and, to judge from the quantities of effloresced salts incrusted on the grass about it, highly mineral in its character. The predominant ones seemed to be magnesia and soda, as well as I could judge. This spring is on a branch of the Comanche warpath; here they stop to repose their cavyards of stolen horses. The natural scarcity of wood in this region and the frequent use as a camping place

245 Comanche spring, which was at the present Fort Stockton, Pecos county.

by these Indians has rendered it difficult to find enough for cooking purposes without going off the trail for a half mile or more. We remained here the rest of the day, as, not knowing when we would again meet water, it was judged best to start from it with refreshed animals.

WEDNESDAY, MARCH 14. Finding this morning the traces of Connelly's wagon trail to Presidio,[246] we followed it for eight or ten miles, until it became so overgrown and washed that it was impossible to distinguish it. Its general direction here was S. 65° W. and W. About eleven o'clock we came upon a spring of similar character with the Awache. We did not discover it until we were directly upon it; surrounded by a reedy lake from which issues a creek concealed in the grass, this spring when found is a gem. Its basin was some thirty feet across and its sides sloping down like an inverted cone; but clear as the water is, we could not see the bottom. This we named the "Basin" and stopped at it to rest a few moments. Our march continued until five, over a rolling prairie, the traveling upon which was generally very good. We were forced to camp without water. During the night three of our animals got loose; there was nothing, in fact, but shrubs to tie them to, and, contrary to their general habit of staying about camp, they took a straight course for water and, in spite of the guard, got away. It was a serious loss, for one of them was a favorite and hardy pack mule. Twenty-five miles.

THURSDAY, MARCH 15. I sent the Mexican boy Poli out to hunt for our missing mules early this morning, and the rest went on. We still followed a westerly course along the base of the mountains. We now came nearer

246 A trail made by Henry Connelly's trading expedition from Chihuahua to Fort Towson and return in 1839 and 1840.

this range. The whole face of the country changed; instead of the long, level, monotonous tables of sandstone and limestone, peaks of every fantastic shape met the eye, and high hills overlooked us, crowned with dark masses of basalt. Their columnar structure and dark red, black color was in superb effect with the yellow grass and dark green hue of the live oak and mountain cedar. By now the last ridge of the stratified rocks was passed, and we were fairly amid the rugged evidences of fire. Towards evening we came joyfully upon a little brook of running water. This, likewise, similar to the Awache, makes its way to the prairie, there to sink. The grass here was good and we called the creek "Dark creek." We have marched about twenty miles.

FRIDAY, MARCH 16. A range of hills of no great elevation (the spurs from the mountain), which here put out into the prairie, lay directly by our camp. I ascended one. It has the same trap formation noticed yesterday as characteristic of this region; but when on top I was surprised to find rude walls of rocks evidently piled by hand for purposes of defense. They crowned the brow of the hill and were very crude in their construction and arrangement. My conjecture was at [a] loss to know by whom and when they were made. From this hill, a little to our west, we could see the clear waters of a pretty stream. As it was no more than three miles, hardly that, I determined to move camp over towards [it] and rest the remainder of the day. Upon its banks lined with the green cottonwood and the hackberry, in pleasant shade and listening to the music of its rushing waters, we forgot the hardships of the last few marches. I named it the "Perdido," for, following it a few miles down, it was found to sink, disappearing entirely.

We were now beginning to be on quite short allowance of provisions, and the quantity of fish in this stream helped much – trout (very fine), suckers and catfish were caught in any abundance. This, however, was not the first time that our fishing lines had assisted our commissariat. All the way up the Pecos we had subsisted on catfish, the only fish I believe that inhabit its turbid waters. We had become uneasy for Poli, but tonight he made his appearance. After a long and faithful trailing of the missing animals, he had been forced to give up the search, and we concluded some roving party of Indians had picked them up. This boy Policarpio is one of the most valuable members of my party, a patient and untiring hunter, an unerring trailer with all the instinct and woodcraft of the Indian, combined with the practical part of surveying which he has learned from Howard – moreover, a capital hand with the mules. I don't know of any person whom I would rather have in the woods.

SATURDAY, MARCH 17. We left the Perdido this morning at half past seven on the course of N. 73° W., which we continued for two hours, and then, still among the round-top hills at the base of the mountains, bore N. 88° W. for a gap which gave promise of a pass. The travel was rather rough, and we crossed the beds of three dry arroyos, or creeks, very stony and composed of pebbles of sandstone of every variety of color, and fragments of the feldspathic and porphyritic rocks of the higher elevations, washed down by the waters. At twelve we fell in with an Indian trail apparently but lately traveled, and on this about two we suddenly met an Apache family coming towards us. We descried them first, however, and they were somewhat startled, but there being no chance to escape, they showed no fear. An Apache warrior on foot with his bow and arrows and in the costume of the model artists, two squaws on the same horse, and a very old, withered Indian man and woman on another animal composed the party. We held some talk with them. They said we were going wrong for Presidio, and the warrior pointed the course. We gave them a little tobacco, and they went on their way well pleased, but not before the old Indian had set the grass afire. This looked ominous and we proceeded cautiously, Smith, Howard, and the Delaware scouting in advance.

At three we left this trail and took another nearly on our course southwest, but at four o'clock I spied in a fresh burn at some distance beyond, a large *caballada.* The valley in which we were was narrow; the hills prevented an extended view. Upon this the train was halted, but before any preparation could be made our scouts came galloping in from the front closely pursued by a large band of Apache, and simultaneously we were enveloped front, rear, and left flank by five different parties.[247] Issuing from every gorge hard by, the painted devils came crowding up at full speed, and looking about us we could see them on every hill. They advanced upon us with bows strung and brandishing their lances, [and] appeared as if they wished by their hostile gestures and wild cries to frighten both ourselves and our animals. On our right was a little recess between two spurs of the boundary ridge of the valley. Wishing to avoid, if possible, a collision, yet if obliged to fight, to do it to the utmost, I remained alone among them, while Smith and Howard with the party moved gradually to this point, extricating themselves coolly from their dangerous neighbors. They crowded close upon

247 Whiting encountered the Apache at a point which is probably within the present Reeves or Jeff Davis counties.

me and upon the party. To gain a little time for the men to tie their mules together and make their few preparations, I called out to the chiefs to stop and parley. They came out, one an old and portly man, his hair in long plaits, his countenance the only one amongst the painted ugliness that had anything pleasing in it. He appeared influential; he was not so fierce in his demeanor. Another, Gómez [248] by name, the terror of Chihuahua and a byword in Mexico, a well-made fellow, apparently about thirty or thirty-five years old, dressed something like a Mexican and speaking excellent Spanish, was hostile and insulting and evidently desirous to fight us.

They sternly demanded who we were and whether we came to the Apache country for peace or war. I answered Americans, *en route* for Presidio. We came peaceable; if we remained so, depended on them. In the meantime the mules had been tied up, their heads together; and in front of them appeared the Texans, squatted to the ground, their rifles cocked, their mouths filled with bullets, and their faces showing every variety of determined expression from the angry flush on the face of the younger men to the cool indifference of the veteran of San Jacinto and the men of Mier and Monclova. They waited but a signal. Howard, more fluent in Spanish than myself, came down to interpret.

We were enveloped by an angry crowd of the painted devils. On our right and left, parties stripped to the breechclout, with bows strung and fingers full of arrows, were ready to take us in flank. The remainder, enclosing Dick and myself, were ready to charge. Their numbers were upwards of two hundred. The prospect

[248] Early in 1853, Julius Froebel, then in the city of Chihuahua, described Gómez as "the most dreaded chief of these savages [Apache] in northern Mexico." Julius Froebel, *Seven Years' in Central America, Northern Mexico, and the Far West of the United States* (London, 1859), 363.

was gloomy. Gómez insisted we should go to their camp, and adding if we didn't move, he'd make us; [he] called out: "You are afraid." But the defiant reply of our intrepid young guide and interpreter and the significant cocking of pistols and rifles which accompanied it, changed the tone of the cowardly and treacherous crowd. The position taken up by Lieutenant Smith with the escort – the best our circumstances afforded – and his judicious arrangements had also their effect, and the chiefs, to Gómez's great dissatisfaction, agreed to my demand that before conference they must call off their people and come up unarmed. They did so. It was decided that they should precede us to the springs hard by, where they were encamped; we would follow, take our position, and decide our future relations by a council.

Cautiously and with much apprehension on the part of my men of treachery from the savages, we followed the yelling bands. It was an exciting and picturesque scene. Two hundred Apache, superbly mounted, set off by their many colored dresses, their painted shields, and hideous faces, galloping to and fro at full speed and brandishing their long lances, moved in advance down the valley. Behind, at some distance, mounted humbly on jaded mules, close together and watchful, [came] the little band of Texans. This swart and bearded party, with their resolute and rugged aspect and cautious advance, was not the least impressive feature of the scene. Between the two parties rode Howard, Smith, and myself, accompanied by the five chiefs. We had made this arrangement in view of treachery, that at the first movement of hostility the revolvers with which unfortunately we alone were armed, might do their work upon the chiefs. Turning to the right, we shortly came upon a spring of clear, cool water issuing from the hillside. Here was the *caballada* of the Indians and their large drove of cattle, all, of course, with Mexican brands.

We took our posts in a little rocky gully which seemed, in the treeless valley, to afford the best chance. Each man, unsaddling his mule with one hand while the other held the rifle, placed his packs together; and closed we sat down, our movements curiously watched by the Indians. Gómez, riding up, insultingly demanded why we made no fires, why we didn't scatter, and collect wood (here very scarce), and go to cooking. But observing his band still mounted, their bows still strung, he was answered that we held wood enough in our hands; and we all remained together, gloomy and almost despondent of escape.

At eight o'clock the chiefs appeared, unarmed, to talk. Through the medium of Mr. Howard and the boy Poli, I explained to them that towards all friendly Indians the intentions of the United States were friendly, that agents would probably be sent among them, and they would, while they continued peaceable and well disposed, be put upon the same footing with other Indian tribes; that we were an advance party of the army soon to appear on the frontier for the purposes of carrying out the United States intentions. They asked if they would be disturbed in the possession of their lands. I told them no, provided they were peaceable. They were curious as to our relations with Mexico. I satisfied them as far as I could, but prudently refrained from touching on all points, for the slightest allusion to that part of our treaty which relates to the restraining of Indian depredations and the restoration of stolen captives and property would have been the signal to fight. I was in no condition to enforce what I said; and when it is considered that we were but thirteen armed men, and five of these provided with but a single shot, our scanty stock of provisions reduced to short allowance, badly armed and mounted, and important public information dependent upon our return, this concealment on my part will be pardoned.

The chiefs, each making a short speech, which one who spoke Spanish interpreted to me, declared themselves satisfied. They spoke to the effect that they wished to be friendly with the United States. The old chief Cigarito, noticed above as prepossessing in his appearance and demeanor, standing up addressed me to this end, as near as I could gather: "Stranger, your words are good. You come of a great people. We have heard of you in Mexico. You have conquered the Mexicans in many battles, and your warriors are many and braver than theirs. We do not believe you speak two ways like them. I live in these mountains; my relations and my tribe is here. We wish to be undisturbed and to be at peace with your people. I and my band are friends to yours." He concluded by requesting a paper, or safeguard, for himself to the great chief (meaning General Worth) who commanded the army. The others said nearly the same thing, with the exception of Gómez, who preserved throughout his fierce and insulting demeanor, proudly declaring he was the greatest man in his country or in Mexico and that he didn't care for Americans or any nation – he was not afraid.

We separated there. Hungry, supperless, and anxious, we lay down on the rocks, our arms in our hands. The chill air of the mountains and the cold wind from the north increased our discomfort. Desperate beggars and accomplished thieves as these Indians are, our tobacco and the small articles which in the darkness of the council they could lay hands on, suffered.

SUNDAY, MARCH 18. On the lookout for attack all night, we learned from a Mexican captive this morning that a war talk had been held by the Indians after the council and that Gómez was only prevented by the refusal of the chiefs Cigarito and Chino Guero from attacking us as we lay in camp. Providing a scanty meal, we saddled up. Part of a beef which we procured from the Indians increased our stock of provisions. The chiefs were now informed that we were about to start. Gómez came down and demanded that we should wait; he was refused. Cigarito offered with his band to guide us as far as his town, whence one of his men would show us a pass through the mountains. This was accepted. Gómez now demanded our powder and balls, for which, he said, as we were friends to the Apache, we had no use. Flatly refusing him any, he left me in an insulting manner.

Our apprehensions of treachery were not yet allayed. Marching in close order, we observed that the Indians with us kept to the rear; and knowing that the trail on which we were now traveling and which took us through the scene of yesterday's surprise had a branch to the right towards the Indian camp, we feared an attack from Gómez in front, while those behind would take part in rear. But the old chief who rode at the head of the train soon reassured us by conducting us farther into the mountains, amid the ravines of which we felt that their mounted force would avail them little. He warned us to beware of Gómez and begged to be regarded as having nothing in common with him. We learned that the latter was but four days from Mexico, with a large *caballada* of stolen horses and drove of cattle, and with plunder and captives taken in a late foray.

Riding now through the superb scenery of the mountains, by two o'clock we reached the Apache town. Twenty-five lodges were situated on the banks of a little creek, sheltered from the sun by a grove of hackberry and cottonwood. Their *caballada,* very numerous, was grazing hard by on the fine mountain mesquite grass. We took our position just above their camp upon a rise of the valley, the creek on one side of us, a clump of trees on the other, and in front the Indian village within range of our pistols. We were in place to defy either treachery or open attack.

In the afternoon I visited their town. The wigwams, or lodges, were generally built of willow withes stuck into the ground, and bent over to form together a round-topped hut similar in shape to the kraal of the Hottentot and about high enough for a man to sit upright in it. This willow framework is covered with skins, buffalo hides, blankets, or other stuff obtained in Mexico. The entrance is by a small hole through which one can scarcely crawl. The chief's house was larger, however, and sufficiently high to allow us to stand up. It alone was conical in shape. A hole in the top let out the smoke from the fire. Entering with Dick Howard, I found the old man Cigarito at home. Stripped to his breechclout, he was sitting in the midst of his family. He motioned to us to be seated and had placed before us some Indian food, a sort of preserve made of the plant commonly known as bear grass. Its botanical name I am ignorant of. Its long, flat, flexible leaves, studded with horizontal spines, present the appearance of the tail of the sawfish. The stem of this plant just above its root is roasted and resembles in its taste the roasted apple. They have another preserve made of the dried flowers and fruit of the common Spanish bayonet, and another from the juice and pulp of the maguey, the plant from which the

Mexican liquor mescal is made – whence their name of Apache Mescalero.

Cigarito warned me to beware of Gómez and begged to be considered by Americans as having nothing to do with him or his band. At his request I gave him a paper to General Worth in case Americans should fall in with him. At night I warned the chiefs that all Indians approaching camp during the night would be shot and directed them so to inform their people. This they did, and the night passed off without disturbance.

MONDAY, MARCH 19. I found this morning that many small articles had been purloined by the Indians, certainly the most accomplished thieves I know. Many of our cooking utensils were taken, in spite of precaution and watching. The buttons of my jacket were cut off and my small India rubber cape carried off. But my most serious loss was that of a bundle of papers, tied up together and taken with some shirts from my saddle-bags. This had been done during the council at the last camp. These papers were important to me and they comprised all my orders, letters of instruction, money vouchers for disbursements at Fredericksburg, the mail for Presidio, etc. They were taken to make *cigarrillos* with.

Inducing with great difficulty one of Cigarito's men to lead us to a trail where we would make our way through the mountains, we set out from this village. These villains have an enormous *caballada* of horses, some of them very fine and all with the Mexican brand. Each lodge also has a Mexican slave, a boy or girl stolen in infancy and brought up by the blows of the women to very severe labor. Literally do the Mexican race thus become hewers of wood and drawers of water, bondsmen to the Indian. Our guide, a strapping young fellow, who sat the beautiful animal he rode (wild as the scenery of his own mountains) as if he were a part of him, evinced a great distrust to go with us, afraid that we would kill him when he was separated from his people. His cupidity overcame his fears, and the offer of two blankets led him to take the risk. How superbly the fellow rode! The animal he bestrode had evidently never been saddled before – a wild young colt with long flowing mane. The creature pitched in frenzy, but it might as well have tried to shake his mane off as to disturb even the easy grace of his rider's seat. He led us through the hills, still at the base of the loftier ranges, until twelve, when, pointing to a lofty mountain peak of notable appearance, [he] told us the road went by that, and there was plenty of water, and started with his coveted blankets, at full speed, for his people.

At half past one we reached the headsprings of the Perdido, where that pretty creek issues from the mountains. Here we stopped to noon on fine grass. The formation around us is entirely primitive: masses of highly ferruginous rock of the granitic and trap series surround us on every side. At half past four we were again in the saddle, pursuing our way by the old and faintly marked Indian trail. In about an hour's ride, as we were entering a dark gorge, we descried a party of Indians at the other extremity of it. Upon seeing us, they fled in great confusion. We moved cautiously forward, and our path, shortly turning to the west, entered a splendid defile and brought us by the foot of the bleak mountain pointed by the guide. Though night was coming on, our march was still kept up. Water appeared everywhere in great plenty, and at half past eight we halted and encamped.

TUESDAY, MARCH 20. This day and night have been

stirring. We set out from camp early. Our road has been remarkable. The daylight showed us, on awaking, a fine pass. Through the gorge, now running at the base of the dark cliffs of basaltic columns, now winding amid the prettier grouping of trees and in little mountain valleys, is a clear stream. We followed it through the range, delighted at the promise of a successful passage of the road where wood and water should obtain in plenty. Wild roses, the only ones I had seen in Texas, here grew luxuriantly. I named the defile the "Wild Rose pass" [249] and the brook the "Limpia." At twelve we left the valley of the pass for a while and emerged upon a bald, elevated plain. This, still surrounded by hills, is entirely destitute of trees or even bushes. To our left we saw an extensive pond of water. Catching a glimpse off to the right of the green cottonwoods of the Limpia and warned of the dangers of the plains by our recent meeting with the Apache, I directed the march towards them. At about one we came to camp in a grove of lofty *álamos*. The Limpia here forms a clear, deep pool of blue water; and here it issues from the mountains, now on our right hand, in a southerly course and follows hence the pass we have just come through. The large trees are marked with the rude sketches of the Comanche.

We had intended to noon here, but Indian signs became frequent; alarm smokes and signal smokes in the direction we had come, answered off towards the south, began to darken the air. The tract between us and the ravines of the Cibolo beyond, is a bare, bleak prairie. I determined to steal a march upon Gómez, for I had no doubt that he was moving his other bands. Our ani-

[249] A short distance northeast of the present Fort Davis, Jeff Davis county. Mrs. O. L. Shipman, *Taming the Big Bend* (1926), 38, 201.

mals were staked out as if we intended to camp for the night. After the scanty meal of the day was done with, the packs were arranged to be readily disposed of at night. Our arms were thoroughly examined and put in order. Our camp fires were lit. About eight at night we saddled up with great rapidity and stillness. Orders were given that upon alarm the command should close upon the head, and a lariat, passed through the halters of all the mules, was to be tied immediately by the Mexicans. The men were to ride four and five abreast.

Our fires still burning, we issued from our camp without a sound. No man spoke. I may live a long time yet, but I shall never forget the still and oppressive hours of that somber march. The night was clear in its cold starlight. The wind swept by over the bleak plain in fitful and furious gusts from the west; to the eastward above the hills of the pass rose the lurid glare of the gathering fires of the Apache. Anxious and with senses keenly alive to every sound, we moved in close order over the plain, listening each moment for the Indian whistle and the rushing of his horse's hoofs. We had left the trail as an additional precaution and were steering a west course.

About eleven, on our left, a brilliant fire suddenly flashed into light from the summit of a lofty peak. The whispered words "a signal," "a signal" ran through our party. We knew that our movement was discovered. The lurking spies about our camp had found we had gone and made all speed to their signal hill. How intense the excitement of the next two hours! That fire flashing on our left; while every little space the dark figures, distinctly visible, would pass between us and the light, heaping on the brush and feeding the flame. Answering back in the east were the mountains, lit up with a long, red line of fire. I moved upon the dark outline of a hill before us, which promised some shelter from the wind (now blowing a chill gale) and perhaps defense and rest. At half past one we reached it and found the rocks at its base a fine natural work. Here, without water, weary and desperate, we lay down on our arms. No fires were lit, and the tired sentinels kept up their watch undisturbed. Travel eighteen miles.

WEDNESDAY, MARCH 21. The morning showed where we were [250] – at the base of a hill composed entirely of huge, rounded masses of grit, apparently boulders, piled one upon the other in titanic shapes. I named the hill "Volterra." The smokes were rising near the signal mountain to the southeast of us and by which passes the Presidio trail. The Indians had evidently lost us. Expecting us to pass by the direct course, they had gathered in force in that direction. Our night march and our westerly course of last evening had saved us a bloody fight. We were now near the ravines of the Cibolo and would soon be in position to bid defiance to Gómez.

Breakfasting on a little coffee and a spoonful of *pinole* – all we had – we set out on our course, now southerly, for Presidio. The tract we now traveled in was one of hill and vale, favorable enough for us. We soon entered, however, an extensive dog town. These curious little animals, the American marmot, strip the whole vicinity of their burrows of every green shoot, baring the plain and giving a peculiarly desolate aspect to the landscape, the effect of which is not diminished by their dismal squeak as the passage of the *caballada* disturbs them. We should be grateful to them, for they furnished us a breakfast. The Delaware, Jack Hunter, killed a panther just as we reached the gullies

250 They were now within the present Presidio county.

of the Cibolo.[251] Poor as the prospect was, the idea of meat revived our famished spirits. The march was kept up until 4 P.M., when we camped in a secure ravine by a water hole of the Cibolo. The panther was a godsend. Young panther, as my Florida recollections prove, is not bad, but panther very old, very lean, and very tough – without prejudice – is decidedly not good. We had to take it though. The night of the twenty-first was intensely cold, the water near-by freezing over. March seventeen miles.

THURSDAY, MARCH 22. At quarter of eight this morning we left camp, following the valley of the Cibolo in a south course for Leaton's Peak, a notable mountain, which, I am told, can be seen from Presidio. This valley is a remarkable locality. We again see the table formations, through which the great primitive rocks we have left seem elevated. On our right we found large strata of green sand between two distinct beds of lime and clay. The ground is broken into many fantastic shapes, ridges, and tables, all, however, practicable for wagons, and we rejoice in the prospect of success in our reconnaissance. We found today great quantities of milky and smoky quartz, with botryoidal shapes, frequently appearing as if fused and enclosing nodules of clay. Some of these nodules having crumbled left hollows like bottles and vessels. Smith found some beautiful specimens. Several superb cactaceae in bloom were also met. The magnificent cluster of scarlet flowers on some of these plants particularly attracted my attention. I regret much the absence of books prevents my giving a proper description and classification of them. We dined today on our panther meat at a spring similar

[251] Now called Cibolo creek, which flows south through the present Presidio county.

in character to the Awache, but the water, owing to the clay bed, was not nearly so clear as that. At half past three our march was resumed and continued until dark, a day's journey of twenty miles. I had sent the boy Poli in advance to hunt. We found him waiting for us at the water with a deer he had been fortunate enough to kill, and a prairie dog. It was very poor, but it was better than we had had for some time. We demolished it that night. Antelopes abounded in our vicinity all day, but so very wild we could not kill them.

FRIDAY, MARCH 23. We still traveled a southerly course down the valley of the Cibolo, now become monotonous and uninteresting. The course of the creek was marked by reeds and willows. The adjacent bottom was arid and dusty, and clothed not with the green mesquite of the mountain creeks but with chaparral, cactus, and here and there rank sedge grass. We here fell in with Hays's trail out from Presidio. After a march of eight miles we stopped to noon on clear, running water in the Cibolo. The water of this arroyo is not good, as a general thing, except when it is running. When it stands in pools, it soon becomes brackish and unpleasant from its being strongly impregnated with diffused salts. This day has been intensely warm. We left our dinner camp at two o'clock, and at four left the Cibolo on our right hand and ascended from its valley to the higher land. It is very stony. We are now in the peculiar gravel region which marks the course of the Río Grande for a long distance. The ground when we leave the Cibolo is covered with fragments of breccia, but not *in situ*.

On rising the ridge, the welcome sight of the smokes of Presidio del Norte met our longing eyes, defined in long, blue lines against the dark sides of the Sierra Madre. Three or four miles farther we passed the Cottonwood spring and grove. The vegetation appears here much farther advanced than above, and this beautiful grove is welcome to the eye after the dry and barren valley of the Cibolo. Today for the first time I met a curious plant – long stems with a dark, greenish-gray back covered with a hard, curved spine and growing generally in clusters of from five to twelve from the same root, without branches and, at this time of year, without leaves. These stems bend outwards as they rise and are topped with a beautiful pear-shaped cluster of small crimson flowers. After a march of eighteen miles we came to camp on clear, running water and good grass. I determined to rest an hour at camp and then push on with Smith and Howard to Leaton's Ranch, now about twelve miles. We started at seven in the evening and until nine kept the trail very well; but the country becoming stony and sandy and much broken into arroyos, or dry creeks, we lost it. Still keeping our course as far as we thought prudent, at one we lay down in the bed of a gully and slept until morning.

SATURDAY, MARCH 24. At daylight when we awoke we saw we were within two miles of Leaton's place. The little white church of the Norte beyond had a very pretty effect below the dark mountains, with the morning sun shining lightly upon its walls. We soon came in view of the Río Grande with its green valley and cottonwood groves. It was delightful to our jaded spirits to catch glimpses of the adobe houses. At seven we reached Fort Leaton,[252] where we received a warm welcome and

[252] On the Río Grande, near the present Presidio, Presidio county. It was established about 1848 by Ben Leaton, a native of Kentucky. In May, 1853, Froebel described it as "a large building surrounded by a mud wall." Froebel, *op. cit.*, 409; Shipman, *op. cit.*, 10-11, 199. In his report to the chief of engineers on June 10, 1849, Whiting wrote: "I take great pleasure in noticing Mr. Leaton here. His position is in every respect remarkable. Located in a valley of the Río Grande, a little below Presidio, with some eight or ten

great hospitality. Leaton has performed severe labor and gone to much expense in his location. His fort is a collection of adobes, or earth-built houses, with a look-out and a wall which encloses also his corral. The rooms are surmounted by a crenelated parapet wall, and the place would make a strong defense against Indians. He represents those living between this and the Paso as hostile in the extreme, and considers, with the smallness of our force, that we undertake an expedition of great risk. The party made their appearance about ten this morning. Leaton immediately allowed them to camp in his yard, had wood brought and a meal cooked for the rough and hungry travelers, and after an enormous dinner the remainder of the day was appropriated to rest.

SUNDAY, MARCH 25. This morning I had the necessary subsistence for our next march put in a state of forwardness. All that can be procured – and that at high prices – is dried beef, *pinole,* and cornmeal. *Pinole* is parched corn ground and sweetened, a very pleasant and nutritive article of food. But both it and the meal here have to be ground by hand and the beef must be dried. Three or four days will perforce be consumed. Everything brings enormous prices in this vicinity. Mr. Leaton has to supply himself entirely from Chihuahua. The neighboring village is a poor, stricken town, and the journey into Chihuahua is one of no common peril. We will require many new animals, nearly all ours be-

Americans in his employment, he has in a few months accomplished a great amount of severe labor, fortified himself in a good position, secured his stock, and carried to considerable extent his farming operations, his men being all the while obliged to work with their arms at hand. They have been exposed to the incursions of the Indians on one side, and to a series of outrageous impositions and aggressions on the part of the Mexicans on the other, and forced to mount guard day and night." *House Ex. Docs.,* 31 cong., 1 sess., no. 5, p. 287.

ing either sore backed or tender footed and unfit to proceed farther. Leaton is very active and enterprising in his assistance. His endeavors with small resources to promote our success lay me under many obligations.

Smith, Howard, Leaton, and Delacy went over with me today to the Norte. It is a collection of one-story adobe buildings, situated on one of the gravel tables at the junction of the Conchos with the Río Grande. It has a barren and desolate aspect. The soil in the vicinity is sandy and sterile. Indeed, for farming purposes, Leaton has the only soil about, and his tract is confined. Gazed at with wondering eyes by the population as the strangers who had passed through the Apache country, we walked through the streets, and on coming to the Presidio, or Fortaleza, del Norte, we called on the commandant, Don Guillermo Ortiz. This fortress is a rude adobe structure, oblong in shape, without flanking defenses, containing the church and the barracks, and capable of accommodating five or six hundred men. Some miserable, ragged creatures, apparently half starved and called "soldiers," were standing about the gateway. A scarecrow was walking past with a bankrupt escopette. We were ushered into the commandant's room. A few chairs and a pine table were its furniture. He soon made his appearance, a short, slightly built man, dark mustache, and gentlemanly address. We were presented in form by Mr. Leaton [and] afterwards to the alcalde and other officials of the place. The usual compliments passed, and whiskey and Pass brandy from Leaton's were handed round, and then a Mexican dinner brought in, in the usual style, one dish at a time – stewed chicken flavored hotly with *chile colorado; tortillas;* a roasted turkey exceedingly well cooked; and finally frijoles and coffee. We ate to repletion, as might have been expected of men with our late experiences. Adjourning, we visited Don José Rodríguez, recommended by Leaton as the only honest man in the place.

The town of the Norte[253] is said to contain from twelve to fourteen hundred souls but, like all Mexican towns on the frontier, is a miserable, Indian-blighted place. There are several abandoned silver mines in its vicinity, one on the Sierra Rica said to contain fine ore. There are also mines on the American side of the river, but the workers were long since driven off by the Indians. Only an eyewitness can form an idea of the complete stagnation in every branch of industry produced by these terrible Indian depredations. The town of Norte, once a more flourishing place and occupying an important military position, now indeed enjoys in some sort immunity, but it is for the reason that its inhabitants have been stripped of their all, and, in the way of plunder, present no attraction for the Apache robbers.

Fort Leaton will become an important site to the United States in view of the treaty stipulation and the Indian aggressions. It will make a convenient post, or depot, and refuge for the roving camps of dragoons which must be placed upon the great warpaths. Presidio is at the western part of that large bend of the Río Grande where most of these passes into Mexico exist.

---

253 The inhabitants of Presidio del Norte, according to Froebel, were the "allies, spies, powder purveyors, the receivers and buyers of stolen goods, of the Texan Comanches." Froebel, *op. cit.*, 408. In July, 1852, Major Emory wrote: "The Presidio is a miserably built mud town, situated upon a gravelly hill overlooking the junction of the Conchos and the Río Bravo. . . The town, which contains about eight hundred souls, is one of the oldest Spanish settlements in northern Mexico. . . The church is within the walls of the Presidio, or fort, and contains one or two paintings of a better class than are usually found disfiguring the walls of frontier churches. In almost every house is found, in addition to the cross, a figure of our Saviour, which is sometimes so very grotesque that piety itself cannot divest it of its ridiculous appearance." *House Ex. Docs.*, 34 cong., 1 sess., no. 135, vol. 1, p. 85.

It is in convenient striking distance also of the upper passes of the Apache. With a proper and efficient system of mounted troops, heavy blows will at one day or other be struck upon the Comanche from this post. It will also become the customhouse for the Chihuahua trade, destined to pass, henceforth, if I mistake not, not by Santa Fé, but from New Orleans and the southern states. It appears to me one of the most important places on the Río Grande. These suggestions are necessarily brief but they touch upon subjects pregnant with importance. I hope, should they meet the eye of the chief engineer, they may be deemed worthy of more mature consideration. The whole of the neighboring region of the Big Bend requires thorough reconnaissance. The geology, geography, and topography of it are unknown. Important public information may be gained both for military and commercial interests by a judicious system of reconnoitering parties traversing the extensive region lying between the Pecos and the Río Grande.

MONDAY, MARCH 26. Having learned that various outrages have been committed in the neighborhood by the Mexican authorities and the circumstances having been officially made known to me, I made inquiries of them in the matter. Their answers and my report are among the papers addressed to General Worth, and it is not necessary to cumber these notes with them.

TUESDAY, MARCH 27. Ordered a board of survey on the animals of the escort, and procured the necessary mules to supply the place of those condemned. Made up my accounts with Leaton, paying him by drafts on the departments at San Antonio. Hardly knowing what was before us, and all accounts about the number and hostility of the Indians of the Río Grande being so much against us, I judged proper to leave everything not absolutely essential to our progress, in Leaton's care, together with a succinct account of our operations thus far. The provisions now being well forward, I appointed to start on the morrow or next day.

WEDNESDAY, MARCH 28. Most of the day today has been taken up in our preparations of making bags to hold our provisions, etc., separating the packs, arranging the messes, etc. I have secured the services of two additional men to increase our little party, W. F. de Saez and John Spencer.

THURSDAY, MARCH 29. The morning of this day has been occupied in the selection and packing of our train. We left Leaton's in the afternoon and camped four miles from his house on the Río Grande banks.

FRIDAY, MARCH 30. March from Presidio del Norte to El Paso. We left our camp on the Río Grande at eight this morning; Leaton passed the night with us. The hospitality of this man, his zealous endeavors to promote in every way the interests of the expedition, his reckless profusion, and the efforts of both himself and his wife to make my messmates comfortable, I can never forget. And the load of obligation was not a little increased by his insisting at the very last moment on sending his favorite man along with me, in order, as he said, should we get into a scrape some one at least might get out. This morning there were, as usual, the delays and vexations which accompany a start from the settlements: refractory mules, some pitching and others pulling back; gear not properly adjusted; and packs not well arranged. But at length we moved in order through the sandy bottom of the river. Nearly opposite the Mexican town we passed a fine part of the valley where the mesquite, the willow, and cottonwood abound in size, and where some judicious and tasteful clearing would make a pleasant site for the quarters of a post, while hard by is a commanding table, similar to the one on which Presidio is built, where the lookout or defensive works might well be placed. Barracks properly arranged will probably make the only defensive works upon this frontier. They can be cheaply and conveniently built of adobe, the almost universal building material. But our position is offensive with reference to Indians. They will never attack posts garrisoned by American troops, and hence the different sites located along the Río Grande, with those probably in contemplation from this river to the Wichita, should be considered as depots.

Our trail lay over fine, gravelly sand, occasionally intersected by small gullies washed by water. It was between the cottonwoods, which almost everywhere line the banks of the river, and the gravel ridges which put out from the hills, or rather mountains, on the right. We continued until two, the weather very warm, when we camped in a secure grove after a march of about fifteen miles. The precaution of [stationing] sentinels the moment we stopped, was adopted. We are determined that whatever be before us, we shall not be surprised. The Sierra Grande, as I believe the Mexicans called the mountain which for some twenty miles above the Norte lies parallel to the river, is very singular in appearance. A high, unbroken, narrow ridge from one end to the other, seems to form its summit. The side towards the river is very steep and is intersected at short intervals by huge furrows which extend from the summit to the base, terminating generally in ravines which course towards the water; and [it] looks as if, when elevated, the mountain had been combed down by the teeth of some titanic harrow.

SATURDAY, MARCH 31. We moved at eight. On our left on the opposite bank is the north end of the Sierra Grande, while beyond it and farther up the river stand the Pilares, a notable hill of two peaks which has been thus named by the Mexicans. On our right [is] a high and large mountain, which I have called "Mount Barnard." The travel has been much interrupted by chaparral, the cactus in every variety, enormous *palmitos* from fifteen to twenty-five feet high, and every kind of thorn. Our progress was good notwithstanding. We moved with caution. Dick, Lieutenant Smith, and Spencer constituted our advance; they rode at the distance of several hundred yards ahead. I led the train in close order, and Brady scouted in [the] rear at some distance. By twelve we reached a valley opposite the *casa vieja,* or old *fortaleza,* which stands deserted, crowning the bluff on the opposite shore. Built for defense against the Indians, it is, in its crumbling desolation, a mournful monument of Mexican weakness. Two towers at either extremity of the site constitute its lookouts and flanking defenses. These are connected by a long curtain which on top shows the remains of a crenelated parapet wall. Here the Río Grande runs for some distance over a rocky bottom, forming a very good crossing, *vado de piedras,* or rock ford. This point is about thirty-five miles above Leaton's.

We dined here and at half past two moved on. Some little difficulty was found in the travel where the gravel ridges before mentioned are washed at their base by the river. Passed great beds of clay. Beyond the north point of Mount Barnard and near the river stand some notable hills, presenting a resemblance to old feudal castles with the round towers of those days. Horizontal on top, the action of water appears to have scraped the sides of the hills and cut them in the shape of towers. I have named them "Tower hills." Opposite to them on the river bank we came to camp, after a march of nineteen miles.

SUNDAY, APRIL 1. After marching about three miles through chaparral, we came into the formation called by the Mexicans *cajónes,* or boxes. We find our progress interrupted by continual tables of gravel, narrow ridges with steep sides, separated by ravines and, towards the river, terminating in perpendicular escarpment. They are generally composed of distinctly stratified beds of red clay, gravel, and sand. On our right hand, now having passed Mount Barnard, were seen high mountains marked with great patches of white – whether sand, clay, or lime we could not tell. These I called the "White mountains." A little farther on and we entered among high and rough hills crowned with red basaltic rock overlying sandstone. Two of these make notable landmarks, being almost exactly alike in shape. We passed a salt spring this afternoon and soon after, at three, reached a clear creek of pleasant water, where we camped after a march of between sixteen and twenty miles. It occurred to me today to apply to the chief engineer for some engineer soldiers to serve on this frontier, and I make a memorandum here with that view.

MONDAY, APRIL 2. A heavy shower of rain having fallen the past evening, camp was not moved until nine in order that the saddle blankets might be dried. One of the mules was found unfit to proceed and accordingly abandoned. The red hills continue to make down to the river, and our advance was much interrupted by ravines, bluffs, and thickets. Howard, Smith, Spencer, and I were constantly scouting to the right and left, on the lookout for suitable wagon passes. I am of opinion

[that] so far we have met with no obstacle which may not be removed. Generally when we passed with the train over the hills adjacent to the river, a few hours' labor with the ax, picks, and crowbars would enable wagons to pass below, thus much shortening the distance. One place by which we came is remarkable. The trail led us down a very steep hill and passed under a huge, isolated rock of conglomerate which towered above our heads, its peak inaccessible, and seeming as if it would topple over upon the travelers. Its top looks like a dog's head; whereupon I called the pass "Hell-gate" and the rock "Cerberus." We marched beyond this for almost an hour, when, upon finding good grass and the river bank convenient for water, I determined to halt. Our animals have been much fatigued by the severe labors of the morning. I suppose we have made scarcely more than six miles from eight o'clock till half past twelve.

At half past three we saddled up, our road still in the red hills, but this afternoon chiefly by the river bottom. On account of the undergrowth and the willow, our progress was laborious and slow, and in many places we were forced to the hills. One part of our path was notable: a high and craggy hill rose from the water's edge directly opposite a straight stretch of the river, and we wound by a narrow trail some one hundred feet above the stream, along its precipitous side. The sun setting in the west and throwing the hills into strong light and shade, the peaks of Mexico towering in every variety of fantastic position and form, and the Río Grande with its pale green fringe of cottonwoods and willows, formed a pleasant picture. Towards dusk we reached a bottom where, though the grass was poor, we were obliged to camp. Twelve miles.

TUESDAY, APRIL 3. At eight o'clock we were again

in motion, and we continued by the river all the morning, at times with great difficulty. Howard, indefatigable as usual, climbed a high hill, round the base of which I carried the train, and he found there was a pass to the east of it. The country adjacent to the river now appears rather more open; and as we have left the red hills behind us, the valley assumes an aspect similar to that below, intersected with smooth, gravel ridges dividing it into level and sterile tracts. Respecting the travel of the last two days, I am of opinion that it is possible to make a wagon road. I should require, however, at least one company on fatigue duty in advance of the troops, or perhaps two well provided with implements. They should start three or four weeks before the main body. On account of the poor grass of last night, I stopped to graze upon the river bank at half past twelve. The animals suffer extremely with tender feet, so rough is the task of beating out a trail in this rugged country. Two have already been abandoned since we left Presidio, and I fear to lose many more.

At half past three we again moved on through a hard bottom, destitute of trees and surrounded by the clay and gravel hills. At half past five we came to a singular rock, apparently of limestone, which stands to the left of the trail upon a small round elevation. Exactly resembling a sentry box, I named it "Sentinel Rock." Several of us climbed it, and, looking towards the opposite side of the river, we discovered the ruins of an extensive *fortaleza;* the *débris* of the old roofs, the crumbling towers, and the line of connecting curtains of great length could be plainly seen. Half a mile beyond this, after a march of sixteen miles, we came to camp.

WEDNESDAY, APRIL 4. Leaving camp at half past

seven, we followed out an old Indian path, which shortly led us among the gravel ridges. Our course was rather more direct than that of the river, but in many places the travel was necessarily rough, chiefly where we crossed the ridges. These are so steep that it is necessary to zigzag up their declivities, and the loose, rolling stones with which they are covered are exceedingly severe upon the mules. We toiled on, however, watchful as always and observant of all around us. It was plain we were approaching a more fertile and pleasant part of the river banks than is to be found lower down; trails become frequent, some of them with the signs of recent travel; cattle tracks, too, were noticed. All these things indicated that we were drawing near some Indian town. Arms were looked at, and we preserved our customary cautious advance.

Upon rising onto a gravel ridge, a broad and beautiful valley appeared before us, the largest we had seen. Here in every direction were the Apache lodges. It was with feelings of no small satisfaction that we found the population had recently left and, from the signs on the trails, gone to the mountains. Hundreds of lodges in every variety of position, great quantities of cattle, horses, and other remains, and a numerous and greedy flock of buzzards showed how extensive a band dwelt here – enough to have rubbed our little party out. This is a winter town. This nomadic tribe, subsisting almost entirely upon the spoils of the unhappy race which they regard as slaves, move into the lofty region of the mountains during the spring and summer months and, selecting there some pleasant spot on the clear creeks which flow in the hills, where the cottonwood and mesquite give them shade and the mountain grass fatten their *caballadas,* they prepare for the fall and winter campaign. Towards September the winter grass of the Río Grande bottoms is beginning to be good. Then they return to the river amongst these thick groves, and, sheltered by the surrounding hills from the northers, the women and children remain while the warriors ravage Mexico. Their incursions and those of the Comanche penetrate to Chihuahua, Durango, Zacatecas, and even to San Luis Potosi. We stopped for dinner in this valley. The grass was very fine.

At half past two we again moved on. Upon ascending the gravel ridge which separates this from the next bottom, we discovered horses near the river. This put us all on the *qui vive,* but they were soon seen to be loose – probably broken-down animals left by the Indians to recruit. Cattle, too, were spied in the next valley, studded like the last with the lodges of another extensive town. I dispatched Poli and the Delaware to shoot a cow. The former was soon successful, and the train was halted for three-quarters of an hour while the meat was cut up and packed. This bottom is a fine one and of considerable extent. The soil is light, susceptible of cultivation I should think, and affording an admirable site for a post. Here we fell in with the trail of our friend Gómez as he passed down the river on his way to the point where he met with us. We followed it up through a very level tract, passing round the hills lying immediately upon the river, and reaching it again at half past six at a notable place where it forces itself through a narrow gorge between two high and precipitous bluffs of sandstone overlaid with lime. This place I called the "Notch." Our march of today has been about twenty-two miles.

THURSDAY, APRIL 5. We left the Notch at twenty minutes past eight and struck immediately into the hills, here crowded close onto the river. These are of different formation from those below. We entered a dry arroyo, which at first promised well as a pass but soon convinced us that the Notch hills were, unless at enormous expense, impracticable for the passage of wagons. The steep sides showed to us vast strata of compact quartzose sandstone, huge layers of shale, clay, slate, and the kindred formations in every variety of inclination to the horizon. Quarries, too, of compact gray limestone were seen, intersected by white veins of what I presumed to be calc-spar. The trail is deeply worn and passes over places where a chamois goat would pause. Our unshod mules, however, managed well, and after about two hours of severe toil we again came in sight of the river, here forcing its way through precipitous crags. Far away from the giddy height at which we stood, we saw a beautiful valley with its usual clothing of cottonwood, stretching to the northward. Upon descending we found this also crowded with the Apache houses. Under every tree and on every little knoll was seen a lodge. It is another evidence of the good fortune which marked our wanderings that the brutal and treacherous race which dwells in these towns, so far outnumbering us and looking upon us with gloating and hostile eye, had left the river at this time for the mountains. After marching about six miles in this valley, we stopped to dine. To our right now lies, evidently distinct from the lofty formation which stretches from the river, a rugged and high mountain. This I called "Mount Chase." Leaving camp at half past two, we continued on the trail, passing through a succession of valleys, until the river made a sharp bend to the southwest and the trail was lost. Here, not knowing how soon we might strike it again, we came to camp in a secure valley at quarter to six after a march of about fourteen miles.

[FRIDAY, APRIL 6.] The practicability of the route

pursued thus far between Presidio and Paso having been discussed by Lieutenant Smith, Howard, and myself, it was concluded that the group of hills called the Notch was not practicable for the march of the troops with the means which would be placed at the disposal of the conducting officer, and [we] determined to remain at this camp today and dispatch a party to examine the valley to the eastward. Under all circumstances the frontier road between the two points in question should pass by the river to the west of the Apache ranges and through their winter towns. Lieutenant Smith and Howard started this morning, mounted on our best animals, to examine the pass supposed to exist round the Notch hills. I sent with them two men, Conley and Gifford. It was a service of no small hazard but one which they thoroughly accomplished, returning at half past six with favorable accounts. They had met with no Indians in the hills but found several trails. Poli, who, while hunting, had climbed a high hill beyond us, reports that the river still comes from the west, to the left of a high mountain now become visible on our course. We at first supposed Mount Chase was on the Mexican side, until we reached it, deceived by Disturnell's map (a remarkably incorrect representation of the country), and thought the same with regard to the mountain just mentioned. Every day since we left the Pilares we have been making westing, frequently more than and generally equal to our northing.

SATURDAY, APRIL 7. At eight we left camp. In order to get out of the valley in which we were and which is confined on all sides by rugged hills, we followed an old trail leading along the river bank. It shortly brought us to one of the most dangerous bluffs I had yet seen. The hill, here of solid, smooth, and slippery rock, is washed at its base by the water. The hazardous path was at many points inclined, and I often hesitated about advancing. One false step of our animals, and rider and mule would have inevitably fallen headlong into the rushing stream. We at length got so far we could not return and after much trouble passed the bluff without accident, thanks to the sure feet of Mexican mules. We then struck into the bed of a dry arroyo. Its tortuous course at length led us out of the hills, but we saw, after a march of two hours, we were not more than two miles from our camp. The river still appears coming from the west, and, fearing to lose it, we again struck into the hills. They are similar in formation and character to the Notch. Vast strata of shale, tumbled and bent in every variety of curve, beds of lime and sandstone, red and bluish, appeared at the side of the arroyo, and fragments of primitive rocks, not *in situ,* were found in its bed. The trail had been much traveled by Indians, but our advance was toilsome and weary. At half past one we came to a spring. The water [was] clear but warm and slightly impregnated with some kind of salt. Here we stopped to dine. I climbed a high hill hard by and could see for a long distance up the Río Grande. Our progress was to be interrupted no more by hills and mountains. I determined our course northwest, to strike the river for our night camp. We saddled up at four and after a day's march of fourteen miles we reached it.

SUNDAY, APRIL 8. At eight we resumed our march. The aspect of the country is much such as we have seen. Table hills of gravel and occasional beds of shale occur at intervals. Our course was northwest and north up the river. After a march of ten miles we came to dinner at quarter to twelve; and leaving our rest at twenty minutes after two, we had, in an hour's travel, the satisfaction of finding a fine, open valley and good ground. On our right is the last peak of the Monte de la Cola, or Eagle's Tail,[254] and to our left we see mountains which are said to be visible from El Paso. Our progress has been good, and we came to camp after a day's march of twenty miles.

MONDAY, APRIL 9. At seven this morning we left our camp and continued the march in one unbroken valley, the largest we had met with since we left Presidio. The river at length appears, flowing by a course nearly east through broad and level bottoms heavily timbered with large cottonwoods. Traces of ancient beds of this fickle stream appear close to the sand hill bluffs on the American side, but it has now coursed for a long time at the foot of the Mexican mountains, leaving to the United States an extensive and fertile tract of land. We are leaving the blue peaks of the Eagle's Tail behind and bearing upon the last visible mountains on the other side. About eleven, in a small pond hard by our trail, we saw a flock of twenty-five huge white pelicans. Though familiar with the smaller and darker-colored pelican of the Gulf, this species I had never before seen. These are very large and perfectly white, with the exception of the tips of their wings, which are jet black. This variety gives them a very pretty appearance when flying. Three large, black-tailed deer, the mountain species, were wounded by some of the party near this place, but I didn't wish to delay the train to secure them. These deer, unlike the common kind, rarely go in herds but are generally found either singly or in couples. The old bucks have the most superb antlers I have ever seen.

At twelve, holding our course through the mid-bottom, we came suddenly upon an old cut-off of the river;

254 In the southeastern part of the present Hudspeth county.

at the point we struck it, it was so boggy as to be impassable. We were here delayed three-quarters of an hour looking for a crossing. At half past one we came to our dinner camp upon the river after a march of seventeen and one-half miles. At four the march was resumed and kept up during the afternoon, still in the extensive groves of *álamos,* becoming wider as we advance. In this tract the grass is generally poor. Our animals are much jaded, many having given out entirely. Our course has been generally between northwest and west, and the day's march twenty-three and one-half miles.

TUESDAY, APRIL 10. At half past seven we left camp. I directed the course upon the mountains beyond El Paso. Spencer, who has been at that place, showed me the Chihuahua gap and other noted landmarks about. Our trail still lay in the broad, cottonwood bottom. The soil, nearly destitute of grass, here is light and loose and spongy, and, until about half past ten, when we fell in with an old *carreta* track, the march was severe for the mules. The signs of wheels rejoiced the whole party. We had been traveling in a course to cut off the great bend here made by the river; but at half after one, the train being very tired, it was found best to strike into the river for encampment, and after a march of fourteen miles we reached the water. The remainder of the day was spent by the men in shooting at a mark. Some capital shots with the rifle and pistol were shown.

The question of our homeward route has been much discussed among us. We all agree that, as far as known, the valley of the Río Grande presents great difficulties, only to be overcome by time and ample means, to the passage of trains. A march for the column destined for El Paso, which should combine as little labor as possible with abundance of water and grass, is now the main object of the reconnaissance. As we take more northerly routes, the country is more open, and little or no labor is required for the immediate passage of trains; but as we go north, we lose the living water of the rougher country and are forced to depend upon muddy and uncertain pools supplied by uncertain rains. General Worth was earnest in urging the great importance of a road between El Paso and Presidio, going so far as to direct me, should I find a practicable route, to return by it without crossing the country direct from El Paso, and intending in this event to march the column by the lower post. This not being found the case, I am in doubt. Strong reasons obtain to return via Presidio, equally strong to cross from El Paso to the Pecos; and this party, too small of itself, cannot be divided.

WEDNESDAY, APRIL 11. On leaving camp at half past seven, it was found we were in the great bend of the river, laid down on the map of Wislizenus as between the village of San Elizario and Camp Comanche. Its course, however, is not correct in that sketch. We soon fell in with a large *carreta* road, which for the remainder of the morning we followed. This trail lies through a fine tract, heavily timbered – the trees are very large. We saw nothing of the southern chaparral and undergrowth to impede us. At quarter past ten we passed the easterly point of the great bend, which, from the high bluffs of red sand, I called "Sand Hill Bend." From this point one day's short march will bring us in a course little south of east to our camp of the ninth. We shortly came up to some cattle, a rare sight on a frontier so destitute of stock as this. They were herded by some Mexicans, who, on seeing the rough and fierce-looking party approach them, fled precipitately. One Indian would have made them do the same. At twelve we stopped to dine upon the river bank. We are now opposite to the island called "La Isla" and belonging to the United States. A Mexican visited our camp. He declared himself an American, told us we were thirty miles from El Paso, and that our best road would be to take the island which extended nearly to the town.

While we were eating, a heavy shower of rain came on, accompanied by thunder and lightning. At three we resumed the march, all inspirited with the prospect of soon beholding houses. The ford to the island was but a short mile from our camp. The water was not more than three feet at the most, and we readily crossed.[255] To eyes long since wearied of the rugged and desolate scenery of the Río Grande and the Pecos, nothing could be pleasanter than the prospect in this beautiful place. The road wound through cultivated fields of rich and well-irrigated soil, a few cattle and many flocks of goats appeared here and there, kept from the fields of wheat and corn, not by fences, but by herdsmen. Groups of Mexicans and *poblanos,* with their high sombreros, wide and flowing drawers, and leather breeches split at the sides and ornamented with numberless buttons, at work in the fields, completed the picturesque effect. Nor was the little town of San Elizario, though built of the usual unsightly adobe, a blemish

[255] Early in 1851, Bartlett described this island: "About ten miles below El Paso is an island some twenty miles in length; it is one of the most fertile spots in the whole valley, and has been cultivated since the first settlement of the country. On this island, which belongs to the United States, are the towns of Isleta, Socorro, and San Eleazario, chiefly inhabited by Mexicans. Of these San Eleazario is the larger, and was the old *Presidio* or military post on the frontier. It contains many respectable Spanish families, and some few Americans. It is now the seat of the county courts. The church and presidio are in a ruined state; they were, nevertheless, occupied by our troops for a couple of years after the Mexican war." Bartlett, *op. cit.,* I, 193-194.

in the picture. The houses were relieved by the green luxuriance of the fruit trees of the North – pears, peaches, apricots, plums grew in endless profusion. Vineyards, neatly pruned and walled about, appeared side by side with fresh and green wheat fields. As we passed through, the people crowded to the doors to see the rugged visitors but manifested little curiosity. They said they too were Americans. Marching about half a mile beyond the town, we came to camp in luxuriant grass after a day's travel of twenty-one miles.

I went up to the town in the evening. The people were polite and attentive. From them I purchased some eggs and milk, a luxury to us. Their price was four eggs for a picayune; small loaves of excellent wheat bread they sold at a picayune apiece. I was told that great scarcity prevailed in most parts of the Paso valley. No one would part with his live stock. Their cattle, said they, were all milch cows or steers for the plows and the carts, and their goats their sole dependence. I called on the *padre,* whom I found at his house – an obese, sensual-looking, heavy-eyed man with a dull, Father Gorenflot expression of countenance. Presuming on my former companionship with my old friends, the Jesuits of Georgetown, I addressed him in Latin, but for his comprehension it might as well have been Sanskrit. He gave me some information about the country and its resources, but his talk was generally confined to his own grievances. He complained the people didn't pay him sufficiently for the two evils of marrying and burying them, and seemed to regret that La Isla had passed into the hands of the Americans. Well he may!

THURSDAY, APRIL 12. We left our camp at half past eight. By ten o'clock, after traversing an extensive mesquite flat, we came to another little village, called

"Socorro." Though not so large as San Elizario, it resembles it in the cultivation around it and the appearance of the people. Farther on about three miles is a third hamlet, called "Isleta." Misunderstanding the directions given us at this place, we took the wrong road, which brought us to the Mexican crossing over the main, or western, branch of the river. To regain the proper path, we were forced to cross a low and muddy bottom almost overflowed from the Río Grande and the numerous irrigating canals. We at length came to dinner at half past one, having marched about twelve miles. Two Americans traveling down the island met us here, Lucas and Corfield by name. They report great scarcity of provisions at El Paso. Learning from them the place to cross the so-called Brazos, we saddled up at four, and by six the party was encamped near the Santa Fé road, opposite the town of El Paso at a place known as Ponce's Ranch.[256]

[256] The site of modern El Paso, Texas. About 1824, El Paso del Norte (the present Ciudad Juárez, Mexico) granted a tract of land along the left bank of the Río Grande, immediately opposite the town, to Juan María Ponce de León. The owner cultivated the soil and the place became known as Ponce's Ranch. After 1848 it became American territory, but El Paso del Norte remained a part of Mexico. In June, 1849, Benjamin Franklin Coons, of St. Louis, an enterprising Santa Fé and Chihuahua trader, purchased Ponce's Ranch, and in the following September leased the buildings and a part of the ground to the United States government for use as a military post. The troops remained there until 1851, when they were withdrawn to garrison the newly-established Fort Fillmore, New Mexico. Meanwhile, under date of November 24, 1849, Coons inserted an advertisement in the Santa Fé *New Mexican* in which he announced his intention of starting a commission and forwarding business "nearly opposite El Paso." He claimed that travelers to California and traders to Chihuahua would find his establishment "a great accomodation for the repairing of wagons, shoeing of animals, and every description of blacksmithing and carpentering necessary." He informed the public that he had built a fine tavern "supplied with the very best," and that he had completed a ferry boat to carry merchandise and passengers across the Río Grande. He concluded: "Liberal inducements will be offered for American families to emigrate and settle." A flourishing settlement soon came into existence there. At first it was known as Coons' Ranch or Coons'

We had thus reached the terminus of our outward-bound march. For fourteen days we had toiled among the wild mountains of the Apache. Many of our animals, one by one, had given out. Few will ever know, none may realize, that march of this little party, regarded by those behind as moving to certain destruction. No hour of no day but we listened for the yell of the Apache. At no time was any man's rifle out of his reach. The numerous towns we passed upon the river justified the forebodings of the people at Presidio, taught by a sad experience the nature of those who dwell in them. We owed it to their fortunate absence that we now rejoiced in the sight of houses, pleasant vineyards, and green wheat fields. Hence our faces would be turned homewards, and we said but little what might be in our way.

Learning here that Lieutenant Sacket, First dragoons, was stationed at Doña Ana, about seventy miles above El Paso, and finding the accounts of scarcity confirmed, I employed Captain Skillman, a gallant adventurer well known for many daring exploits in this country,

Hacienda, but beginning about 1851 it was called Franklin, which was Coons's middle name. During the middle fifties it was at times referred to as Smithville, after William T. Smith, who appears to have purchased the interests of Coons. Late in 1857 or early in 1858 it began to be called El Paso, Texas, but the name Franklin was occasionally used for a number of years thereafter. In 1859 a municipal government was organized, with a mayor and a board of aldermen. Coons to Polk, Mar. 28, 1847, Letters Received, MSS., O.R.D., A.G.O.; O'Bannon to Webb & Kingsbury, Oct. 14, 1857, Mar. 8, 1858, Webb MSS.; *Senate Ex. Docs.*, 31 cong., 1 sess., no. 64, p. 52; *New Mexican* (Santa Fé), Nov. 28 [?], 1849; *Santa Fé Republican*, Sept. 17, 1847, June 27, 1848; *Santa Fé Weekly Gazette*, Oct. 2, 1858; *Mesilla Times* (Mesilla, N.M.), Oct. 18, 1860; *Telegraph and Texas Register* (Houston), Mar. 5, 1852; *Western Texian*, Mar. 23, 1854; *Western Journal of Commerce* (Kansas City, Mo.), Sept. 4, 1858; *Daily Missouri Republican*, Nov. 12, Dec. 18, 1849, Apr. 28, 1858, June 8, Oct. 4, 1859; Bartlett, *op. cit.*, I, 192-193, II, 383; Carlysle Graham Raht, *The Romance of Davis Mountains and Big Bend Country* (El Paso, 1919), 119, 132.

Plaza and Church of El Paso del Norte about 1852

to ride an express to that place for the purpose of procuring subsistence for our return march. As I went down in the evening with Lieutenant Smith and Howard to cross to El Paso, the first person we met, passing in the dugout, was the celebrated Great Western. Never was anyone more delighted at the sight of American officers than she appeared. Her masculine arms lifted us one after another off our feet. Left sick at Chihuahua by Major Graham's command on its way from Saltillo to California, she had since passed through much privation, suffering, and hardship. She was now about moving to the American side to await the arrival of the army.

FRIDAY, APRIL 13. The town of Paso was, I believe, but little known to the Americans until the march of Doniphan's columns. It is situated at the upper extremity of a long and fertile valley of the Río Grande. Above it the rugged mountains of the pass shut in the river to a narrow bed. To the southwest and southeast stretches an extensive and broken range of mountains. Plainly visible is the great gap, or notch, through which passes the highway of the northern states of Mexico – the Chihuahua and Santa Fé road. The town, situated on this and probably destined to become a stopping place or depot on the great California trail, will in time become a place of resort and importance. At present its business is chiefly in the hands of a few American traders, some permanently residing, others mere passengers. Its settlement was commenced somewhere about 1680, that era so prophetic of the future condition of northern Mexico and still spoken of by the lower classes, when the once victorious Spaniards fled to the south before the revolted Indians. It is quite extensive, larger even than its population would warrant, variously estimated from five to ten thousand. But this is from the numerous orchards, gardens, and vineyards which are attached to many houses, and form not the least pleasing feature in the appearance of the town. Cultivation of wheat, corn, various kinds of vegetables, and of the grape is successfully pursued to an extent sufficient for the wants of the valley. A tolerable wine and a very pure, strong, fiery liquor, called "Pass whiskey," is made here. In their system of agriculture nothing is seen to be admired but the irrigation, and that could be vastly improved by the introduction of American industry and ingenuity. Their excellent grape, in the hands of experienced winemakers, might prove a lucrative product. Their wheat is unquestionably fine. Indolent and improvident, these people rarely raise more than sufficient for their own immediate wants. From this cause and the heavy drains produced by the march of the troops through the place, proceeds the present scarcity, now become painful to the poorer classes. It will probably last until the crop is gathered.

I would pretend to give with tolerable accuracy the latitude of this place, but our watches have long since been out of order. An approximation by Lieutenant Smith makes it about 31° 46′. It is certainly below the parallel of 32°. Disturnell's map,[257] I think, puts it above. Most Mexican maps place all towns north of their true position. Presidio del Norte is a notable instance, this place not being more than twelve miles north of San Antonio and not a great deal north of Chihuahua. Here I fell in with an old man named Dutton, one

[257] Disturnell's map was entitled: "Map of the United States as organized and defined by various acts of the congress of said republic, and constructed according to the best authorities. Revised edition. Published at New York, in 1847, by J. Disturnell." J. Fred Rippy, "The Boundary of New Mexico and the Gadsden Treaty," *Hispanic-American Historical Review*, IV, 715.

of the few remaining Rocky mountain trappers of the old school. He knows, as it is said, the Gila country very thoroughly, and I mention his name here as a memorandum. I find great difficulty in procuring even sufficient for my men to eat. The express has been dispatched to Lieutenant Sacket.

SATURDAY, APRIL 14. I have spent the whole of this day in buying subsistence. Rarely have I been so beset and harassed. I succeeded in procuring enough for one or two days. I learn that animals are equally difficult to obtain. My train is broken down; they can scarcely get grass, and I fear to be delayed here much longer than I anticipated.

SUNDAY, APRIL 15. Express returned this evening with a letter from Lieutenant Sacket stating that his supply train had not yet arrived at Doña Ana, but as soon as it came he would fill my requisition. Until then it is impossible for me to move.

MONDAY, APRIL 16. I have succeeded in purchasing a few animals from Americans hereabouts; the prices are high but are forced upon me. In payment I have given drafts upon Captain Brent, quartermaster at Santa Fé. Today I secured the services of the brave Captain Skillman[258] as a guide and member of my

[258] Henry Skillman, a native of Kentucky, migrated to Missouri some time before the Mexican war and engaged in the overland trade with Santa Fé and Chihuahua. Early in February, 1847, when Colonel Doniphan was marching from El Paso to Chihuahua, the traders traveling with the army were ordered to organize themselves into two companies of infantry; Skillman was elected captain of company B. He also acted as a scout several days before the Battle of Sacramento, February 28, 1847, besides participating in that conflict. Returning to Santa Fé, he was soon employed as interpreter and guide for Lieutenant-colonel Lane's detachment of troops ordered to El Paso. On October 27, 1847, when the command reached Fray Cristóbal, Skillman was chosen interpreter for a scouting party of twenty-two men, commanded by Sergeant Smith, which was instructed to march ahead of the detachment, enter El Paso if possible, and take Ex-Governor Armijo

party. The hostile spirit of the Apache, our purpose to return to San Antonio passing directly through their range and where they now are, and the Indian war existing in New Mexico with these same tribes, all warn me to provide against Gómez. As mentioned before, I had left at Presidio many valuable papers and some necessary baggage, together with several fine animals belonging to the United States. These it is important I should have. Skillman has volunteered on the perilous duty of going for them. He will probably start tomorrow. Ethneye[?], Spencer, and Gifford have likewise volunteered to accompany him. They will endeavor to reach Presidio del Norte, procure there all that is required, and make the best of their way thence, to join me on the Pecos. It is an adventure of no little interest and hazard, and I look forward with great anxiety to its result.

Lieutenant Sacket[259] arrived this evening with our

and other prisoners. Early in November the small party boldly entered the town and captured Armijo, who, however, soon violated a parole and escaped. Once more Skillman returned to Santa Fé, where, in February, 1848, General Price selected him to command a party of fifteen scouts to accompany the army to Chihuahua. In 1851 he signed a contract with the postmaster general to establish an overland mail and stage line between San Antonio and Santa Fé. Despite occasional Indian attacks, he operated his stages fairly regularly until the outbreak of the Civil war, when he joined the southern forces. He was killed near Presidio del Norte on the night of April 13, 1864. *Missouri Reporter* (St. Louis), May 20, 1846; *Santa Fé Republican,* Nov. 27, 1847, Feb. 12, Mar. 18, Apr. 22, 1848; *San Antonio Ledger,* Oct. 30, 1851; *Daily Missouri Republican,* Jan. 5, 1852; Connelley, *Doniphan's Expedition,* 103, 398, 406; Shipman, *op. cit.,* 6, 8-9, 36, 199; Raht, *op. cit.,* 150-152; *Southwest Historical Series,* III, 332, 343, IV, 335, 340.

259 Delos Bennet Sacket, a native of New York, was graduated from the United States Military academy on July 1, 1845, when he was promoted in the army to brevet second lieutenant in the Second dragoons. He was stationed in Texas during 1845 and 1846, and served under Zachary Taylor in the early part of the Mexican war. On June 30, 1846, he was made second lieutenant, First dragoons, and on December 27, 1848, first lieutenant. He was stationed at Santa Fé in 1848 and 1849, and at Doña Ana in 1849 and 1850. During the latter year he returned to the United States Military acad-

supplies. He received from Smith, Howard, and myself that delighted welcome which officers meeting far from their homes always extend to each other, especially when, as now, all four[260] had been companions and classmates at West Point. I busied myself this evening in writing reports for General Worth to be intrusted to Skillman. He has orders in case he does not fall in with us, should he succeed in reaching the Pecos, to make the best of his way to San Antonio. At ten o'clock at night I mounted and rode up to the Pass, which position I proposed to examine in the morning of tomorrow.

TUESDAY, APRIL 17. I arrived at the Paso by the Santa Fé road at twelve last night. The distance is some eight miles from the town of Paso. It is situated nearly opposite a sharp pointed peak, which I have called "Mount Frontera," on the opposite side of the river. The mountains here close onto the Río Grande on both sides; and from this point, now the residence of Colonel White,[261] the channel is rocky and rapid. Here is a suitable ford; a branch of the great road leaves the left bank of the river by it and continues through El Paso to Chihuahua. The ford opposite the town of Paso being not so good, this one is generally preferred by

emy, where he was assistant instructor of cavalry tactics until 1855. He died on March 8, 1885. Cullum, *Biographical Register,* II, 131-132, III, 171; Heitman, *Historical Register,* I, 856; *Santa Fé Republican,* Sept. 12, 1848.

260 Sacket, Smith, and Whiting were classmates at the military academy, but Howard was not a graduate of that institution.

261 T. F. White issued a circular, dated Frontera, August 7, 1848, which announced his removal to that point: "The Subscriber having established a House at the town of Frontera, opposite El Passo, on the American side of the Río del Norte, for the transaction of a General Commission and Forwarding business, offers his services to his friends and the Public. He also has on hand a well assorted Stock of merchandise, consisting of Lienzos, Manta, Prints, Hardware, Queensware, Groceries. . . Traders passing to and from Chihuahua, will find at his establishment, Corn, Provisions, and all other articles usually required by a Train of Wagons." *Santa Fé Republican,* Aug. 8, 1848.

traders. I find the position suitable for defense and eligible as a military post, as commanding the great highway [at] the ford [of] both branches of the road. It is, I think, above the boundary line and will probably be a point upon the California trail. These considerations have induced me to recommend it as a site for the encampment and permanent location of the troops destined for Paso. After an examination of the ground, known hereabouts as Frontera, I returned to Ponce's Ranch and, having completed preparations, sent off Skillman and his party. Lieutenant Sacket left for his post this evening.

WEDNESDAY, APRIL 18. This day has been spent in preparations for our departure tomorrow. Two of my men, Conley and Johnson, applied for discharge. As I had increased my party, and moreover had with me the express rider Love, charged with dispatches for San Antonio and whom General Worth directed me to bring with me on my return, I consented and paid them off.

THURSDAY, APRIL 19. This morning we turned our faces homewards. Leaving Ponce's Ranch at eight, we cut off some of our upward march by striking a course through the river bottom direct to the ford. The weather has commenced to be very warm, and during the march it will be necessary to spare our animals in the heat of the day. Crossing the Brazos, by 12 M. we had marched thirteen miles, and we stopped to dine upon one of the irrigating canals which intersect the island. I noticed the lightness of the soil and the ease with which even the rude agriculture of the Mexicans produces crops. American plows substituted for their sharp sticks, and one horse for two or three yoke of oxen, would do wonders. About half a mile above Ponce's Ranch the

Mexicans have made a rude dam by piling stones in the water; and by this an irrigating canal is watered, and supplies moisture to the whole Mexican side for a long distance and drinking water to the town itself. A well-built American structure at that point would amply irrigate the whole of the American side and greatly improve the beautiful valley below.

After dinner I mounted my horse and rode in advance of the train to make some commissary purchases and to endeavor to obtain some information about the Pecos country. I arrived at San Elizario about 5 P.M. The alcalde brought several Mexicans professing to be acquainted with that region. Their accounts, however, were generally confused. There are several trails to the Pecos; most of them, however, strike towards the Salinas, or Salt ponds,[262] whence much of the salt consumed in Chihuahua is derived, and their course is north of east. I received such a description of the country as would enable us to travel that way, but the distance to San Antonio would be greatly increased; and I have noticed that the farther north one goes in that region, the less wood and permanent water is found. Gómez certainly came direct from the Río Grande with a large *caballada*. We know the point he left the river; and as its direction from El Paso to that place is not much off our course, I shall follow the advice of Mr. Howard, who proposes to take Gómez's trail to the Sierra Diablo and thence strike for the Las Moras hill.

FRIDAY, APRIL 20. It was necessary to remain at San Elizario all day to await Lieutenant Smith and Howard, who had remained in El Paso in order to bring on some mules lately purchased and some horses which

[262] In the northeastern part of the present Hudspeth county.

were left to be shod. Early in the morning a heavy shower of rain came on, and I moved camp to the old *presidio* of the town, a ruinous structure built in the form of a square and formerly used as barracks for the Spanish troops. The alcalde, Santos Lucero by name, has been very polite, and attentive to the wants of the command. I obtained from him the Mexican names of the mountains in the vicinity of Paso. The large rampart-looking mount which stands on the American side over against the town is known as the Sierra Colorada. Beyond it and farther to the northeast is the Soledad, a lone peak and a notable landmark. Bearing N. 30° E. and apparently rising from the plains, appears the Sierra Alta.[263] Blue in the distance and a little to the south of it is the Hueco, or Hollow, Mount.[264] Looking to the southeast, we may see the symmetrical shape of the Sierra Blanca,[265] and beyond it the fantastic peaks of the Cola del Águila.[266]

I derived from him some interesting particulars relative to the island and its inhabitants. The first town which the traveler meets on La Isla in his way from El Paso is called "Isleta," and is an ancient pueblo (as the settlements of the remnants of the old Indian tribes long since reduced by the Spaniards are called). There is another opposite this town on the Mexican side. The inhabitants of the two speak different dialects. Their costume differs somewhat from the Mexicans. They wear the same wide, flowing drawers, but confine them from the knee down with buskins and moccasins. Their

263 Now called Cerro Alto, in the northwestern corner of the present Hudspeth county.

264 Now called Hueco mountains, along the western boundary of the present Hudspeth county.

265 Near the present Lasca, Hudspeth county.

266 Now called Eagle mountain, southwest of the present Mica, Hudspeth county.

women also wear the buskin. Still speaking their old language, still holding many old customs, time has not diminished their fierce animosity to the Spanish race. Their religion is a crude mixture of savage rites and Catholic ceremonies. All retain the tradition that one day the great Aztec emperor will reappear, and reinstate the suffering descendants of that people to their ancient power and glory. Patient farmers and herdsmen as they are, the general dread with which the ruthless Apache inspires the Mexicans does not extend to them. They meet him with his own weapons and are rarely worsted.

The town of San Elizario may contain about a thousand inhabitants, a frugal and peaceable race. There is far greater appearance of plenty and comfort here than in El Paso. It is possible that at certain seasons of the year La Isla may be unhealthy on account of its low grounds, subject to overflow from the river; yet it is a valuable acquisition; and I have seen no Mexican towns where the people appear as industrious and their little farms as thriving as they do here.

SATURDAY, APRIL 21. We left the town this morning, the day bright and clear. Taking a road which led us to a crossing lower down than the one we had used before, we were not long in reaching the Brazos. From the ford we entered a fine grove of lofty *álamos.* Here Howard stopped to make a location. We proceeded at a brisk walk and by quarter to eleven reached the Sand Hill Bend. Near here is an arroyo, at this point dry. But looking off to the left we could see cottonwoods upon it, far into the hills, an almost unfailing sign of water. Our course was now directed upon a point a little to the left of the southern Soledad; by this we cut off much of the distance lost in our upward march.

Passing the sand hills, so laborious for the animals, we entered the fine grazing bottom, in which we continued until twenty minutes of three, when, upon reaching a bend of the river, we stopped to dine. We found this place a pleasant camp; it is at the edge of a cottonwood grove, bounded by a steep sand bluff, doubtless formerly a bank of the old river bed. It is thickly grown with underbrush and contains very good and clear water. Leaving this spot at half past five, our course for two miles lay directly east and bearing upon the Sierra Blanca – this in order to avoid a tract of thick chaparral and cottonwood, wherein progress is hindered by old beds of the river now overgrown, and by much fallen timber. It then became more southerly, and we finally entered an extensive and beautiful tract covered with green, luxuriant grass and adorned with trees of great size in graceful groups and clusters. There is no unsightly dead wood to mar the scene, and I know of no better place for the encampment of the troops on their march. We came to camp upon the river at this place after a day's march of twenty-four miles.

SUNDAY, APRIL 22. We started on an easterly course this morning, knowing it would shortly intersect our old trail upon which better traveling would be found. Low hillocks of sand abound hereabouts, reminding me much of those produced by the winds upon the Florida coast. The Río Grande valley, too, for some distance is very sterile, producing but little grass, and that of poor quality. A march of nine miles brought us opposite our former camp of the ninth. I rode down there, for I recollected having left my spurs under the tree when I spread my blanket, and spurs are somewhat essential to the man who rides a mule. I was fortunate enough to find them, together with some tobacco which

Smith had forgotten at the same place. It, too, is an article indispensable to the frontiersman. Give him coffee and tobacco, and he will endure any privation, suffer any hardship, but let him be without these two necessaries of the woods, and he becomes irresolute and murmuring. After a hard day's march I, for one, can imagine few luxuries more pleasant or more tempting than a bowl of strong coffee, hard by a bright camp fire and followed by a pipe of good Cavendish flavored with a little kinnikinnick.

We still moved on in the same sandy soil and through dead forests, once green when the shifting river ran through them but now perished for lack of moisture. The day was intensely warm, and at length, about twelve, upon finding a small patch of the common sedge grass of this region, which was quite green, we stopped to dine. The river banks are not steep at this point, but are low, flat shores covered with a dense growth of willow switches; and the stream breaks, forming many small and barren islands. The Sierra Blanca glistens today in the sunlight and, towering above the surrounding hills, is a notable landmark. This afternoon a wild pack mule, which carried the provisions of Allen's mess, stampeded, spilled the pack, and smashed the saddle. This accident delayed us half an hour. With the readiness of a man who has lived for nine years between Fort Leavenworth and Chihuahua, Allen soon contrived to arrange his packs, and we proceeded, reaching, in a little while, the cut-off which had so hindered our march before. Although we struck it much higher up, it was still impassable, and we were forced to head it, moving for that purpose round by the high red bluffs which once formed the river banks. We met several deep washes in our way, which we were likewise forced to head. At length, however, we found clear water and excellent grass in an old cut-off lying between the Sierra Blanca and the high point of the Soledad notch, and upon this [we] encamped. Our day's march has been but twenty miles, owing to the excessively heavy traveling.

MONDAY, [APRIL 23]. No great dependence is to be placed on our timepieces. Mine has long been out of order, and Smith's presents the singular phenomenon of going too fast for local time when we are traveling east and too slow when we are going west. This has long deprived us of our customary approximation to the longitude. This morning we passed Pelican pond, now perfectly dry, and here we once more saw many of the birds which gave it its name. Proceeding on our old trail, we crossed the extensive plain of grass which lies between the cottonwoods and the hills. The day has been very beautiful and the ground excellent, but Allen's refractory mules have twice delayed us. When we had marched about ten or eleven miles, we reached a point on the river opposite to the pass of the Eagle mountain and here we halted to dine. While occupied in preparing our meal, some fire carelessly carried from one mess to another caught the grass, and the wind being high, we had a furious fight with it. Several of us got our hair and beards scorched, but at length with water and blankets we put it out. These accidents are very dangerous, both from the alarm they always give (by the smoke) to Indians and the risk to packs, arms, and animals.

We set out this afternoon, moving up a dry arroyo lying between two spurs from the mountains. This would apparently lead us to the south point of the Eagle mountain, where, from the difference of formation between it and the more southward range, we were led to believe a narrow pass might exist. It soon became evident that we had mistaken the canyon, and we were forced, in order to get into the right one, to cross a very steep, high, and rough ridge. Here was the home of many beautiful varieties of the cactus family. Most of them being in flower at this time, my attention, always alive to such things, was strongly attracted, and in the hope of one day adorning the gardens of my friends, I noted such peculiarities of the plants and the place as might enable me to find either. I regret being unable to bring one specimen with me, as it appeared both in flower and leaf a solitary instance of beauty, which, many varieties of the family as we had seen and were constantly meeting, might be found here alone. The pass is the bed of a creek now dry and affords the means of making a tolerable road through these rough hills. It is not very long, and half an hour's march brought us to a broad and ascending plain where the traveling is excellent. Upon reaching its highest point, we could see directly in front of us the splendid peaks of Mount Chase, lit up by the setting sun. Northward appeared the symmetrical heights of the Sierra Blanca, and far away to the northeast, valleys and mountains which we had never seen but promised ourselves one day to explore. The wind came up with the twilight, chill and damp, and we halted at length without water, sheltered by a round-top knob hard by. I should think that tonight we are about ten miles from the river.

TUESDAY, APRIL 24. Upon rising in the morning, the word "to saddle" was given early, as being without water, we had no breakfast to cook. As we wound through the chaparral of the valley, Mount Chase lay on our left, easily recognized in his cloudy grandeur by the dark crowns of basalt which capped the knobs at his base. The traveling was very good over level, firm sand, free from stones. The creek, now dry, which is found in this valley is lined with hackberry and mesquite; their green foliage deceived us into the idea that we were near water, of which, from the heat of the day and our lack of it last night, both men and animals stood in great need. We reached the Río Grande at half past three after a march of about twenty-five miles, and halted about a mile and a half below our camp of the fifth and sixth ultimo, whence Lieutenant Smith and Howard had gone out to explore a pass. That through which we had just come, although with probably thirty-five miles distance between watering places, we consider as fortunately found, as it enabled us to avoid the steep and rough hills which so much impeded our upward march. From it I think a direct road may be made to the Pass which will pass above Mount Chase and thence above the Sierra Diablo to the Iron[?] hill. If this be the case, there will be a great saving in distance and labor.

WEDNESDAY, APRIL 25. The pass discovered by Howard lies between the southern extremity of Mount Chase and the adjacent hills. It is the bed of a creek, where we found pleasant water and sufficient grass for our animals. Our path followed the little brook, which finds its way between great walls of sandstone and breccia. The traveling is very rough, and much preparation will be required here to make even a tolerable road. The chief obstacles are: fragments of rock which, while they offer no trouble to horsemen, would interfere with wagons; a gravelly or pebbly ground, very severe upon the feet of the animals; [and] several points where shelving and scooping are required. But if the Río Grande is struck as low down as this, there is nothing else but to pass this way, as the Notch hills are with common means impracticable.

From our noon halt the trail continued between precipices of sandstone and breccia until it at length came out into a narrow valley lying between table ridges on the eastern side of Mount Chase. As we reach this, we find the spurs, or hills, on our right crowned with dark gray sandstone in bluffs, while to the left are seen mounds of red clay and gravel. We passed a large bed of green sand hereabouts in the arroyo, and the bluffs of sandstone soon terminated, giving place to banks of yellow, argillaceous earth. Farther on, the sides of the tables are laid bare, showing the same earth overlaid by a stratum of cemented gravel or drift, detached fragments of which are found rolled down to the valley in heavy masses. I have named some hills off to the eastward, crowned with dark-colored rock, "Organ hills," and farther towards the north the "Red pyramids," three bright red knobs notably marking the country. In the ravine here we found water in holes and some Apache camps. Far off to the north and east I saw a dark mountain, probably the Sierra Prieta,[267] and another east of it similar in appearance to the Sierra Blanca. This may be a part of Mount Guadalupe.[268] It was late in the evening when we reached our camp at the Notch. The traveling had been heavy and wearisome, the gravel under foot in the arroyo being loose and yielding. Here, as when marching up the river, we fell in with Indian cattle, and as one of the

267 In the eastern part of the present Hudspeth county.

268 The Guadalupe mountains are in the northwestern part of the present Culberson county.

people shot a cow, we were regaled round our camp fires with beefsteaks and marrowbones. We have made about twenty-five miles today.

THURSDAY, APRIL 26. We were once more among the Apache towns. A march of seven or eight miles brought us to Gómez's trail. In the beautiful valley at this point I determined to remain the rest of the day to recruit our weary animals. This locality may be known on the north and northeast by numerous small hills of red earth, some of which, two in particular, have been washed along their sides into columns, presenting a notable appearance. The cottonwood grows in fine groves with the rapid river winding among them; each pleasant spot has been chosen as a site for Apache lodges. We encamped west of the Red Column; tomorrow we leave the Río Grande. This afternoon a heavy shower appeared to the eastward, and shortly afterward the hills in that direction were spanned by a superb and complete double bow. The whole scene was of remarkable beauty. There were dark and somber clouds in the south and east, piled in threatening masses but relieved by the brilliant colors of the arch; the hills below were lit up by the setting sun. The southern mountains frowning grimly, the green clothing of the river in smiling contrast, and the picturesque camp fires with athletic forms stretched about them in every variety of attitude and grouping, completed the pleasing picture.

FRIDAY, APRIL 27. Following a great number of lately traveled trails, we were led to an opening of the hills, a narrow gate just above the columns, between two white bluffs over- and underlaid with red clay and occasional green sand. Above all appeared the conglomerate in heavy masses and strongly cemented.

This formation continued for some distance. Quantities of red sandstone (the new) appeared along the bottom of the ravine but not *in situ*. The whole aspect of the hills, as we entered from the river, showed that some great convulsion, in which water was the agent, had forced a passage. The pioneers will find hard work here, particularly at a hill about four miles from the river and at a rock gap still nearer. We shortly entered a large basin. Parallel ridges of red sandstone (dip 45°; strike runs north and south) bounded the passage to the north. To the southeast is a range of lofty table hills marked by a single peak resembling a crown. We have called them "Crown hills." These make the southern limit of the valley, which is distinguished by patches of whitish earth. It is barren and desolate. A little creek, which cannot be seen until the traveler is upon it, winds its way, destitute of trees or bushes, through its lowest parts. Here we found plenty of water and sufficient grazing for our train. Scarcely any wood, however, is to be found in this place. It is a residence of the Apache, whose lodges are seen here in great numbers especially about the "Needle," a singular rock coming sharp up to a point and apparently a column of basalt.

We crossed the winding ridge of this valley at two this afternoon and upon reaching its summit, to our great joy, the Sierra Diablo unexpectedly broke upon our view, distant about thirty miles from us with a level prairie extending to its base. One of the peaks visible, most of us declared [it] to be the place where we met Gómez. This prairie is part of a very extensive valley lying between the Río Grande range and the sierras, and extending from the Cibolo below to a high range of mountains to the northward, probably the

Guadalupe. Its appearance in that direction confirms the idea of a pass towards the Sierra Blanca. A sharp peak off to our left, belonging to the spurs of Mount Diablo and surrounded by a group of cones, makes a fine landmark. We called it the "Sphinx and Pyramids." After we had crossed the prairie, we halted for an hour upon the side of a hill where we found good grass, in order to rest and graze our train. In the bright and beautiful moonlight we pushed on, expecting to make Gómez's camp this night. But mistaken in the distance, we were forced to encamp without water when the moon went down. Twenty-five miles.

SATURDAY, APRIL 28. Instead of proceeding directly to the eastward as we should have done (as this would have brought us above the Sierra Diablo and by the Perdido on a direct route for the Pecos), we made the mistake of plunging directly into the hills. We were suffering for water and supposed we would thus sooner strike Gómez's camp, where there are springs. All of these hills are covered with dark basaltic rocks. After a very thirsty and weary march this morning, it was with great delight that we hailed the discovery by Lieutenant Smith of springs of cool and delicious water far up in a ravine, among huge rocks and overhung by large Spanish oaks. This grove is surrounded by frowning cliffs of the dark rock which everywhere tells its tale of fire. Under the shade of spreading trees, the thick foliage of which made a perfect screen, we rested from a troubled march. We called the spot the "Spanish Oaks" and left it in the afternoon with regret. With natural reluctance to go back upon our trail, we found ourselves involved in a labyrinth of inaccessible hills, and, following a faint trail, endeavored to extricate ourselves through the ravine by which it passed.

This was soon found impracticable; and retracing our steps for a mile, we shortly fell in with another path leading in a more southerly direction. This took us over a very high and rough hill into a part of the great western valley. In the high range on our left were two ravines thickly clothed with Spanish oaks. Judging from their appearance that water was hard by, we entered one of them. In it an abundance was found, and we encamped amid thick trees and under huge beetling cliffs.

SUNDAY, [APRIL] 29. There were several old trails leading up this glen. Following them, we were shortly brought to a very steep elevation. An old and much worn path went up the side by zigzags; direct ascent was impossible. The climbing was very severe, and as we neared the top after many halts, the mules could only advance a few paces at a time. Arrived at the summit, while resting our strained and weary beasts, we looked out upon the magnificent view which was spread before us. It opened through the gorge of the ravine whence we had just climbed, and we caught a sight, far as the eye could reach, of the great yellow level of the western valley, and beyond of the blue mountains of the Río Grande in clear and beautiful outline. This picture, seen between two lofty walls of dark volcanic rocks, seemed like a great painting set in a giant frame. Far, far beneath our feet at a fearful depth lay the dark glen with its Spanish oaks and glittering water, seen here and there and bounded by the rugged grandeur of the surrounding cliffs. Turning around, we beheld the stupendous pile of rocks so singular in form and of which the similarity to that which towers over the Apache valley had led us here. Loudly discussing our position, we moved on through a beautiful valley bountifully timbered with the mountain pines and with oaks of many varieties. A short march convinced [us] that we were in a region entirely new to us. The growth of trees, the plants, all bespoke a more northerly or colder clime than belongs to the locality where we had met the Apache. We found that we were upon one of those great tables of the Diablo mountains, which are so common in Mexico. From this again rise high hills and lofty peaks. The trail is made up of pleasant dales and glens, covered with green grass and watered by cool springs which are found in the ravines between the heights.

We came now to a well-worn trail running towards the north. A branch was discovered by which we could follow our course. The grass freshly turned and now springing up green and the signs on the path showed that at no distant time the Apache had passed this way. While dinner was being prepared at a fine spring of water, I climbed a high hill to try and make out the country. All seemed strange. The so much talked-of peak which we passed this morning rears its rocky head in solitary splendor from the enchanting valley of pines. Its gray cliffs resemble the turrets of a vast structure. I have called it "Cathedral." Though very mountainous, the land is well timbered with oak and pine and, as we proceeded, presented a succession of pretty views. The trail wound from hill to valley, through glens and groves in endless variety, until we halted for the night upon the bank of a pretty creek.

APRIL 30. We followed the little brook this morning, and before long found it making a sharp bend toward the north. Here it appeared to me best to leave it and take our southerly course in the direction of some distant mountains which had been discovered yesterday to the southeast from the top of a hill; but influenced by more experienced judgment, we kept to the creek, now a running stream. There were traces of Indians having passed at some distant time, but it soon became so rocky and the mountains closed in upon us in such stupendous bluffs of trap, basalt, and syenitic granite, etc., that we were fain to halt. Dick and I climbed to the top of a high peak with great labor. Arrived at the summit, what a rugged poem was spread out before us! To the north and east the mountains appeared interminable, but southward and southeast was open country and some blue hills which had a familiar look. We made up our mind to retrace our steps and try and get out in that direction, according to my opinion of the morning. We passed back then, through this terrible canyon, which, as we had stumbled upon a skull in it, the people called "Deadman's pass," affirming that but one man had ever got into it before and he, *ecce signum,* had never got out. We arrived by 4 P.M. at the bend of the creek. Allen's pack mule had got separated from the train this morning in some intricate grove and he, together with Love and the Cherokee Rodgers, had started off to hunt for it. They joined us here, successful but with broken-down animals. Leaving the encampment here, Dick and I started out to try and find a pass from this terrible prison. Fortunately, after some hours' search and severe climbing, we were successful, and upon our return the spirits of all rose with the intelligence.

TUESDAY, MAY 1. Nine of our mules strayed off last night. Francisco the old muleteer and Poli were sent after them while breakfast was being prepared. They were successful in their errand. We took our way out of this strange place by the pass which had been reconnoitered yesterday. We experienced no difficulty in getting to the other side of the mountains which shut in the Deadman's pass, and we found ourselves on a similar elevation to that near Cathedral peak. After a little consultation it was decided to follow a well-worn trail of the Apache leading in a southerly direction. This shortly brought the party to a steep and perilous descent like that mentioned on the twenty-ninth. Far down below us we saw the green trees and sparkling water of a pretty creek. Our mules, sure-footed as goats, managed the rugged path well. Upon the creek an ever varying succession of beautiful landscapes occurred. Oak, hackberry, willow, and wild cherry made pleasant groves; the yellow grass of the hills contrasted well with the dark red crowns of volcanic rocks.

Gradually the appearance of the country became familiar. It was suggested that we were upon the headwaters of the Limpia. Large and recently made trails led down the valley, telling us that great bands of Apache had passed within a few days. These we followed with the oft expressed hope that we might be fortunate enough to see Gómez. We were determined to hang him. At first the bluffs on the right and left looked natural; then appeared the tall cottonwood groves, the first we had seen since we left the Río Grande. Doubts were at length removed by our coming upon the "Painted Trees." But how changed from the fresh, green, quiet spot we had left the evening of our gloomy and anxious march! To be sure, it was as still, but the grass had been trampled by the hoofs of hundreds of horses. More than two hundred lodges had been placed around our camp fires. Their frames met the eye in every direction. The whole force of

Gómez's bands had gathered here the morning after we left, called in by the signal smokes and beacon fires which then sprang on every hill. It was with mixed feelings of wonder at our escape, and a burning desire for vengeance and a hope that before we left these mountains we might fall in with Gómez, that we looked at this scene. The collection of Comanche paintings had received some rich additions of Apache designs. Several rudely done in charcoal represented Indians on horseback at the pleasant pastime of lancing ourselves on mules, and one which roughly portrayed our running away roused the ire of some of my Texans. Entering now the Wild Rose pass, we soon halted for the night about a mile below the Painted Camp.

WEDNESDAY, MAY 2. We are now satisfied as to the practicability of a road from the Pecos to the Presidio del Norte and the Paso, and [are] greatly encouraged thereby. To be sure, considerable labor will be necessary here and there, but we have found the great desideratum – water; and future and better-provided parties in reconnoitering will greatly diminish the amount of labor now recommended. I wish I had either time or means to examine immediately from the Pecos, starting at a point somewhat above where we left it, say the Great Comanche crossing, and passing above the Sierra Diablo and Mount Chase, reaching the Río Grande by Eagle pass. I am strongly of opinion that this is practicable, and know that it will much shorten distance and diminish labor. I make this memorandum here to recommend, on our return, an advance by it from the train for this purpose. We traveled down the Limpia today upon the trails made by the big war parties of the Indians. It is a beautiful little brook, and its waters flow clear and cool over its pebbly bed. Conjecture was set on foot this morning by our discovering in the pass the trail of a party of American-shod animals *en route* to Presidio. It had been made but two or three days. The tracks looked as if made by public-shod horses, and many of us were inclined to think that the general, weary of our long absence, had sent out another party. Our noon halt was made about a mile below our camp of March 19. The wild pea vine, which grows luxuriantly in the pass, made a refreshing food for our animals.

This afternoon we passed one of the camps of the party mentioned above. The Delaware, carefully examining it with the curious and minute observation of his race, reported six fires of white men and one of Delaware Indians. Our march was briskly continued until we were struck from the north by a terrible storm of rain and hail accompanied by lightning. Its fury forced us to seek shelter by the willows and cottonwoods which grew here and there upon the creek. The hail was very large and hurt severely, and the rain came down with pitiless violence, wetting everything thoroughly. Kindling a fire with great difficulty during a short lull of the storm, we cooked our supper. The blaze and the hot coffee were very grateful to the chilled and tired party, and we soon wrapped ourselves in our wet blankets and lay down to sleep as best we might through one of the most uncomfortable nights I have ever spent. The rain continued to beat on us until nearly morning. We lay near the lone mountain which stands before the Wild Rose pass, concealing it from view in the plains and giving two entrances, one on either side of it. On our outward march we came in by the northern one from the Perdido. We got out by the other.

TUESDAY, MAY 3. After carefully examining and

recharging our arms this morning, we moved down the valley, pursuing an east course. The sun came out very bright and warm about nine o'clock, and I ordered a halt to dry the saddle blankets of the train. This is very essential when marching in warm weather, nothing making a mule's back sore sooner than a wet pad in a hot sun. Upon resuming our march, we found on all sides evidences that the violence of the preceding day's storm had been much greater towards the east. The grass was cut to pieces, and the leaves, bark, and branches of the scattered chaparral entirely stripped. The ground too was soft and mushy, and our mules, in passing several valleys, bogged heavily. At 4 P.M. we halted upon quite a pond of water, most of it [having] gathered during the late storm. Here we were astonished at the sight of a large mass of ice about two feet thick composed entirely of hailstones. These had been washed down from the neighboring slopes and frozen together, and although they had lain all day in the sun, they were still very large. I measured their circumference and marked it on the margin of the page. It was very fortunate we came no farther last night, for we could hereabouts have found nothing strong enough to have secured our mules during such a storm as this has been.

FRIDAY, MAY 4. We found ourselves today, after a march of fifteen miles, too far to the southward and below the Awache spring. The cause of this error was the substitution in our course of the bearing of Apache peak for that of Mount Cholula, as I have called the peak on the north of the Wild Rose pass. The country traversed is open, generally sterile, and destitute of timber, presenting a tedious succession of low ridges with intervening dales. We made our dinner camp at a very large water hole from which the Iron hill bears N. 40° E. A dark cloud hung over us all the time we lay here, and, though the surrounding country was bright and dry, we were wet through by a heavy shower. This afternoon Poli and I had an exciting chase after a drove of wild hogs. We singled out the fattest; every now and then he would stop, turn, and gnash his tusks at bay. We soon secured him, and his hams and ribs were taken along to make our supper. At six we camped at the Awache spring.

Weary after our long march of twenty-eight miles, we sat round our camp fires, eating our meal of roasted ribs of the wild hog. We had appetite, and with that, spite of a wild, strong flavor, the supper was very savory; but it was rudely interrupted. We had come late to camp and the night was very dark. We were startled by something falling near us as heavily as if a stone had been violently thrown. Another and another followed. Smith shouted, "It is hail"; and we dropped our supper and rushed to our saddles. An awful storm came suddenly upon [us], accompanied by such hail as put us in fear of our lives; for, on the bleak plain which surrounds the spring, there are no trees or shelter of any kind. Holding our saddles over our heads for protection, we sat shivering until the hailstones ceased to fall. The rain continued all night with great fury. By this time, however, this party care but little for the severest exposure incident to these climates, and I believe we all slept as soundly as if under a roof. The three tents which we took with us from San Antonio have been long, long since cut up to make saddle pads, and when we had them it was generally voted less of a bore to lay in the rain than to pitch them.

SATURDAY, MAY 5. The morning was rainy. Everything had been wetted. We scattered through the chaparral and gathered wood, here so scarce – finding, with search, enough to build large fires. At these we dried our blankets and at length set out, following the old trail of Connelly's wagons. This took us below the Iron hill. The traveling proved very good, and after ascending the divide beyond the Altar, a hill a short distance east of the Awache, we entered a valley bounded by table hills. The white, lime-capped bluffs of the Pecos began to appear. We stopped to dine hard by some excellent grass, distant some five hundred yards from a large water hole. The general aspect of the part traversed this morning is very sterile, shrubs and grass growing only in scattered clumps. This afternoon, after passing a small thicket of hackberry, we came suddenly upon a clear and beautiful spring gushing from the limestone bluff on the north side of this valley. The grass around, which had been burned off when we were marching up the Pecos, had grown again in great luxuriance, and here we encamped. This is the place at which the Lipan tribe was encamped at that time, and called by old Capote the "Clear Water." They have been here very lately, as appears from the signs.

SUNDAY, MAY 6. We traveled this morning down the right bank of the creek which takes its rise at our camping place, the Escondido spring. Fresh horse tracks were soon discovered before us, crossing and recrossing the valley. Some thought them signs of a mustang or loose horse, but Poli, who followed for some distance, declared that the animal had a rider – he had seen no grass cropped along the trail. Shortly afterward, while approaching the Table hill, which stands by itself in the valley, I discovered several Indians riding at full speed. In a few minutes, more were discovered advancing toward us. The train was halted, mules tied, and preparations made to fight. Howard rode on to meet them, followed by Lieutenant Smith. Having rapidly completed my arrangements, I started to support them. The gestures of the savages were very hostile. The cold demeanor and contemptuous language of our friend Howard quelled the dogs very quickly. Drawing his revolver, as I rode up he remarked to one who appeared very fierce that he would listen to no such language, and if he uttered another word of war he would kill him there. Upon this they declared they only wished to talk and proposed going up to my men. This I would not permit. We found them to be Lipan. There were not more than thirty of them altogether, under an old chief called Capote, who, upon being made to understand (as he was, very decidedly) that upon any bad behavior on the part of his people we would rub him and his band out, became very humble. They begged hard for tobacco and other presents; but we would give them nothing, none of us being very well disposed towards Indians, and many of my men desirous of paying the Lipan for the treachery of the Apache. We then moved on and the Indians cleared out. The creek, owing to the late rains, was at this time running all the way to the Pecos. The spring is situated about eighteen miles from the river, which we reached early in the evening. During the night no one slept, since the mosquitoes were worse than I had ever seen them even on the lower Mississippi. The mules could not graze, and we sat by our fires and smoked, talked, and fought them until a breeze relieved us near morning.

MAY 7. We were now once more upon our old trail and briskly marching down the right bank of the Pecos.

The desolate aspect of its valley we found somewhat improved by the spring vegetation. The stunted mesquite had put out its leaves; the cones which fringe the river banks were green, the cacti were in flower, and thus something of the barren and tedious monotony was removed. During our march this morning the mosquitoes and gnats were intolerable. They kept our hands and pipes in active service. At ten o'clock we reached the bluff near which we had halted on our outward march. Here we stopped to rest. The river at this point takes a sudden bend something north of east, and by passing behind the bluffs which limit the valley, we are enabled to strike it again in its southerly course. This cut-off makes a good road of level and pleasant traveling. After a brisk march from our dinner camp, we reached the river bottom at half past 3 P.M., and here a severe storm of hail and rain fell upon us. The rain was bad enough, for it wet us all thoroughly; and the hail, which fell very thick and of the size of a musket ball, was no pleasant accompaniment. Halting under some hackberries, we waited until the violence of the shower had passed, and moving on a few miles farther, encamped on the river bank after a march of twenty-four miles.

MAY 8. We started early this morning. Moving on the several trails which pass up the valley, we saw no signs of the march of Skillman and his party, about whom we had become anxious. By 9 A.M. we reached the camp where we met the Lipan. The trees hard by and the little thickets were so green and flourishing that the place looked strange in its new dress. From this point to Live Oak grove even the Pecos looks well, and the landscape has something of beauty in it. By midday we reached our old crossing, called "Solomon's ford." The encampment was placed upon the high bluff which overlooks the river, at a spot evidently a favorite resting place of the Comanche. I strolled down to examine the trails leading to the crossing. No sign of any kind appeared, to show that anyone had been here since last March. Our little bridge has been washed away by a slight rising of the stream, but otherwise all was as when we left. It was at this place that I had agreed to leave a note for Skillman in case I should reach it first, and push on.

Dick, Allen, and myself started out this afternoon in different directions in search of practicable passes down the river. From what we had suffered between the San Sabá and the Pecos, it had been deemed best to make as much southing as possible on the latter stream. Bearing a little west of south and entering an extensive ravine, I fell upon the great Indian warpath, the continuation of that noticed in Live Oak valley. The great number of deeply worn and oft traveled trails tell forcibly the use which is made of this road. It appears to me important that all of their great thoroughfares should be well examined. They almost always pass by convenient watering places and over country readily traversed, and such reconnaissances would add much to the efficiency of our troops and conduce greatly to the protection of this extensive frontier. Allen reported that the route by the river bank is practicable.

MAY 9. This morning, leaving a note for Skillman in the designated spot, the party marched down the right bank, following an old and long-disused trail. The appearance of the scenery became, as we continued, more and more interesting. Groves of live oak and of hackberry, mesquite of greater size, thickets and shrubbery of great variety occurring every here and there, relieved the sameness of the limestone bluffs. The stream approached so near to several of these that we considered the opposite side the best for the road. This valley, regarded merely as a military route, is very fine, a single ponton or a trestle bridge sufficing for its passage at any point, and this affording the advantage of choosing either side, as most convenient. A march of sixteen miles brought us to a fine mesquite flat surrounded by a pretty grove. Here the river makes an abrupt bend to the right, and passing between two abrupt cliffs our further progress along its banks was stopped. We encamped at this place. Stripping, I plunged with Poli into the rapid stream, and we soon discovered a practicable crossing for the animals.

MAY 10. Our arrangements for crossing our baggage were very simple. A couple of stout poles were cut and set in the ground on either side, strongly braced with pickets. A lariat was stretched from one to the other. To this a packsaddle was slung, with two hauling lines for either bank; and by this contrivance all our baggage was readily passed in a short time. Some small articles were lost, however. The more adventurous and better swimmers of the party took to the water, but it was a feat which, from the very great rapidity of the current, was not easy. The others preferred to be pulled across in the slings; and as the ropes had slackened a good deal, much laughter was caused by the [ ] [269] engaged in hauling, by dangling each passenger in the water. While busy with this matter, we were rejoiced by the sudden arrival of Skillman and his party with our *caballada,* baggage, and provisions. These brave fellows had safely accomplished their daring and perilous service. We spent the remainder of the day in di-

269 Illegible in the manuscript.

viding the new store of eatables, in arranging packs, etc., and listening to the detail of the captain's adventures. He had met with our friend Gómez, and we learned that the wily chief, outwitted by the events of the nineteenth and twentieth of March, had, after our escape, moved down to the vicinity of Presidio. Well knowing that he deserved but little at the hands of Americans and fearing our approach with stronger forces, he made a treaty with Leaton and permitted Skillman to pass through his whole tribe unmolested. He manifested great anxiety on the part of his people to be friendly with the United States, and begged to be recommended to General Worth's consideration. He will be!

MAY 11. The canyon by which we left the Pecos, bearing off to the southeast, was rough and difficult. Chaparral (here very thick), cactus, and the various stony gullies made the march for a few miles very severe. At length, by a difficult ascent, we reached the elevated tables; here the route became better, and we proceeded briskly. Our noon halt was made on fine grass but without water. Of this our gourds and canteens supplied sufficient to make our coffee, the great essential in a prairie bill of fare. We find the country to consist of a vast table elevation cut up by some great convulsion of old time into numerous ravines or canyons. The great difficulty here is the passage from the ravine to the table, for by either, as long as they can be followed, the traveling is good. These valleys are rendered pretty by groves of live oak and cedar, with occasional groups of other trees whose names I do not know. We were rejoiced to find abundance of water for ourselves and animals in the holes of the limestone rocks. We encamped upon quite a pool, exceedingly thankful for the good fortune which seems our constant companion.

MAY 12. As we advanced upon our course, we were surprised and pleased to find the country less rough. We were approaching the divide between the Pecos and the Devils river, and met a succession of valleys and hills – the valleys covered with luxuriant crops of fine grass and the hills no longer obstructed by the limestone bluffs which hindered our march yesterday. The hope of reporting a route revived. Provisions are getting low, and today I dispatched the hunters right and left. Our noon camp we made after a march of eleven miles on an east course. We discovered abundance of water in the rocky bed of a small creek and quantities of excellent grass. The same course was continued this afternoon until we had passed the divide, when we commenced making southing by a canyon of the Devils river. Our march was kept up until six, when we came to camp at the foot of a precipitous bluff stretching nearly east and west. At the foot of this was abundant water, and as the boy Poli came in with a fine fat doe, a rich supper compensated the fatigues of the day.

MAY 13. Still following the valley, which now began to widen, a march of two miles brought us suddenly upon a still and beautiful lagoon of clear blue water, half hidden by a dense grove of lofty pecans. The picture was enchanting and I longed for the pencil of Weir – our animated and eager party wishing to look at this oft talked-of spring; this spring which the Indian alone knew – the water so still and silent in its soft light – around it the somber green of the superb pecan, and above all a frowning background formed by the huge, dark gray cliffs of limestone. Hard by were the frames of the Comanche lodges, and many a deep-worn trail we now discovered coming in by the direction of the heads of the Texas rivers. We followed one of these which led down the valley. By it we passed around a couple of bluffs and then found the traveling very good in a sandy mesquite flat. Our course upon this path was south by west. At eleven we again fell in with the river, now bending still more to the westward; and here, having crossed to the right bank, we determined to dine. Our march this morning has been ten miles. Its monotony was varied by the pastime of shooting rattlesnakes, great numbers of which were met and slain. This afternoon, after following the Comanche trail for about a mile, we had the satisfaction to find it leave the river by a course east by south. It ran up a canyon for a short distance and then passed to the table elevation by ascending a very steep and rugged hill. From this we gained a view of the rolling country to the southward; and traveling by a southeast course upon the plain, in an hour and a half we descended by another ravine towards the river. Here we found a very high red bluff of limestone and at its base an abundance of water. The march this afternoon having been very rough and severe, I decided to halt here for the night. We have made sixteen miles.

MAY 14. Leaving camp early and continuing for an hour upon the Indian path, which here passes a very stony tract of country, we came suddenly upon a magnificent pecan grove which enclosed a bright blue lagoon. The landscape, which was very beautiful, is similar to that at the head of the river. Huge cliffs hem in the scene, and dark green trees throw a pleasant shade in the valley. This is the head of the running water of the so-called Devils river. Crossing the stream and gaining the right bank, our path wound through the dense groves and passed the relics of recent Comanche camps and fires. It then emerged upon a succession of broad, flat limestone rock tables which formed the bank of the river, now a bold running stream. From south by east it turned gradually south, and after a rough march through some mesquite and hackberry groves, we again crossed the water to the left bank. Still following the trail, it led us up a rugged ascent, whereon the sharp pointed plants and jagged flints gave great trouble to our mules. From this height we could again see the silver line of the river running a course north of east. We had cut off a bend. This afternoon, after leaving our dinner camp and again passing to the right bank, our progress was slow and toilsome down the river valley. Without the advantage of the Indian paths, we forced our way through dense masses of undergrowth. This painful march was continued until towards sunset, when Dick, ascending a high hill, halloed from its summit for us to encamp. Owing to the obstacles in our way, we have made but eleven miles today.

MAY 15. Adopting Dick's advice, we ascended the tables this morning; and falling on a spur of the divide which intersects this bend of the river, we continued upon it until we fell in with a trail which soon led us by a southerly course to fine traveling upon an elevated and rolling plain. Our march this morning was enlivened by an exciting bear hunt. Five of these animals were discovered and, in spite of the jaded condition of our animals, we put spurs in chase and continued firing balls into them from our pistols until all were secured. Our stock of provisions had fallen to almost nothing, and this spoil, with a fat doe which Dick had shot, made a most welcome supply. This morning we crossed Hays's trail to Presidio, and at length, about noon, stopped to dine upon some rain water in the rocks. We reached, early in the afternoon, a low range of hills, upon which our course had been directed in the morning. To these I gave the name of "Hope." Ascending one, we could descry from its top the magnificent group of the San Agustín mountains in Mexico. These, from their fantastic shapes, are very notable landmarks. The Cordelaria peak readily distinguishes the cluster by its symmetrical, sugar-loaf form. The hills, too, lying immediately on the Río Grande were here distinctly to be seen.

Keeping now a course between south and southeast, at about two miles from the Hope hills we struck the head of the Arroyo de los Palos Blancos, a singular brook which I hardly know whether to characterize as permanent. Its water has a strong sulphurated odor but is drinkable. Here we encamped. I decided that Smith, Dick, and Skillman could proceed in advance from this place to carry into San Antonio the earliest intelligence of our approach, and wrote the necessary orders and a brief summary of our labors to be transmitted by them.[270]

MAY 16. They left very early this morning, furnished with the best animals we had. We followed them rapidly. The trail upon which we moved yesterday was now lost amid the many old Indian camps on the creek. I therefore took a course about south by east, passing through a rolling country similar to yesterday's travel and leaving the arroyo on our left. This course I gradually altered until it became southeast. I bore upon the

270 They arrived at San Antonio on Monday evening, May 21. *Nacogdoches Times,* June 16, 1849.

point of a distant ridge, evidently on the other side of the San Pedro. The country now became more rugged, indicating our approach to the river once more, and we shortly entered an extensive canyon remarkable for its large pools of water. One of these was nearly as large as the Lake of the T.O.S. in the San Sabá valley. To our great satisfaction the trail lost above was discovered here, and we were delighted with the chance thus given of finding a crossing without difficulty, a singular piece of good fortune. Perpendicular walls of limestone here commence to take the place of the steep hillsides of the ravine. These cliffs are notable for the numerous caves which are hollowed in the face of them. Upon seeing them, Old Francisco, the muleteer, recognized the canyon as a famous Comanche pass, to which he said he had been a long while ago in pursuit of some Indians out of San Fernando. He added that if we would examine the larger caves on our right hand, we would find their walls covered with Comanche paintings. It was as he said. In a vaulted chamber upon the rock, the Indians had drawn in colors rude pictures of adventures in Mexico. Here we halted to dine, and I gave to this pass the name "Painted." Just below the caves and set against the face of the cliff appear several regular and notable pilasters which would always identify this place.

Crossing the creek by the trail, it led us over an elevated plain of no great extent and shortly brought us by an easy descent to the San Pedro,[271] here a beautiful stream. The crossing [272] we found to be exceedingly good, and the ascent on the other side equally so. This river San Pedro is put down upon some maps as much

271 Devils river.

272 They crossed to the east bank of Devils river in the southeastern part of the present Val Verde county.

more extensive than it really is. After a running course of about sixty miles, it empties into the Río Grande fifteen miles east of the mouth of the Puerco, the old boundary between the states of Chihuahua, Coahuila, and Texas. The old Spanish adventurers appear to have had some knowledge of it, as several maps locate near its head a fortress called "Fort del Altar." The formation on its banks is, I think, beyond a doubt a part of the great range of Silurian and metalliferous limestones, which has been noticed in Mexico opposite to this part of the country, and which, like this, finds its northwestern limit in the basaltic and porphyritic mountains of Chihuahua (a continuation of the formation of the Chinati Sierra noticed above), and its southeastern in the cretaceous formation of Texas and Mexico, through which the Río Grande makes its way. There may therefore exist in this section many deposits of ore. The alleged existence of this fort would point to this. However, we saw no traces of it; but as we cut off the great bend of the river we might well have passed it without observation.

This river, like the lower Puerco, makes its way with little or no valley, or bottom, through the great table formation between huge perpendicular cliffs. These become the more remarkable as the traveler proceeds south, and below our crossing, the steep ravines and rugged canyons render travel almost impracticable. It was here that the party under Hays got lost and spent so much time attempting to ascend this river. Leaving it, we came upon an extensive and rolling prairie dotted here and there with little thickets of mesquite,[273] of less elevation than the great table formation of the

273 They were traveling a short distance north of the present Del Río, Val Verde county.

upper prairies, and bounded on the north by their southern slope and on the south by the Río Grande. Here commences the cretaceous formation of Texas. Consulting my map, I assumed a course southeast by east for the Las Moras hill; and steadily holding to this, we came to camp after a march of twenty-two miles, at the San Felipe creek, a clear, running stream of pleasant water.

MAY 17. We passed the brook this morning about a mile north of the Loma de Andrade, a hill named after a Mexican captain who distinguished himself against the Indians in this vicinity. Last night I had taken an observation on the North Star for latitude, and judging from that, I assumed the course of S. 85° E. for the Las Moras spring, and in the course of the morning had the satisfaction, on rising the ridge of the west branch of the Pedro, to see the hill itself, a notable landmark, directly ahead of us. The country hereabouts is extremely beautiful to eyes long since weary of the sterile monotony of the upper limestones. Here the land is rolling, covered with fine crops of grass, and relieved by numerous groves of live oak and mesquite. The travel is very fine and water is had in abundance. Our march was continued until night, when we came to camp in a beautiful spot on the west branch of the Zoquete about a mile above its forks. We had passed, during the day, all the creeks laid down on De Cordera's map as situated between the San Pedro and the Zoquete. They are pretty little streams of clear, blue limestone water and, like most of the Texas waters, are generally shaded by groves of superb pecans. Game we met in great abundance, and many deer were brought into camp tonight.

MAY 18. A march of eight miles today brought us

to the Las Moras spring.[274] This, hidden in a dense grove of pecans and mulberries, is the head of the Las Moras river. About three miles off stands the hill, a remarkable feature in the country. It is of no great elevation, not being higher than the table formation farther to the north, but it rises solitary with its two eminences from the midst of a beautiful plain of great extent. It is a favorite lookout of the Indians, and many trails for Mexican depredation come by this point from the upper Nueces, the Llano, and the San Sabá. Southeast from this mound and distant about ten miles is a low range of hills running east and west, and extending to the Nueces. In this neighborhood we discovered the fresh trails of a party of dragoons, evidently, from their direction, a scouting party from the Leona camp, a post which, when we left the settlements, had not been established. We encamped tonight on a branch of Elm creek after a march of eighteen miles.

MAY 19. We passed through some of the finest mesquite land this morning I have ever seen. The luxuriance of the vegetation and the crop of grass is beyond any idea I had previously formed. We profited by it in the abundance of fat and tender venison which was taken on all sides. Camping for dinner on the Paisano, a little creek which heads in this range of hills, Poli discovered a bee tree. Nothing but cutting it would satisfy my men; and although it was a huge live oak and they had but a hatchet to work with, they perseveringly pecked away until they succeeded in obtaining as much honey as they wanted. We enjoyed here the famous frontier meal of a side of venison roasted on a ramrod, basted with bear's oil and dipped in honey. This afternoon we passed the extreme point of the

274 Near the present Brackettville, Kinney county.

Paisano hills. The Leona mound, similar to the Las Moras in position and shape, appeared before us, distant about twelve miles. Close by was the great Nueces bottom, heavily timbered with elm, ash, oak, and pecan. We crossed about a mile below the point taken by Lieutenant Smith and halted for the night on the other side, having marched twenty-seven miles. The Nueces here flows over a pebbly bottom and seems easily passed in most places.

MAY 20. About three miles from the river, falling in with the trail to Leona, we found Skillman's hatchet hanging to a limb over the path. This surprised us, but the mystery was explained shortly by our meeting a scout, the sergeant in command of which informed us that the night before last, Lieutenant Smith's party was robbed of all their animals on the Nueces. They were compelled to leave their saddles and foot it into camp. The scout was sent to recover them if possible. We arrived about nine o'clock at the camp, where we received a warm welcome from Captains Eastman and King of the First infantry. We had left the former at Fredericksburg on our outward march. We were overwhelmed with the intelligence from the settlements. The cholera was raging in San Antonio, and we learned that the accomplished soldier, whose orders we had executed, had fallen before it.[275] Our own fate had been long decided – we had been given up. With the natural joy consequent on our return to the settlements dampened by this news, we remained in camp all day to rest. Howard and Lieutenant Smith had left just before we arrived.

275 Major-general William Jenkins Worth died of cholera at San Antonio on May 7, 1849. Heitman, *Historical Register*, I, 1061; *Daily Missouri Republican*, May 26, 1849.

From this point to San Antonio the route is by the well-known Woll [276] road, so called from the Mexican general who, marching a heavy column by this way, surprised the town of San Antonio during the Texas war. General Wool's [277] column afterwards followed it on the march to Presidio Río Grande. Accomplishing the distance of ninety miles in three days, early on the morning of the twenty-fifth of May [278] we entered San Antonio after an absence of one hundred and four days.

This meager outline of our labors is now closed, but I cannot part from my brave companions without expressing here my gratitude for the resolute and unmurmuring courage with which they invariably followed and supported me, and which was equally conspicuous as well in the presence of a numerous and treacherous enemy as in enduring the privations of hunger and thirst. Skillful in the use of their arms, careful of their animals and their provisions, watchful, cautious and daring, these hardy frontiersmen of Texas combine all the qualities which make the successful border soldier. For service of this kind I know none that I prefer. Well calculated as they were, however, to form an escort for Lieutenant Smith and myself on the duty assigned to us, I must say that their number was far too small; and thus, while the interests dependent upon the expedition were in continual jeopardy, its objects were not as well attained as they might otherwise have been.

276 General Adrian Woll.

277 John Ellis Wool. See *Southwest Historical Series,* III, 118.

278 On June 10, 1849, Whiting reported to General Totten, chief of engineers: "We made our appearance in Béxar on the 24th of May." *House Ex. Docs.,* 31 cong., 1 sess., no. 5, p. 291.

DIARIES OF FRANÇOIS XAVIER AUBRY, 1853-1854

DIARIES OF FRANÇOIS XAVIER AUBRY, 1853-1854

DIARY OF 1853

TEJÓN PASS. JULY 10, 1853.[279] As the country between this point and San Francisco is well known, I have kept no minutes of my journey thus far. We crossed the Sierra Nevada at the Tejón pass, which is in about the thirty-fifth parallel of latitude and about fifty miles south of Walker's pass. From this point we will travel

[279] Aubry's diary of 1853 is published from the *Santa Fé Weekly Gazette* (Sept. 24, 1853), where it was first printed. On September 15, 1853, James L. Collins, editor of the newspaper, asked Aubry's permission to publish the journal. Aubry replied: "Your favor of this date has just been handed to me. I cannot refuse to comply with the request it contains, at the same time that I much regret the meagreness of my notes, and my inability to give a more accurate and scientific account of the country over which I have just passed." Commenting editorially on Aubry's diary, Collins wrote: "We have the satisfaction of laying before the public Mr. Aubry's notes of a trip from California to New Mexico by a route hitherto but little known. In fact the route pursued by Mr. Aubry has never before been explored by any one. The belief which has long existed in the public mind of New Mexico, in regard to the existence of an excellent route for a wagon or railroad from the central part of the Territory to California, has received ample confirmation from this exploring expedition of Mr. Aubry. From this enterprise of noble daring, the most interesting and useful information is furnished to the world, on a subject, which at this time, engrosses the attention of statesmen and capitalists to a degree perhaps unknown in any former period of our history. This information too, although unofficial, is not the less authentic or the less worthy of credence on that account. To those who know Mr. Aubry it would be superfluous for us to say a word in behalf of his veracity and good judgment. His friends all know him to be a man absolutely without a parallel in physical qualities, and unsurpassed in all the noble traits of human character. We confidently give assurance to our readers that the journal of this gentleman may be relied upon to the letter, and that we have reason to believe that the modesty which always attends real worth, has caused him to under-value the usefulness of his labors, and the accuracy of his judgment." *Ibid.*

east until we reach the Río Grande at Albuquerque, New Mexico. It is well to remark that unfortunately there is no one with us who knows anything of the country through which we must pass, and we could not obtain any information in regard to it. My party consists of eighteen men – twelve Americans and six Mexicans. Messrs. Tully,[280] of Santa Fé, and Adair,[281] of Independence, have joined us for a pleasure trip. We use pack animals entirely, having neither wagon nor carriage.

JULY 11. Left the pass [282] and made twelve miles east over a level, gravelly, and sandy soil, and found a spring of good water.

JULY 12. Traveled twenty miles eastward, the country similar to that of yesterday. We met with no timber, but found several springs of fresh water. There is

280 During the fall of 1853, Lieutenant Whipple interviewed Tully at Albuquerque. Whipple wrote: "Mr. Tully, a companion of Mr. Aubrey in his recent trip from California, has given a description of the country over which he passed. Mr. Aubrey himself has since confirmed the statements of his friend, cautioning us to avoid his trail as being unsuitable for our operations." *House Ex. Docs.*, 33 cong., 2 sess., no. 91, vol. III, p. 48.

281 Abner E. Adair was probably born in Missouri about 1832. "My recollections carry me back to 1835 and onward in the western frontier of Missouri," he stated in July, 1916. Early in 1917, when Adair wrote his recollections of Aubry's fastest ride, he asserted: "In 1853 and 1854 made two trips with him [Aubry] from New Mexico to California, driving sheep to that golden land, messing with him; and black Pompey who had been his cook and carriage driver was our cook." *Odessa Democrat* (Odessa, Mo.), July 14, 1916, Feb. 23, 1917.

282 Tejón pass is near the present Lebec, Kern county, California. Early in September, 1853, Lieutenant R. S. Williamson, of the topographical engineers, examined the pass for a possible railroad route. He then wrote: "Near the eastern extremity of the Tejón is a break in the mountains, known as the Tejón Pass. Through this break a wagon-road has been made leading to Los Angeles, and it is one of the worst roads I ever saw. This pass had been much and favorably spoken of as a railroad pass. . . The Tejón Pass is a peculiar one. The altitude is quite great; but the ascent and descent appeared to be gentle, except very near the summit. It was hence supposed that, by means of a tunnel, the pass might be found to be a good one." *House Ex. Docs.*, 33 cong., 2 sess., no. 91, vol. V, p. 21.

François Xavier Aubry

timber in the mountains about the Tejón pass, but none on the eastern side of them.

JULY 13. Traveled today thirty-five miles east [283] and struck the Mojave river,[284] where we found plenty of good water. This river sometimes disappears in its course, whilst at others it contains as much as two feet of water. There is a little cottonwood timber upon its banks, and canebrakes in great abundance. The cane is not of the large species. The Mojave takes its rise in the San Bernardino mountains, which lie to the south of us, and after pursuing a northern course to a point a little north of our present camp, turns suddenly east, and soon south of east to empty into the Great Colorado. Found good grass for our animals.

JULY 14. Made twenty miles east along the Mojave and found water, timber, and grass abundant.[285]

JULY 15. Continued along the river about eighteen miles farther, in a direction nearly east; then leaving the Mojave to our right, we traveled fifteen miles northeast. Met with an abundance of grass, a little timber, and a few miles of fertile land along the river. There is no water in the bed of the stream, but it may be had by digging a few feet. Found wild cane from time to time. Encamped without water, grass, or wood.

JULY 16. Still pursuing a northeastern course, we traveled today thirty-five miles over a level, gravelly soil. We have deviated from our due east course in order to avoid a region of sand hills that lie to our right and directly between us and the Great Colorado. The weather is very hot, and no rain has fallen since we left the pass. So far we have met with neither Indians

283 This day they crossed the Mojave desert.

284 They reached the Mojave river near the present Bryman, San Bernardino county.

285 The party camped near the present Barstow, San Bernardino county.

nor game of any kind. We obtained a little water about halfway in our day's journey, but saw no timber or grass.

JULY 17. Made thirty-three miles northeast over a level, gravelly country; about halfway obtained a little very bad water. No grass or timber in sight during the day, but at night we obtained good water, grass, and wild cane. Prairie mountains lie on both sides of the trail.

JULY 18. Traveled twenty miles, still northeast, over a level country. Saw but little good land and no timber. After traveling about five miles, we found good spring water, but encamped without any.

JULY 19. Course still northeast, distance thirty-two miles, country level, soil inferior, grass and water, but no timber.

JULY 20. Made twenty miles northeast over a level, gravelly country and obtained good spring water and grass. Saw no timber.[286]

JULY 21. Were detained in camp all day by the sickness of one of the men.

JULY 22. Traveled twenty miles east southeast, most of the distance through a little canyon, where we found good grass, water, and cane in abundance, and struck the Great Colorado of the West. The river at this place is over three hundred yards in width, and has from ten to fifteen feet [of] water in the channel. Its banks are entirely destitute of timber and grass; in fact no vegetation is met with except a small shrub, called *chamiza* by the Mexicans and I believe artemisia by botanists. We were very fortunate in striking the river at a point where there are neither canyons nor mountains, although the country appears very rough and mountainous both to the north and south of us. To the north the

286 Aubry was now traveling through the present Clark county, Nevada.

rocks are black and irregular and seem to be volcanic, whilst the cliffs to the south are of red sandstone. The banks at the crossing are low, rocky, and unchanging, and the current exceedingly rapid.

We followed the river up for five miles, and selected a crossing where it is some two hundred yards wide and twenty or twenty-five feet deep. We succeeded in finding a little driftwood, of which we made a raft. Four men took charge of it, and it was carried some three miles with the current before it could be landed. The heights were covered with Indians, in readiness to shoot us down. I started down with four men to follow the raft and protect the men who were upon it, having ordered the camp to move down in haste. Having unloaded the raft upon the eastern bank, the men recrossed the river, and we selected a camp opposite the place where the baggage was deposited, and during the night kept up a constant fire with our rifles across the river, and in this manner protected it from the Indians. The animals were taken to the crossing I had first selected, to swim the river. I took them up with three men on the west bank, and four men received them on the opposite side. This detained us half a day, and altogether we were detained five days in crossing the river.[287] The driftwood of which we constructed our little raft appeared to have been cut by beavers. These animals must be exceedingly abundant, as they destroyed during the first night the ropes with which our raft was bound together, and carried off the timber. The loss of the ropes was a great inconvenience to us. We set a guard afterwards at night over our second raft, to protect it from a similar fate. The river showed

[287] They crossed the Colorado river a short distance south of the present Boulder Dam.

signs of having been some fifteen feet higher than when we crossed it. It is here a grand and magnificent stream, swift like the Mississippi, and apparently as well adapted to navigation. The place of our crossing is well suited to bridging, or ferriage by steam or otherwise. We saw no waterfowl about the river, and only a few antelopes and black-tailed deer. East of the river [288] we encountered a great many rattlesnakes of an uncommonly large size. They seem to be a new species, as their tails are covered for some six inches from the point with alternate white and black rings of hair or bristles about a quarter of an inch long. According to my observations the Colorado of the West is set down upon the maps greatly too far to the east, perhaps as much as one hundred and fifty miles. The Indians were constantly in sight and watching our movements. They could not be induced to approach us, but assured us, across the river, that they were Mojave.

On one occasion whilst at rest for a few minutes in a deep gully about a mile from the crossing on the west side of the river, a Mexican mule boy discovered something glistening upon the ground, which on examination proved to be gold. We at once commenced washing sand in our tin cups, and in every one discovered particles of gold. This gold was discovered in a dark, coarse sand, and a black, heavy sand was found in the cup after washing away the gravel. The sandy soil was so compact that we could not dig it up with our fingers. The Indians being still on the heights near us, and our party being separated by the river, the danger was so great that we could not remain longer at this spot. I intended to return again, but the Indians became so

[288] After crossing the Colorado, the party entered the present Mojave county, Arizona.

numerous that it was impossible to do so. This gully is on the right bank of the river, and the head of it is in a very rough and rugged mountain.

JULY 27. We washed sand on the east side of the river and found gold in greater abundance than on any previous occasion. I myself washed a tin cup full of yellow clay and found about twenty-five cents' worth of the pure metal. A Mexican boy, on washing a frying pan full of coarse sand, found from forty to fifty particles of pure gold, some of which were as large as the head of a pin. We took the clay and sand from the top of the ground without digging. The appearance of the country also indicates gold. I made no further examination, as our animals had subsisted for five days upon the *chamiza,* without a blade of grass, and our provisions had been damaged in the Colorado, which must cause us to travel several days without anything to eat. Today we made ten miles east. The country is without wood, water, or grass.

JULY 28. Two of our men being sick, we were compelled to return to the river on their account. Struck it some fifteen miles below the crossing and found that from near that point it makes a considerable bend towards the east. The country here does not indicate gold, nor could we find any on washing the sands.

JULY 29. The condition of our sick men obliged us to remain in camp all day. Our animals were in a starving condition, as there is not a particle of grass on or near the river.

JULY 30. Left the river and traveled fifteen miles east and five miles northeast. A sick Mexican was so much exhausted that we were compelled to make for a mountain north of us which indicated water, but we found neither water, timber, nor grass.

JULY 31. Traveled eight miles northeast and struck

a large stream, but much smaller than the Colorado, coming from the east southeast and running west northwest. This stream may be what the Mexicans designate as the "Río Grande de los Apaches," and what the Americans have recently called the "Little Red river."[289] One of my Mexicans followed this stream a few miles and says that it empties into the Colorado seven or eight miles below camp, and that there is below us a valley of good soil, and grass in abundance. Where we struck this stream there is neither timber nor grass. In the evening we traveled five miles south, to avoid mountains, and as many east. The country was level but without grass or timber. The mountains, or perhaps more properly hills, that we have thus far met with are nothing more than elevations of various forms and dimensions, dispersed in a detached and irregular manner over a vast and otherwise uninterrupted plateau. Hence I have constantly termed the country level, and very properly, as it may be traversed in all directions among the solitary and detached elevations or mountains without the necessity of crossing them.

AUGUST 1. Traveled twenty miles east and found a spring of good water,[290] the grass was abundant, and cedar trees were seen on the highlands. The country is level and the soil inferior.

AUGUST 2. Made ten miles east, crossing a mountain or ridge, where we found a fine pass, grass, and timber (cedar and piñon) abundant.

AUGUST 3. Traveled twenty miles south of east over a country somewhat broken; timber and grass abundant. Indians were around us in numbers all day, shooting arrows every moment. They wounded some of our

[289] This stream may be the one that flows into the present Red Lake, Mojave county.

[290] Probably at or near the present Peach springs, Mojave county.

mules and my famous mare Dolly, who has so often rescued me from danger by her speed and capacity of endurance.

AUGUST 4. We moved ten miles south to avoid mountains, and struck a valley[291] which we left a few days since, and which extends to the Colorado. The mountains which we left are covered with timber. Grass and water were found in plenty. The Indians commenced firing on us at sunrise and continued until we reached camp. Arrows passed through the clothes of several of the men, and three passed through my own clothes; and I was slightly wounded by two others in different places. An arrow passed through the collar of Dick Williams.[292] We killed several of the Indians and wounded more. Peter Prudom accidentally shot himself in the right knee.

AUGUST 5. Traveled ten miles southeast in a valley; no water; grass and timber in abundance on all the mountains.

AUGUST 6. Continued ten miles southeast in the same valley in which we traveled yesterday; found no water, but good grass, and plenty of timber on and below the mountains. As our sick men are unable to travel, we are suffering for water, having been nearly three days without any, and indications are not now favorable. Indians still around us.

AUGUST 7. Traveled ten miles southeast, half the distance in the same valley, and then went to a mountain and found good water, grass, and timber. All the mountains in this country are covered with cedar, pine, and piñon. The grass is good in all the prairies, but none of them have any water. The soil is sandy and

291 This may have been the present Aubrey valley, which extends along the boundary line between Yavapai and Coconino counties, Arizona.

292 Richard M. Williams. *Daily Missouri Republican,* Nov. 4, 1854.

full of particles of mica. Indians are numerous and continue to fire upon us.

AUGUST 8. Made fifteen miles east southeast, crossing a little chain of mountains, where we found a level pass, and timber, grass, and water in abundance. Crossed a stream running from northeast to southwest, which I think goes to the Colorado. After crossing the mountains, we passed through a fine valley with an abundance of good spring water, and timber near it. The Indians attacked the camp several times last night but without success, and continued fighting us during the day but with less boldness and resolution.

AUGUST 9. After proceeding eight miles east, we found ourselves surrounded by canyons apparently from one to four thousand feet deep; at least we sometimes could not see the bottom. We were compelled to return to the same camp. The country is high and level, and well supplied with timber, grass, and water.

AUGUST 10. Moved ten miles southeast over a somewhat broken country. Crossed a stream of good water (with timber along its course) which is evidently a tributary of the Gila. The country indicates gold in abundance. We crossed a little chain of mountains, where we found a great quantity of silver ore in flint rocks.

AUGUST 11. Traveled southeast over a country a little broken, but well supplied with water, grass, and timber. Indications of gold still exist.

AUGUST 12. Made fifteen miles southeast, crossing the bed of a large stream now dry, with plenty of timber along it. Struck the valley which we left some five or six days ago, having crossed a few days ago the headwaters of a stream which passes through it. This valley will be of the utmost importance in the making of a wagon [road] or railroad. Today, for the first time on this trip, we ate a dinner of mule meat. It was a new dish to most of our men and made some of them sick. To me it was an old acquaintance and I feel well. It only served to remind me of hard times on other journeys. The quality of the meat depends on the appetite of the man. Several of us are now on foot.

AUGUST 13. Marched twenty miles east, leaving to our right the great valley so often mentioned and which extends to the Colorado. Passed through a little valley between two mountains, where we found timber, grass, and water in abundance. The soil was excellent. We here met Indians, who professed to be very friendly, with papers of recommendation from the commanding officer of Fort Yuma, on the Gila trail.

AUGUST 14. We left early, and after traveling five miles in an eastern direction, stopped to breakfast near an Indian camp of Garrotero. They professed friendship; but having no faith in their professions, I selected a camp on the top of a small hill, which would give us an advantage in case of a fight. All went on well until our mules were saddled and we were ready to start, when, at a given signal, some forty or fifty Indians, apparently unarmed, and accompanied by their squaws, children, and babies (tied to boards) in their arms, very suddenly charged upon us and attempted to destroy the whole party with clubs and rocks. The signal of attack was the taking of my hand in farewell by a chief, which he held with all his strength. So soon as these first Indians commenced the fight, about two hundred more rushed from behind a hill and brush, and charged upon us with clubs [and] bows and arrows. I thought, for a few minutes, that our party must necessarily be destroyed; but some of us having disengaged ourselves, we shot them down so fast with our Colt revolvers[293] that we soon produced confusion among them and put them to flight. We owe our lives to these firearms, the best that were ever invented, and now brought, by successive improvements, to a state of perfection. Mr. Hendrey, an American, and Francisco Guzmán, a New Mexican, greatly distinguished themselves.

Twelve of us, just two-thirds of the party, were severely wounded. I, among the rest, was wounded in six places. Abner Adair, I fear, is dangerously injured. It was a very great satisfaction to me to find that none of my men were killed, nor any of the animals lost. We bled very much from our numerous wounds, but the blood and bodies of the Indians covered the ground for many yards around us. We killed over twenty-five and wounded more. The bows and arrows that we captured and destroyed would have more than filled a large wagon. Before the attack commenced, the squaws kept the clubs, which were from eighteen to twenty-four inches long, concealed in deerskins about their children. When put to flight, they threw their babies down into a deep, brushy gully near at hand, by which many of them must have been killed. This is the first time I ever met with a war party of Indians accompanied by their wives and children. The presence of the latter was evidently to remove from our minds all suspicion of foul play on their part. I was never before in so perilous a condition with a party in all my life. On this occasion, which will be the last, I imprudently gave my right hand, in parting, to the Indian chief. The left must answer for leave-taking hereafter.

We have thus far had so much ill luck to encounter

293 For a history of Colt's firearms, see *Southwest Historical Series,* II, 103-104.

that our arrival at our destination must be much delayed. First, our men fell sick; then our provisions were damaged in the Colorado; latterly a man shot himself through the knee; our mules' feet, for want of shoes, are worn out; and to crown all, today two-thirds of the party are badly wounded, and all have barely escaped with their lives. We are now subsisting entirely on mule meat and do not get as much of that as we want. We are without salt and pepper, and in their absence it requires a stout stomach to digest our fare. But nobody complains, and the possibility of not doing what we have set out to do has never entered the minds of my party. We traveled five miles this afternoon, with the Indians at our heels shooting arrows at us every moment.

AUGUST 15. Traveled ten miles east amongst mountains, where we found water, grass, and timber in abundance. Indians around us all day shooting arrows. I omitted, in the proper place, to say that I brought away from the mountains we passed through on the tenth, a little black sand, less than a cupful, and found in it, on washing, twelve or fifteen particles of pure gold.

AUGUST 16. Made ten miles east and found no water; plenty of grass and timber seen on the mountains north of us. Indians still numerous and troublesome. Today met with copper in very great quantities. A vein of the pure native metal, about an inch and a half in diameter, was seen sticking out from a rock, which must have worn away by time and left the copper exposed. I think there is gold in the ore but am not certain. Our condition at present is bad enough. I have eight wounds upon me, five of which cause me much suffering; and at the same time, my mule having given out, I have to walk the whole distance. Thirteen of us are now wounded, and one is sick, so that we have only four men in good health. We are unable to travel faster on account of Adair's condition. Our canteens, etc., having been broken or destroyed in our fight with the Indians, we cannot carry water enough for more than half a day. This loss caused us to suffer more than can be imagined. Our animals were broken down by this traveling, which could not be avoided. We would come across an abundance of water every day if we could march some twenty-five or thirty miles, but our condition is such that it requires three days to make that small distance. In addition to all this, we are now on half rations of horse meat; and I have the misfortune to know that it is the flesh of my inestimable mare Dolly, who has so often, by her speed, saved me from death at the hands of Indians. Being wounded some days ago by the Garrotero, she gave out, and we are now subsisting upon her flesh.

AUGUST 17. Moved today about ten miles east, over a country rather rough. Suffering much for want of water. In crossing mountains we have to select the highest places instead of the regular passes, as when caught in canyons or gullies we are not strong enough to fight the Indians. Today, from the top of a little mountain, I saw the great valley so often mentioned, extending to the Colorado, not over twenty miles south of us, and it now seems to turn more to the east. I intend to make for it. I entertain fears that Adair and Baskerville[294] are in danger from their wounds; all the others are getting better.

AUGUST 18. Moved only five miles south of east. Found water, grass, and some timber.

AUGUST 19. Went five miles today in the same direction as yesterday and came to the great valley that

294 William Baskerville. *Daily Missouri Republican,* Nov. 4, 1854.

extends to the Colorado. Encamped on a creek of good water and grass; Adair being sometimes unable to travel, we are waiting on him. Indians around us shooting arrows. We never return their fire without being certain of our shots.

AUGUST 20. Traveled twenty miles east over a level, gravelly country; crossed a creek; found good grass; no timber in sight.

AUGUST 21. Moved ten miles east over a level, gravelly country and struck a large stream which is, no doubt, a branch of the Gila. The mountains to the north of us are very rough and without timber. There is no grass on this stream, which is thirty yards wide with three feet of water in the channel. Its course is from north to south.

AUGUST 22. Made ten miles southeast to a mountain. Country level and without grass or timber.

AUGUST 23. Moved about the same distance and in the same direction over a low, gravelly country. Struck a stream of good water, but without grass or timber.

AUGUST 24. Went about eight miles northeast and encamped in the mountains, where we met with the Tonto Apache. No timber seen today.

AUGUST 25. Crossed the mountains where the Tonto Apache live; found water, timber, and grass in abundance. Traveled fifteen miles northeast from the top of this mountain, from which we saw the Sierra Blanca mountains, which are near the pueblo of Zuñi. Saw a prairie extending from the east end of the Garrotero mountain to the upper end of the Sierra Blanca. I saw this prairie when we were at the east end of the Garrotero mountain, but we were not in a condition to examine it. Fifty miles is nothing with good animals, but ours were broken down; and our wounded men were unable to travel over ten miles a day. But I saw the country sufficiently well to convince me that there will be no obstacle whatever to the making of a rail-[road] or wagon road. The mountains which we crossed today are impracticable for either. I should like to return to the east end of the Garrotero mountain and pursue the route I indicate; but it is utterly impossible to do so, as we are now living on berries and herbs. We would rejoice to have mule meat, but we have so few animals, and so many wounded men, that it would be unsafe to kill any more. I have the good fortune of having true men with me, otherwise it would be uncertain that the party could get through; but I have confidence in my men, and I feel positively certain that we will make the trip. It will take us some ten or twelve days to reach Zuñi, where we expect to procure provisions. I shall travel near the mountains, as heretofore, on account of the certainty and facility of getting water, but shall remain in sight of the prairie extending from the Garrotero to the Sierra Blanca mountain.

AUGUST 26. Moved ten miles east northeast, most of the way along a creek, where we found grass in plenty, and some timber. The Tonto Apache are numerous and troublesome.

AUGUST 27. Made fifteen miles east, crossing two streams, which are branches of the Gila. We met Indians today who, I think, are not Tonto Apache, as they do not speak any Spanish and refuse to answer our questions. We obtained from them over fifteen hundred dollars' worth of gold for a few old articles of clothing. The Indians use gold bullets for their guns. They are of different sizes and each Indian has a pouch of them. We saw an Indian load his gun with one large and three small gold bullets to shoot a rabbit. They proposed exchanging them for lead, but I preferred trading other articles. Whether the Indians made these balls themselves, or whether they were obtained by the murder of miners in California or Sonora, I am unable to say.

AUGUST 28. Traveled ten miles east over a good country, met with more Indians, and traded for some horse meat by giving articles of clothing in exchange. We traded also for a few hundred dollars' worth of gold. Today a mule broke down, and an Indian gave me for it a lump of gold weighing a pound and a half less one ounce. The Indians are so numerous they would destroy the party if we allowed them the least chance. But we are very vigilant and select camps on elevated places; consequently we are unable to make any examinations for gold in the sands of the country. The Indians call themselves "Belenio."

AUGUST 29. Traveled some twenty miles in an eastern direction; the country quite level and the land good, with plenty of grass and water.

AUGUST 30. Traveled today about fifteen miles east over a country a little broken. Water and grass abundant.

AUGUST 31. Moved about twelve miles north of east over a country similar to that of yesterday. Found water, grass, and pine timber.

SEPTEMBER 1. Traveled fifteen miles over a country a little broken and well supplied with water, grass, and timber. The soil was good.

SEPTEMBER 2. Traveled the same distance northeast to the Sierra Blanca. Followed Indian trails all day and found grass, water, and pine timber in great abundance; and most of the soil is of a superior quality.

SEPTEMBER 3. Pursuing the same course, we traveled some fifteen miles among the same mountains. Today we passed through valleys of good soil, and we found the pine timber in greater abundance than yesterday. The trees are generally from two and a half to five feet in diameter and over two hundred feet high. We have seen timber enough today to make a railroad from the eastern states to the Pacific. The passes through this mountain are level and can be traveled by wagons without any difficulty whatever.

SEPTEMBER 4. Made twenty-five miles northeast, crossing the Colorado Chiquito after traveling about two miles. The land is level and good, and water and wood are plenty.

SEPTEMBER 5. Made twenty miles east northeast and got out of the mountains after traveling five miles; struck the prairie, where we found good soil, grass, and water.

SEPTEMBER 6. Continuing northeast over a good and level country for twenty-five miles, we reached the Indian town, or pueblo, of Zuñi,[295] where we met with

295 On August 29, 1857, Lieutenant Edward F. Beale described the pueblo of Zuñi as follows: "Arrived at Zuñi, an old Indian pueblo of curious aspect; it is built on a gentle eminence in the middle of a valley about five miles wide, through which the dry bed of the Zuñi lays. As we approached, cornfields of very considerable extent spread out on all sides, and apparently surrounded the town. This place contains a population of about two thousand souls; the houses, although nearly all have doors on the ground floor, are ascended by ladders, and the roof is more used than any other part. Here all the cooking is done, the idle hours spent, and is the place used for sleeping in summer. Each house or family has a little garden, rarely over thirty feet square, which is surrounded by a wall of mud. Inside of these, and completely encircling the town, are the corrals for sheep, asses, and horses, which are always driven up at night. We saw here many Albinos, with very fair skins, white hair, and blue eyes. The Indians raise a great deal of wheat, of a very fine quality, double-headed. The squaws are more expert at carrying things on their heads than our southern negroes. I saw one ascend to the second story of a house by a ladder, with an earthen jar containing a full bucket of water, without touching it with her hands. It was quite amusing to see the men knitting stockings. Imagine Hiawatha at such undignified work. The old Jesuit church is in ruins." *Uncle Sam's Camels* (Leslie, ed.), 188.

a hospitable and civilized population from whom we obtained an abundance of good provisions, over which we greatly rejoiced. We have subsisted for a month on mule and horse flesh, and for the most of that time on half or quarter rations. But as I have reached this place with all my men, I feel satisfied. I shall take no notes of the country from this town to Albuquerque on the Río Grande, as a level and much traveled wagon road exists between the two places, and is familiar to the people of New Mexico. It has been described by others and is well known to present no difficulties to the construction of a railroad.

SEPTEMBER 10. At Albuquerque, New Mexico. Before laying aside my pencil, for the use of which I have no fancy, I shall set down a few ideas that are now prominent in my recollection. I set out, in the first place, upon this journey simply to gratify my own curiosity as to the practicability of one of the much talked-of routes for the contemplated Atlantic and Pacific railroad.[296] Having previously traveled the southern,

296 On June 20, 1853, when Aubry left San Francisco for New Mexico, he wrote a letter to a friend in St. Louis: "I leave this city to-day to join my party, and shall start in a few days from Stockton for New Mexico. I shall pass through the Tulares Valley for nearly the whole distance. Thence I shall go through the Tejón Pass, leaving Walker's Pass about fifty or sixty miles to the north. Beyond that I can obtain no information whatever about the country lying east. I shall endeavor to travel east from the Tejón Pass to the Del Norte. Major Cross, of the army, informed me that the Tejón Pass and Peralta are in the same latitude; and if the route I take is found practicable, it will probably be the one advocated for a railroad. The best route on the east side of the Del Norte is from Independence, Missouri, which is the best in North America. But a route which would cost more can be had from the Del Norte to Springfield, Missouri, passing through the Mansana mountains, or from Algodones to Delgado's ranche, Galisteo, Anton Chico, and thence along the Canadian, striking it some distance below the Santa Fé road, and crossing it one hundred and fifty or two hundred miles above its mouth; thence a little north of east to the south-west corner of Missouri. You can rely that one of these two routes must necessarily be adopted. Your citizens can rely upon it they can never make a railroad to Texas, and they

or Gila, route, I felt anxious to compare it with the Albuquerque, or middle, route. Although I conceive the former to be every way practicable, I now give it as my opinion that the latter is equally so, whilst it has the additional advantage of being more central and serviceable to the Union. I believe the route I traveled is far enough south to be certainly free from the danger of obstruction by snows in winter. The route, in all its length, may be said to pass over a high plateau or generally level country, for the most part thickly studded with prairie mountains, or detached elevations, seldom so linked together as to deserve to be called a chain of mountains. Numerous mountains were at all times in sight; but being for the most part isolated peaks, a detour of a few miles would always supersede the necessity of crossing them. To the south of our route from the Great Colorado to Zuñi, the country was more level than on the north, and for the greater part of the distance a valley extends nearly due east and west to the Colorado.

The existence of so many mountains along the way must be considered, in reference to a railroad, as a very fortunate circumstance instead of a disadvantage, as it is the mountains alone which furnish the timber and never failing water. The plains are the only deserts and barren spots (if they are to be called so after the fashion of the day) which exist in all that vast region of country

cannot get a route south of the Canadian river. You will find, if you will remember, that one of the two routes I have indicated above will be adopted, if ever they make a railroad to the Pacific. Of course we take no instruments with us. I shall take forty pounds of flour for each man, and we will rely upon our rifles for meat. I shall write you the result of the expedition as soon as I reach the Del Norte. I expect to remain in New Mexico two or three months, and return to this country next winter. I am willing to travel in search of railroad routes, at my own expense, but am not sure that I shall live to see a road built." *Daily St. Louis Intelligencer,* Aug. 9, 1853.

which lies between the Gila on the south and the British possessions on the north, and the Río Grande on the east and the Sierra Nevada of California on the west. The plateau, or table-lands, must of course furnish the track upon which the road is to be laid; but the mountains adjacent must furnish the timber to make it, and the water for the use of men and animals employed in its construction and for the use of the depots afterwards. It is well for the country over which I passed that these mountains exist, as without them it would be in reality one vast and repulsive desert. It would be a disadvantage for a railroad to have to cross them, as, although not difficult to cross, it would much increase the expense. But I saw nothing that rendered it at all probable that they would have to be crossed. On the contrary, I am satisfied that a railroad may be run almost mathematically direct from Zuñi to the Colorado, and from thence to the Tejón pass in California. The section from the pass to San Francisco should leave the Tulare Lake to the west, and should pass through the Coast Range of mountains, say in the neighborhood of San Juan, and thence to San Francisco and by a branch to Stockton. The west side of Tulare Lake is unfit for a road on account of its miry nature. The section of the route from Zuñi to Albuquerque is plain sailing. That from Albuquerque to Independence or St. Louis or Memphis is equally plain by two or three well-known passes through the Sandia mountains, which lie east of the Río Grande.

Certain slight deviations from the track which I pursued would improve the route. For instance, it would be better to leave my trail to the north at a point say one hundred and eighty miles east of the Sierra Nevada, and intersect it again some fifteen miles west of the Colorado. On the east side of the Colorado the road should pursue a directly eastern course for seventy-five miles, and thence take an east southeast course for nearly two hundred miles at the foot and on the south side of the mountains inhabited by the Garrotero Indians. Thence northeast for fifteen miles in a prairie between those mountains and a range of mountains which seem to extend to the Gila. From this point the road should run easterly to the Colorado Chiquito river, and thence northeast to Zuñi. The distance from the east end of the Garrotero mountain to Zuñi is about two hundred miles. This route, as I indicate it, will pass at all times in sight of my trail and through as practicable a country as any railroad route of the same distance in the United States.

The proposed route by the Sangre de Cristo, north of Taos, I take, if practicable at all, to be very objectionable on account of the vast elevations the road must ascend to, and the large quantities of snow which fall and remain there so long during the winter months. This route has also the additional disadvantage of crossing two rivers, the Grand and the Green, either of which would be as costly to bridge as the Colorado.

A route has been somewhat spoken of just north of the Gila, with the view of having a route wholly on American ground. That, I am satisfied, is altogether out of the question on account of mountains alone, if no other objection existed. The Gila route proper, passing in part through Sonora, is objectionable on several accounts besides its situation. In the first place there is no timber upon the plains, nor upon the volcanic mountains that lie along the way. A considerable part of the route, too, lies over a country destitute of vegetation, which, when dry, is a white powder resembling flour, in which the feet of men and animals sink several inches. This same clay, when wet, is the most treacherous of quagmires. Some parts of the road are also very sandy. Don Ambrosio Armijo, who took sheep to California last year, lost as many as eleven hundred among the sand hills west of the Colorado by sinking in the sand and being run over by those behind. Another serious objection to the Gila route is the great desert which lies west of the Colorado, and [which] has an extent of one hundred miles without wood or water.

I have no interest in recommending one of these routes more than another. I took sheep and wagons to California last year by the Gila route, and I am about to return that way to California again with sheep.[297] Upon the route which I have just traveled I encountered many hardships and dangers, and met with serious pecuniary loss; yet I say it is the best for a railroad and would be excellent for ordinary traveling but for the Indians.[298] A large portion of the trail over which I passed – say some two hundred and fifty miles west from the Río Grande – is, for the most part, admirably adapted to farming and stock raising.

DIARY OF 1854

SAN JOSÉ, CALIFORNIA, JULY 6, 1854.[299] We leave

297 Aubry returned to Santa Fé on September 14, 1853, and left there for California about three weeks later.

298 In January, 1854, the *Daily Missouri Republican* published a transportation map of the United States which included Aubry's route. The map was entitled: "Map of the United States Showing the principal Steamboat routes and projected Railroads connecting with St. Louis. Compiled for the *Missouri Republican* Jany 1854." *Annual Review. History of St. Louis, Commercial Statistics, Improvements of the Year, and Account of Leading Manufactories, &c. From the Missouri Republican, January 10, 1854* (St. Louis, 1854), 1-48, and map.

299 Aubry's diary of 1854 is published from the *Daily Missouri Republican*

this place today for New Mexico with a party consisting of sixty men and fitted out at an expense of about fifteen thousand dollars.[300] Judge Otero,[301] Mr. Chávez,[302] and Mr. Perea [303] are my companions. The object of the expedition is to locate a wagon road from this valley to Albuquerque on the north side of the Gila, in the thirty-fifth parallel of latitude or as near it as practicable.

JULY 22. Today we struck the Mojave river, having crossed the Coast Range mountains near San Juan, and the Sierra Nevada at the Tejón pass. The pass through the Coast Range is low and easily practicable for a railroad, and it can be continued at the foot of the Coast mountain to the Sierra Nevada without the least difficulty, as it is all level. The land on the west side of the Tulare Lake is very inferior and forever uninhabitable.

(Sept. 26, 1854), where it was first printed. The editor wrote: "We publish to-day the traveling notes of Mr. Aubrey, taken during his late trip from San José to Santa Fé. They contain much valuable information in regard to the nature and resources of the country through which he passed, and they possess a melancholy interest as a record of the last journey which the daring adventurer made."

300 On June 15, 1854, shortly before Aubry left San Francisco for New Mexico, he wrote a letter to a friend: "I shall leave for New Mexico in 10 or 12 days, and fear that circumstances will prevent me from going to your city. I shall cross the Coast Mountains near San Juan, and the Sierra Nevada at Tehón Pass or Cañon de las Uvas. I take a wagon and a boat. My object in taking a wagon is to make a trail which can be travelled at once, and the boat will be of immense advantage in crossing the Colorado. I shall at no time be more than 50 miles from my trail of last year, and frequently follow it; will pass through Zuñi, and strike the Del Norte at Albuquerque or Peralta. The party will consist of over 50 men, and hope we will have an opportunity of punishing the Indians we met last year." *Daily Missouri Republican,* July 15, 1854.

301 Antonio José Otero, one of the three judges appointed by General Kearny to the superior court of New Mexico in September, 1846.

302 José Francisco Chávez, of New Mexico, a young man of twenty-one. Twitchell, *Leading Facts of New Mexican History,* II, 400.

303 Francisco Perea, of New Mexico, a young man of twenty-four. *Ibid.,* II, 399.

It was oppressively warm; the thermometer marked 112 degrees in the shade. The Cañon de [las] Uvas (or Grape pass)[304] is the lowest pass in the Sierra Nevada and the best for a railroad, and thence the route should come direct to the Mojave river.

JULY 30. We arrived today at the Great Colorado river, where we struck last year. We came from San José to the Sierra Nevada in ten days, and from that mountain to this place in eight days, counting traveling days only. We were delayed in making attempts to find a route to cross this river some fifty miles below this point, but could not succeed. The country south is either filled up with low mountains or sand hills. However, I think a level route can be had by going east to this [crossing?] from a point where the Mojave river turns abruptly to the northeast. But this country is barren and indicates no water. I had intended to pass through it, but Judge Otero objected to it so strongly that I abandoned the project. We brought our boat on a wagon to this place without the least difficulty, and a rail route can be had with the greatest facility. The country most suitable for a rail[road] or wagon road is to leave the Old Spanish trail twelve miles from the Agua Tiomese, and traveling northeast to this place. There is an extensive *vega* about forty miles southwest from here, which will be of great advantage to travelers. On this route there is no sand whatever.

The distance from the Cañon de [las] Uvas to this place is less than three hundred miles, and the whole distance from San José will not quite reach six hundred miles. Also, travelers can reach this crossing by taking the Old Spanish trail to the Vegas Callatana, leaving

304 Near the southern boundary of the present Kern county, California, not far from the Tejón pass.

it to the north and traveling twenty-five miles southeast. Springs will be found at halfway, with grass in abundance. Recent observations show that this crossing is very nearly in latitude 35¾ degrees, as the Vegas Callatana is in a few minutes less than 36 degrees. We found the Colorado river some fifteen feet lower than last year and anticipated no trouble in crossing. The river, as low as it seems, is still navigable for the largest class of steamboats; and this may be the head of navigation, as there is a canyon just above us. This will, no doubt, become a landing for the people of Salt Lake.

JULY 31. We crossed the Colorado in ten hours without any loss whatever. Our boat worked admirably under the management of Perea and Chávez, who are better navigators than any others in the party. We delayed half a day in searching for gold and without much success. We found some small particles in sand obtained near the river. Our two miners say that indications are much better in a little mountain near the river which we crossed the next day.

AUGUST 1. We marched twenty miles southeast [and] crossed a low mountain where there is a good pass; but there are on this side a number of gullies from three to fifteen feet deep. Of course they can be easily made level for a rail[road] or wagon road. We struck the Colorado where it turns to the south.

AUGUST 2. Made fifteen miles east, near our trail of last year. Country level and gravelly; no timber.

AUGUST 4. We traveled fifty miles southeast yesterday and today in the same level valley, which is well supplied with lakes and springs of good water and with an abundance of timber on the mountains. There is a plaza, or dry lake, in this valley, about twenty-five miles in length and ten miles in width. This valley or prairie extends all the way to Zuñi, but, as it makes a bend to the south and afterward to the north, we will attempt to find a more direct route to the Del Norte. It seems that the presence of our large party has created great confusion among the Indians. We found several rancherias they have abandoned, where they left their crops, consisting of watermelons, pumpkins, and a little corn. Also, in some places, they left bows, arrows, etc. Our men regret not having an opportunity of bringing punishment upon them for the treatment they extended to us last year. It would be useless for us to follow them, as they have gone into rugged mountains.

AUGUST 5. We were detained half a day in search of a pass through a high table mountain, and found one entirely level and one to two hundred yards wide. We traveled two miles north and eight miles east; passed two springs of good water and plenty of grass and timber. Today Chávez, Perea, and a few men met some Indians and exchanged a few shots with them.

AUGUST 6. Marched twenty-five miles over a high, level table-land, with great abundance of grass and timber. We saw deer and antelopes, and found rain water in many places.

AUGUST 7. Traveled twenty miles over the same level country; found grass, timber, and water in abundance. We passed during the day several branches of Williams's Fork, or Big Sandy, and encamped near the head of the main stream. I went on top of a high peak and recognized the Garrotero mountains, near our trail of last year.

AUGUST 8. We started in an eastern direction and crossed Lieutenant Whipple's trail after traveling three miles. We continued the same course, and after traveling ten miles we struck heavy and thick timber of pine, cedar, and piñon, where we were detained hours without being able to get through it; and it is barely possible to pass it on foot. In consequence of this we went south and traveled eight miles on Lieutenant Whipple's trail.

AUGUST 9. We left Lieutenant Whipple's trail to the north and proceeded east. We passed near a valley fifteen miles wide and twenty miles in length, and passed through another about ten miles in length and seven or eight miles wide. We found several springs of good water yesterday and today. The whole of this country is well supplied with grass in great abundance, and we saw timber enough today to make a thousand miles of railroad; the trees are from one to four feet in diameter, and from one hundred to two hundred and fifty feet high. There are mountains north and south of us, covered with timber. We traveled twenty miles east and fifteen miles northeast. This evening I went on top of a mountain and discovered, from the formation of the country ahead of us, that there is a stream not over twenty-five miles from our camp; it may be the Colorado Chiquito.

[AUGUST] 10. We marched twenty-seven miles northeast and struck the Colorado Chiquito. According to one of Perea's men we are opposite the villages of the Moqui. We have so far succeeded most admirably in accomplishing the main object of the expedition, *i.e.,* finding a wagon route to this place; and it is clear sailing from this camp to Zuñi, as the valley of this river may be followed all the way without the least obstacle. The country today was level and well supplied with timber and grass. This stream is about twenty yards wide and one and a half feet deep. The valley is narrow with coarse grass in it and unfit for cultivation;

there are a few small cottonwood trees along the stream. We came from the Great Colorado to this place in nine traveling days; distance 225 miles.

[AUGUST] 11. We came to the falls of Colorado Chiquito after traveling eight miles, and made twenty-two miles in the afternoon. We are traveling up the river in a south southeast direction. We discovered today that a distance of thirty or forty miles can be avoided by coming directly east from our camp on the seventh instant and striking the river at this camp. There is a higher mountain, covered with fine timber, which must be left to the north, and some low hills to the south.

[AUGUST] 12. Marched thirty-five miles east along the river, where we found wagon tracks, plenty of cotton trees, and grass.

[AUGUST] 13. Traveled twenty-five miles east on [the] north side of the river, and two miles near a little creek coming from the east. Today we went in the hills and found several very large petrified trees; one was six feet in diameter and two hundred and fifty feet in length. This morning we saw the Sierra Blanca and recognized other mountains on my trail of last year.

[AUGUST] 14. Marched twenty-five miles east over a level country with gravelly soil, good grass, and some cedar and piñon. We are about fifteen miles north of the Colorado Chiquito.

[AUGUST] 16. Traveled twelve miles east and struck my trail of last year thirty-five miles from Zuñi, which we will pursue to that place and travel the wagon road to the Del Norte.

THE SOUTHWEST HISTORICAL SERIES

Comprises the following volumes printed direct from the original unpublished manuscripts, and rare originals

Volume I. (1844-1847)

Webb (James Josiah), Adventures in the Santa Fé Trade, 1844-1847

From the original unpublished manuscripts

Volume II. (1854-1861)

Bandel (Eugene). Frontier Life in the Army, 1854-1861; translated by Olga Bandel and Richard Jente.

From the original unpublished manuscripts

Volume III. (1846-1847)

Gibson (George Rutledge). Journal of a Soldier under Kearny and Doniphan, 1846-1847

From the original unpublished manuscript

Volume IV. (1846-1848)

Marching with the Army of the West, 1846-1848. Comprising the following original unpublished journals:

Johnston (Abraham Robinson) Journal of 1846

Edwards (Marcellus Ball) Journal of 1846-1847

Ferguson (Philip Gooch) Diaries, 1847-1848

Muster roll of Company D, First Regiment of Missouri Mounted Volunteers, June, 1846

Volume V. (1849)

Southern Trails to California in 1849

Early news of the gold discovery

Advertising southern trails and routes

Routes through Mexico to California

Routes from Texas to the gold mines

Routes through Arkansas and along the Canadian

The Cherokee Trail

The Santa Fé Trail

From various contemporary newspapers

Volume VI. (1846-1850)

Garrard (Lewis H.). Wah-To-Yah and the Taos Trail.

From the rare original edition of 1850, with extensive additions by the editor

Volume VII. (1846-1854)

Exploring Southwestern Trails, 1846-1854

Cooke (Philip St. George) Journal of the march of the Mormon Battalion, 1846-1847

From the original unpublished manuscript

Whiting (William Henry Chase) Journal of 1849

From the original unpublished manuscript

Aubry (François Xavier) Diaries of 1853 and 1854

From the original published 1853, in the *Santa Fe Weekly Gazette*

Volume VIII. (1687-1873)

McCoy (Joseph G.) Historic Sketches of the Cattle Trade of the West and Southwest

From the rare original edition of 1874, with extensive additions by the editor

Volume IX. (1859)

Pike's Peak Gold Rush Guidebooks of 1859

Tierney (Luke) History of the Gold Discoveries on the South Platte river; and a guide of the route by Smith & Oaks

Parsons (William B.) The new Gold Mines of Western Kansas: a complete description of the newly discovered gold mines, different routes, camping places, tools and

Volume IX. (1859) *(Continued)*

outfit; containing everything important for the emigrant and miner

Summary by LeRoy R. Hafen of the other fifteen Guide Books including those of Allen; Byers and Kellom; the Complete Guide; Eastin; Gunn; Gunnison and Gilpin; Horner; Marcy; Oliver; Parker & Huyett; Pease and Cole the Pike's Peak Guide Book; Pratt and Hunt; Redpath and Hinton; and The Traveler's Guide

The appendix includes the Statement of Dr. Levi J. Russell; the Cherokee Expedition of 1858 by Philander Simmons; the letter of William McKimens from the South Platte gold mines; the account of the Company from Bates County, Missouri, by James M. Edmonston; Letters of William B. Smedley of the Ray County Company; letter of William B. Parsons, october, 1858; report of William B. Parsons; the Diary of Augustus Voorhees

From the rare originals, with extensive additions by the editor

Volume X. (1858-1859)

Colorado Gold Rush: Contemporary letters and reports, 1858-1859

From many contemporary and rare newspapers

Volume XI. (1859-1860)

Overland Routes to the Goldfields, 1859. From contemporary diaries.

The Arkansas River Route – the diary of Charles C. Post

From the original unpublished manuscript

The Platte River Route – the diary of E. H. N. Patterson

From the original unpublished manuscript

St. Joseph to Fort Kearny – the diary of Edwin R. Pease

From the original unpublished manuscript

From Texas to Pike's Peak – the diary of A. M. Gass

From the original published, 1859, in *The Standard* (Clarksville, Texas)

Leavenworth and Pike's Peak Express Route – the diary of Albert D. Richardson

The Smoky Hill Trail – contemporary letters and reports.

From various contemporary newspapers

The Great Central Route to the gold mines of western

Volume XI. (1859-1860) *(Continued)*

Kansas – E. D. Boyd's Notes on the First Parallel Road

From the *Atchison Weekly Champion,* June, 1859

The log of Sir Richard F. Burton's Stagecoach Trip, 1860

Pike's Peak and back: Notes of a Returned Pike's Peaker – John H. Edwards.

From the original published in the *Nebraska City News,* 1859

Letters from Travelers on the Arkansas River Trail:

From contemporary newspapers

Volume XII.

The Analytical Index to the series